G000114837

THE US LABOR MARKET

QUESTIONS AND CHALLENGES FOR PUBLIC POLICY

Dean Baker

George J. Borjas

Richard V. Burkhauser & Mary C. Daly

Peter Cappelli

Miles Corak

Tyler Cowen

Martin Feldstein

Jason Furman & Betsey Stevenson

Harry J. Holzer

Glenn Hubbard

Melissa S. Kearney

Robert Z. Lawrence

Bhash Mazumder

Robert A. Moffitt

Casey B. Mulligan

Pia M. Orrenius & Madeline Zavodny

Timothy M. Smeeding

Justin Wolfers

Edited by Michael R. Strain

AMERICAN ENTERPRISE INSTITUTE

ISBN-13: 978-0-8447-5007-1 (hardback)
ISBN-10: 0-8447-5007-7 (hardback)
ISBN-13: 978-0-8447-5008-8 (paperback)
ISBN-10: 0-8447-5008-5 (paperback)
ISBN-13: 978-0-8447-5009-5 (ebook)
ISBN-10: 0-8447-5009-3 (ebook)

American Enterprise Institute
1150 17th St. NW
Washington, DC 20036
www.aei.org

Contents

Acknowledgments

I thank Rachel Ayerst Manfredi for pushing me to edit a volume on the labor market, and for reminding me that there would be consequences if I didn't come through. I'm very grateful to Harry J. Holzer for his advice in the early stages of this project, to Jon Rodeback and Sarah Crain for their excellent work in editing the papers in this volume, to Claude Aubert for taking Word documents and turning them into a beautiful finished product, to Judy Mayka Stecker for her hard work and support, and to all the others at the American Enterprise Institute who contributed to this volume. And I am grateful, in advance, to the AEI staff who will promote this volume far and wide.

Bradley Wassink is due special recognition. He played a key role in this project's conception and in shepherding that idea to its final form. It is quite fair to say that this volume would not exist—at least not as you see it in these pages—without him.

Preface

If I asked you to tell me about yourself, there's a good chance you'd begin with your job. "I'm a teacher." "I'm a nurse." There is something noble behind the impulse to lead with your occupation: we want to contribute to society, and for many of us employment is a key avenue for social contribution. Especially in a market economy—where comparative advantage is rewarded and incentives exist to discover yours, nurture it, and apply it—who we are is, to a large degree, how we choose to contribute.

Work allows us to provide and care for our children. (That the national income statistics don't reflect much of this work says nothing about its immense value.) Work fosters community—there is something unique and edifying in enjoying the company of your coworkers after that long, hard project is finally completed or the work week has come to a close. The best antidote for boredom and vice is often a good job. Among other features, the expressiveness inherent in work—its creative element—is, or at least can be, deeply spiritual.

Indeed, work is central to the flourishing life. And public policy, in its effort to promote the common good, is properly interested in helping to create a vibrant labor market in which individuals can earn their own success, realize their potential, and enjoy the dignity that hard work provides.

This effort is challenged, of course, by the realities and evolution of the labor market. There are short-term challenges, to be sure. But the labor market faces longer-term, slower-burning challenges as well—a long-standing decline in workforce participation among working-age men, high unemployment among minority youth, low rates of employment among the less educated, changes to the structure of family and community, the effects of technological change on the structure of occupations and earnings, the globalization of labor and product markets, the economic and social effects of immigration, persistent poverty, changes and challenges in skill acquisition, unintended consequences of existing public policy, changes in the relationship between workers and firms, and so much more.

How should policy respond, adapt, keep up? How should we know whether a new or changing feature of today's labor market is a problem that merits concern, or is just a reality to be accepted?

A good way to start is by asking the right questions. This volume asks some (though far from all) of the most important: Should we be concerned about economic mobility in the US? Is productivity the most important determinant of compensation? How can we make work pay? Would cutting corporate tax rates increase jobs in the US? Do public policies that reduce the reward to work significantly diminish labor supply? How can we build workers' skills? Does lesser-skilled immigration hurt lesser-skilled native workers? What should we do about workers who are especially difficult to employ? Should we be concerned about inequality?

These are hard questions, without clear or obvious answers. To make progress on them, let me advance an argument: a competitive market in ideas is the best way to figure out the world, and to find the best solutions to our problems.

This volume makes manifest that argument. In its pages, each of the questions outlined above is answered by economists—twice. Two papers address each of the questions above, each with a different point of view and a different emphasis.

These challenges aren't going anywhere anytime soon—the essays in this volume will be relevant for many years to come. But these essays can inform policy, helping it to move in a better direction—in a direction that will help the economy, sure. But more importantly, in a direction that will help all of us to contribute, to realize our potential, to lead lives of dignity and fulfillment.

M. R. Strain
Washington, DC
June 2016

I

Should We Be Concerned About the State of Economic Mobility in the US?

How Much Social Mobility? More, but Not Without Other Things

MILES CORAK
University of Ottawa

Shania Twain is one of my favorite musicians. What's not to like? Her powerful voice, heartfelt songs, and unstoppable energy propelled her to the top of the charts during the 1990s and early 2000s. In fact, that's an understatement. She was among the best-selling country-pop singers of all time, album after album winning award after award. Twain's sales were astounding, propelled by what was then a relatively new distribution technology, the compact disc, to give her music global reach.

Her success is all the more appealing because she started life with odds that were stacked horrendously against her. In fact, that's also an understatement. Anyone interested in social mobility who reads her autobiography can't help but pause and marvel.[1] She had raw talent, no doubt about it, but her family could not afford to pay for any formal musical training. Just the opposite. Her skills were honed as a minor, playing in seedy bars after closing time to help pay the family bills.

To say that life was not easy is to be charitable. Twain was raised as one of five children who had three different biological fathers. Her stepfather was of aboriginal origin, whose strong sense of independence always led him to refuse government income support. Her mother, loving and full of ambition for her daughter, suffered repeatedly from what may have been depression. The household was continually uprooted, always moving, barely one step ahead of the rent, with the children witnessing verbal and physical abuse, and ultimately being left on their own at too young an age when both parents died in a car accident. It fell to Ms. Twain to care for and raise her younger siblings.

The aspiring singer must have surely felt that just making it to Nashville for a tryout as a backup singer was a major success, never mind seeing a couple of lucky breaks—with a good deal of energy and perseverance—turn into hit after hit. Shania Twain went from the very bottom of the socioeconomic ladder to the very, very top.

Only in America.

But what's even more astounding, she's not even American. Twain was born in the Canadian province of Ontario, and raised in the northern hinterland where the children of miners and loggers aspired to finish high school and follow their parents to the mines and mills, looking forward to one day owning a house and maybe, as a real badge of success, a rustic cottage on a lake with good fishing. Twain certainly has that and much more, including a palatial home on the shores of Lake Geneva, where she lives between shows in Las Vegas.

Truly, only in America.

I tell Shania Twain's story because it has all the elements to help us think about just what social mobility involves: innate talent, personality, challenging and enriching family environments, and luck, but also new opportunities associated with economic growth, the computer revolution, and globalization, all coming together in some hard-to-define way to create the possibility of upward mobility if individuals seize opportunities even when a good deal is required of them, including picking up and moving, and in the extreme even crossing national borders.

Should we or should we not be concerned about the rate of social mobility in the United States? It is not straightforward to know, and there are certainly different points of view. But the first step in addressing a question of this sort in a way relevant for public policy is to think about what Americans really desire, and just what social mobility means, both as an aspiration but also statistically. The capacity to move from "rags to riches" is certainly a central part of a policy relevant definition of social mobility, but it is inherently related to other concerns like absolute income mobility, which in turn brings into play the importance of economic growth, and the need for security and the capacity to weather life's inevitable uncertainties.

My own view is that, yes, Americans should have more social mobility, particularly when this is a call for breaking the intergenerational cycle of poverty and promoting upward mobility. But a call for more mobility in this sense is also a call for other things: more economic growth that is inclusive and improves the general standard of living for the relatively disadvantaged and, at the same time, more income security that offers the broad majority, as well as the potentially downwardly mobile, a sense of certainty about their material well-being.

Rags to Riches, Relatively Speaking

A common way to think about social mobility is in terms of the "rags to riches" movement personified by Shania Twain, a type of mobility that is central to the great defining metaphor of the United States, "the American dream." Indeed, policymakers often frame their discussion of social mobility in these terms, as in a recent speech by the chairman of the Council of Economic Advisers.[2]

Going from the very, very bottom of the economic ladder to the very top is a rare event, even for the most talented and motivated, and it is appropriate to think somewhat more broadly in giving this notion statistical traction. A common practice is to focus on moving out of the bottom fifth of the income distribution to the top fifth. If our statistics are framed in terms of a five-fold division of parents and children depending upon rankings in their respective income distributions, then the natural benchmark in judging whether or not social mobility is high enough would be a one-in-five chance of moving from rags to riches. If there were no relationship at all between parent and child incomes, then each child would face an equal probability of standing on a particular rung of a five-rung income ladder regardless of the rung upon which their parents stood. Whether your parents were in the bottom fifth or in the top fifth, or anywhere in between, the probability you will end up at the top—or for that matter in any of the five slices of the income distribution—would be 0.2.

One-in-five chances should not in any way be thought of as optimal or as a goal for public policy, but rather as a first cut for appreciating whether mobility is as high as we could possibly imagine, or extraordinarily low.[3] And another important thing to keep in mind is that these probabilities need to add up in a precise way: the chances of moving from the bottom to the top can't keep increasing and increasing without some give at the top, requiring downward mobility for those who started life in the top 20 percent. Just as in the tale of Garrison Keillor's fictional hometown of Lake Wobegon, where "all the children are above average," there is an adding-up constraint that prevents more than one-fifth of the population being in the top 20 percent! In other words, we are being forced to think of social mobility entirely in relative terms, which is both a strength and a limitation. It is a strength by clarifying that the chances of moving up are interconnected with those of both being stuck in the bottom and of falling out of the top. Richard Reeves of the Brookings Institution skillfully relates this perspective.[4]

There is more give if we look at subnational geographies, the transition probabilities governing position in the national income distribution for children raised in particular communities. The interlocking relationship between the probabilities of moving between income ranks is looser the smaller the level of geography. Some communities may experience significant economic growth that will lift their children up the national rankings, while other communities may better prepare them to move and seize opportunities elsewhere. The upshot is that there can be significant differences in rags to riches movement, and intergenerational cycles of poverty and privilege across regions of the country. But also, for any particular community, upward mobility from the bottom need not be tightly constrained by little downward mobility from the top.

These subnational indicators of social mobility are available at the level of commuting zones from the online tables accompanying the paper by Raj Chetty et al.[5] They are depicted in Figure 1 using the 709 commuting zones for which information is available. The

Figure 1. Rags to Riches Movement and Its Correlates in More Than 700 Commuting Zones Across the United States

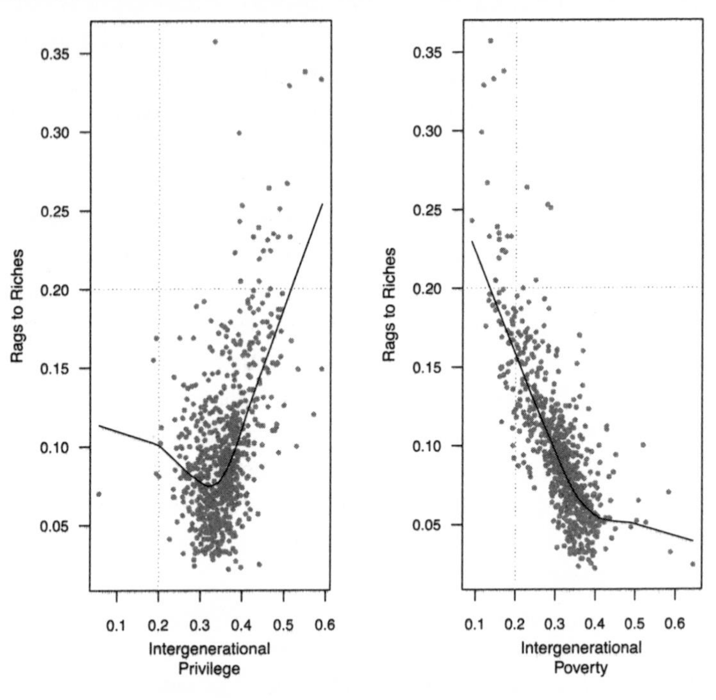

Source: Author's analysis of data from Raj Chetty et al., "Where Is the Land of Opportunity? The Geography of Intergenerational Mobility in the United States," *Quarterly Journal of Economics* 129, no. 4 (2014): 1553–623.

left panel plots in the vertical direction the probabilities of a movement to the top quintile for children raised by bottom-quintile parents—labeled as "Rags to Riches"—against the probabilities of staying in the top for children raised by top-quintile parents, labeled as "Intergenerational Privilege." The right panel again plots the bottom- to top-quintile probabilities, but this time against the probabilities of staying in the bottom for children raised by bottom-quintile parents, "Intergenerational Poverty." The horizontal and vertical dashed lines are drawn at 0.20 for reference, and the general tendencies in the relationship between the indicators are summarized by the curved lines.

The first thing to note is the pervasiveness of intergenerational cycles of privilege and poverty. Virtually all commuting zones show a greater than one-in-five chance of staying in the top given top-earning parents. Basically, no matter where you live in the United States, the most likely way to get to the top is to start at the top. This kind of intergenerational stickiness is mirrored at the other end of the income distribution: 92 percent of these communities (649 of them) have bottom-to-bottom probabilities greater than 0.2, with the chances of an intergenerational cycle of poverty being greater than one-third in 43 percent of these more than 700 communities. These two facts are the foundation of my call for more social mobility. They set the bounds for upward mobility of the least advantaged.

In fact, it is rare that the chance of moving from bottom to top is higher than one-fifth. This is the case in only 22 of 709 commuting zones, and less than one-in-seven have a probability above 0.15. That there is a pretty clear negative relationship between "rags to riches" and "intergenerational poverty" should not be a surprise. This tells policymakers that promoting broad-based social mobility is about more than just an efficient cream-skimming of the most innately talented children of the least-advantaged parents. It has to involve raising the chances of escaping low income across this entire population of relatively disadvantaged.

At the same time, it is important to note that, perhaps surprisingly, there isn't a strong negative relationship between "rags to riches" and "intergenerational privilege." Just the opposite. The top echelon has not been cornered by the children of the rich. Many communities with rather strong stickiness of high status across generations are also communities with higher movement into the top from the bottom. As the chances of intergenerational privilege rise above about one-third, the chances of upward mobility from the bottom tend to be higher, not lower. This tells policymakers that not everything about social mobility has to do with relative standing. Some communities offer children a start in life that allows them to benefit from strong growth of absolute incomes. For children from these communities, economic growth proves to be an upward escalator not just for those with an advantaged family background, but also the well-placed children of the least advantaged who are also able to ride this escalator to higher incomes, and hence higher rank. For many this most likely means moving to other communities with higher growth rates and more economic opportunities. Being forced to think of social mobility entirely in relative terms is a limitation in the sense that it does not fully capture the role of absolute income mobility in both our sense of well-being and as a lubricant for relative mobility.

Social Mobility Is Both Absolute and Relative

There is a natural retort to a call for more social mobility based entirely on the observation that the chances of upward mobility fall short of some arbitrary threshold. In part, the counterargument reasonably questions the value of a benchmark like one-in-five as an indicator of "too high" or "too low," but more poignantly it questions the value of any relative benchmark. At the risk of caricature, the story goes something like this. The simple fact is that America is a much richer place than it was a generation or two ago, average incomes are higher, and almost all children will live a life of affluence that probably could not be imagined by their grandparents. And even if incomes have not grown lately as much as we would have liked, the ever-growing variety of goods and the fall in their prices adds significantly to our welfare in a way that official statistics often fail to capture. Who even listens to compact discs anymore, never mind watching films on video cassette recorders? Social mobility is already very high in America. If you don't believe it, ask any potential immigrant in almost any country of the world; the higher per capita income of the United States being a continual draw for those who also wish to live the American dream. After all, Shania Twain didn't stay in Canada to make it big. In other words, it is not position or rank, but rather the overall level of income, its growth, and the resulting absolute mobility in our material standard of living that give meaning to social mobility.

It is indeed a mistake to ignore economic growth and absolute living standards in discussions of social mobility. But this argument implicitly makes assumptions about the benchmarks citizens use to gauge both individual and social progress that may not reflect how people actually behave. In the extreme it implies that absolute comparisons across our individual lifetimes—or even over longer periods spanning past generations—entirely trump relative comparisons between individuals at a point in time. This is a difficult argument for economists to support because economic theory offers very little guidance in helping to understand at what rate individuals trade off absolute gains in well-being in order to maintain or increase their relative standing. Welfare economics is almost entirely based upon a utilitarian framing of well-being that leaves little or no room for inequalities of outcomes. We can't rely on standard theory because the issue of relativities is assumed away. Furthermore, in some important measure the concern over social mobility is a concern not about outcomes but about process, about "equality of opportunity." Economists know less than public policy makers need in adjudicating trade-offs between relatives versus absolutes, and between outcomes and the process producing them.

At the same time it is hard to deny that both absolute and relative comparisons matter in the way that citizens actually lead their lives, and the lives they value. Americans say so. For example, the sociologist Leslie McCall exhaustively examines polling data to bring into focus the way Americans actually feel about inequality and opportunity, suggesting, among other things, that "beliefs about economic inequality are shaped by views about the rich and not the poor."[6] Whether policy advocates like it or not, relativities matter.

An equally careful discussion of these issues from first principles is offered by the Harvard University economist Benjamin Friedman, who persuasively makes the case for inclusive economic growth as a central ingredient in understanding public policy directed to social mobility. Friedman suggests that attitudes and behavior are governed by two separate benchmarks: an individual's past experience, but also experiences relative to others. Inclusive growth is central to the first benchmark. Friedman claims that making material gains over a lifetime, and believing that one's children will be even better off, takes the bite off of having to make gains relative to others. Inclusive growth and a vision of a prosperous future are, in other words, substitutes for having to maintain relative standing.[7]

But the standards by which individuals judge their well-being evolve. While we look naturally to our past experience to judge whether we are better off, we do not look too far into the past, particularly when what it takes to participate normally in society changes more rapidly. It is cold comfort to be told that your standard of living is much higher than the vast majority of others on the globe, or than your grandparents or even parents. These might be benchmarks appropriate for potential immigrants, or for our parents and grandparents. But young adults must live and engage in the society of today, which entails a different understanding of what are necessities and luxuries. And so economic growth is not only improving our absolute standard of living; it is continually changing our relative standards.

A call for more social mobility as upward mobility in relative terms is also a call for more flux, uncertainty, and potentially downward mobility for the children of those with higher relative standing. As Friedman puts it,

> taking steps to move a society toward greater fairness or more equal opportunity typically does impose risks, as well as costs, on at least some people. The importance of economic growth for this purpose is that rising incomes make people more willing to accept these risks and costs in the interests of what they take to be a better society for themselves as well as others.[8]

When growth slows, when it is not inclusive, when it has a winner-take-all dimension, when it stalls for the majority but favors the top 1 percent, then the concerns over relative shares are heightened in people's minds. This is one reason why social mobility has moved up the policy agenda so significantly in the United States, and why it is increasingly paired with inequality. The Census Bureau reports that median family income, measured in 2014 dollars, doubled during the 30 years between 1947 and 1977 from just above $28,000 to almost $57,000. But the data also show that there has been little headway since then. In 2014 the median income stood at $66,600, increasing by less than $10,000 in the more than 35 years since the late 1970s. This is a long-noted and disconcerting trend that more recently has been coupled with greater uncertainty. The typical family saw its income fall by almost 10 percent in the aftermath of the Great Recession, and the recovery has witnessed a sustained stagnation in incomes.[9] At the same time, top income shares continued to trend up. It is little wonder that this period of limited growth and greater uncertainty has made Americans more concerned about their relative standing, and just as importantly, if not more so, about the prospects for their children. In this sense, an agenda to improve social mobility needs to be more than an agenda to improve the relative prospects of the least advantaged; it needs also to inspire a sense of prosperity for the broad majority and offer a sense of security to those who may not gain in a relative sense.

Major Messages

A natural and policy-relevant way to think about social mobility is as movement from the bottom to the top or more generally as upward movement. Individuals experiencing this sort of change in their economic and social standing over the course of their lives are more likely to be pleased than not, more likely to feel that they have become all that they can be, and certainly likely to wish as much for their children. Policymakers may also be inclined to view social mobility in this way. It appeals to a common set of values surrounding the American dream, and in part it also speaks to the potential for greater growth and efficiency, to the idea that talents are being fully nurtured and human capital fully exercised for greater prosperity.

Social mobility as upward mobility is part of the American dream. But the meaning we give to "bottom" and "top" conditions our understanding of just what social mobility is, how to judge whether it is high enough, and ultimately what—if anything—to do about it.

I argue that social mobility has an inherent relative dimension, and that when focusing on this dimension bottom-to-top movement is likely, at a first look, lower than we could imagine because too many children are disproportionately caught in an intergenerational cycle of relative poverty. But I also suggest that social mobility is not entirely relative; inclusive growth and effective social insurance are also important elements of any policy agenda to promote movement from the "bottom" to the "top." Inclusive growth is valued in its own right for the higher standards of living it promises, but in some measure it is also a balm, relaxing the importance of rank, offering both aspiration and insurance, and influencing whether citizens take an optimistic or a pessimistic view of their future and that of their children.

Acknowledgments

This article was written for the American Enterprise Institute while I was a visiting professor of economics at Harvard University. I am grateful to Benjamin Friedman and Richard Reeves for their helpful comments on the first draft, while at the same time accepting entire responsibility for the content. I can be reached at MilesCorak.com and @MilesCorak.

Notes

1. Shania Twain, *From This Moment On* (New York: Simon & Schuster, 2011).

2. Jason Furman, "Equality and Efficiency: A Global Perspective," prepared remarks, Council of Economic Advisers, White House, May 2, 2016.

3. Miles Corak, "Economic Theory and Practical Lessons for Measuring Equality of Opportunities" (working paper, OECD Statistics, 2016); Christopher Jencks and Laura Tach, "Would Equal Opportunity Mean More Mobility?" in *Mobility and Inequality*, eds. Stephen L. Morgan, David B. Grusky, and Gary S. Fields (Stanford: Stanford University Press); and John Roemer, "Equal Opportunity and Intergenerational Mobility: Going Beyond Intergenerational Income Transition Matrices," in *Generational*

Income Mobility in North America and Europe, ed. Miles Corak (Cambridge: Cambridge University Press, 2004).

4. Richard V. Reeves, *Dream Hoarders: How the American Upper Middle Class Is Leaving Everyone Else in the Dust, Why That Is a Problem, and What to Do About It* (Washington, DC: Brookings Institution Press, 2016).

5. Raj Chetty et al., "Where Is the Land of Opportunity? The Geography of Intergenerational Mobility in the United States," *Quarterly Journal of Economics* 129, no. 4 (2014): 1553–623.

6. Leslie McCall, *The Undeserving Rich: American Beliefs About Inequality, Opportunity, and Redistribution* (Cambridge, UK: Cambridge University Press, 2013), xi.

7. Benjamin M. Friedman, *The Moral Consequences of Economic Growth* (New York: Random House, 2005), 79–102.

8. Ibid., 95.

9. US Census Bureau, "Historical Income Tables: Families," 2016, Table F-7, http://www.census.gov/data/tables/time-series/demo/income-poverty/historical-income-families.html.

What Should Be Done to Increase Intergenerational Mobility in the US?

BHASH MAZUMDER
*Federal Reserve Bank of Chicago**

For much of its history, Americans have viewed the United States as a distinctive society due to its promise of economic opportunity. There has long been a deeply held notion that anyone can succeed and move up the ladder, irrespective of one's origin. Over the last few decades, the idea of American exceptionalism when it comes to social and economic mobility has been profoundly challenged. There is mounting evidence that, if anything, economic fortunes are more tightly connected across generations than in most other advanced economies, calling into question the view of America as the land of opportunity. The well-documented rise in inequality in recent decades coupled with the economic setbacks experienced by millions of Americans due to the Great Recession have pushed mobility and opportunity to the forefront of the policy agenda.

If it is the case that America suffers from a lack of equality of opportunity relative to other countries, then it raises the question of what, if anything, should be done about this. That is the central question that I will try to address in this article. But before discussing policy recommendations, it is useful to take a step back and reexamine certain aspects of the literature on intergenerational mobility. What exactly do we mean by mobility, and how

* The views expressed here are those of the author and do not reflect those of the Federal Reserve Bank of Chicago or the Federal Reserve System.

is it measured? To what extent do mobility measures tell us about equality of opportunity, and is there an optimal amount of mobility? Are measures of intergenerational mobility telling us something useful about current policies, or are they more informative about the past? What does current research suggest are the key drivers of intergenerational mobility?

What Do We Mean by Intergenerational Mobility?

Mobility researchers typically measure the degree of association between a person's socioeconomic status and that of his or her parents. When that association is relatively low, mobility is thought to be high as it implies that parental status only goes so far in determining child success. In this case there is rapid "regression to the mean."[1] A very tight association, in contrast, suggests that there is low mobility and the pecking order in one generation replicates itself in the next.

Sociologists pioneered the field by examining intergenerational associations in occupation, and many observers continue to refer to "social mobility" when describing intergenerational associations more generally. Starting in the 1980s economists began to focus on intergenerational associations in traditional economic outcomes such as labor market earnings. Over time economists introduced innovations in methodology around measurement that led to gradually higher and higher estimates of intergenerational associations in income, implying much less mobility than previously believed. In one week in May 2005, both the *New York Times* and *Wall Street Journal* ran front-page stories highlighting the more dour view of economic mobility in the US.[2] Since that time, the vast majority of studies have confirmed this view.[3]

It is important to keep in mind that the measures of intergenerational mobility based on parent-child associations are only *indirect* indicators of economic opportunity. We presume that, if the associations are very high, especially relative to some baseline expectation, it must be because opportunity is lacking even if we cannot directly observe the barriers. While it is sometimes argued that other explanations such as genetic associations, which have nothing to do with opportunity, can explain high degrees of intergenerational associations, it is challenging for such alternative stories to explain how mobility differences can be so large either among countries, among areas within a country, or at different points in time.[4]

If we are really interested in equality of opportunity, wouldn't it be better to directly measure it rather than inferring it from mobility statistics? Some have argued for a framework in which inequality of opportunity is measured by the degree to which disadvantages are due to circumstances beyond the control of the individual.[5] Here differences in parental or neighborhood characteristics might count toward inequality of opportunity, but differences in individual effort would not. In this case, lack of mobility due to effort might be viewed as perfectly appropriate and wouldn't require action by policymakers. In that sense we might have a clearer idea of the "optimal" amount of mobility.

While such a framework is appealing in theory, in practice it is difficult if not impossible to operationalize because we probably cannot cleanly separate circumstances from effort. Increasingly, psychologists and economists have focused on certain "noncognitive" capacities such as "grit" as being critical for success. But what if it turns out that whether or not you develop grit is partially a function of whether your parents are able to make sure your basic needs are met or are able to provide you with the right enrichment activities? In that case we would not be able to cleanly divide the amount of mobility that is due to circumstance versus effort, and we would mistakenly tolerate more inequality of opportunity than is desirable. Because a multitude of factors interact in a complex way to determine our capabilities for success, I don't think we currently have a satisfactory framework for determining the optimal amount of mobility.

Relative Versus Absolute Mobility?

We should also be fully cognizant that most measures of intergenerational mobility are about relative mobility and not absolute mobility, and this might be at odds with what the public has in mind when it thinks about mobility. The measures of intergenerational association provide statistics about the relative success of descendants of some families versus others but not about whether individuals will actually enjoy a higher absolute standard of living than their own parents. If the US economy is growing 2 to 3 percent per year on average, then we would generally expect to see the average person experience upward mobility. In that sense as long as the gains from economic growth are more or less equally shared by families, absolute mobility will basically be captured by the kinds of statistics on average family income growth reported yearly by the Census Bureau.

Given that there is now fairly clear evidence that the benefits of growth are not equally shared across families, it may be more salient to focus on measures of absolute mobility as well as relative mobility, and some studies are beginning to do that.[6] It seems clear that focusing on absolute mobility in an era of stagnant income growth is likely to further bolster the case that mobility is not optimal. Irrespective of the results, it would probably be useful for policymakers to consider an array of mobility measures as a guide. Since absolute mobility may be the most transparent and easily interpretable measure by the public, there is a strong case for considering it.

Measurement Issues and Limitations of Intergenerational Mobility Measures

The data challenges for measuring intergenerational economic mobility are enormous. Ideally researchers want to measure the entire lifetime stream of income over two generations for a large sample of families. In practice, we might be content to measure income over a 10-year age range when parents and adults are in the middle of their careers, perhaps from age 36 to 45. That means that the most recent birth cohort that is old enough to have completed its mid-career was born in 1971. If you believe as I do that the most important determinants of an individual's earning capacities are skills that are developed by adolescence, then many of the important influences on this person's experienced mobility took place in the 1970s. Intergenerational mobility, therefore, is in many ways a backward-looking measure. We will not be able to understand how the circumstances affecting a girl born today will affect her mobility until the middle of this century. Of course, this is taking a somewhat extreme view since there are certainly reasons to think that contemporaneous labor market policies and institutions can affect mobility for workers of all ages. For example, to the extent they exist, eliminating discriminatory hiring or promotion practices could improve mobility for affected workers.

This suggests a need for early-warning indicators of mobility. Natural examples of this would include a variety of measures taken from birth though college with an emphasis on how these outcomes differ by socioeconomic status. For example, Reardon shows that the test-score gap between families whose income is at the 90th percentile and those at the 10th percentile has risen dramatically for cohorts born between the mid-1970s and 2001.[7] Bailey and Dynarski have demonstrated that the gap in college attendance by family income has risen between cohorts born around 1960 compared with those born around 1980.[8] These kinds of statistics may actually be as important, if not more so, for policymakers as measures of "completed" mobility for individuals born decades ago.

Overall, while measures of intergenerational mobility are not perfect and there is no one right measure of mobility, the studies to date give us more than enough confidence to know that the rates of economic mobility experienced by Americans are probably too low, certainly compared with citizens of other advanced economies.

What Does Theory Tell Us About Intergenerational Mobility?

Economic models of intergenerational income mobility tend to focus on how human capital investments on the part of parents and the public sector shape the intergenerational associations between parents and children.[9] In these models low rates of income mobility can arise if poorer families face "borrowing constraints" and are unable to invest optimally in kids, leading to a poverty trap. Public-sector investments, such as provision of day care centers or schools, can potentially offset suboptimal private-sector investments. From this perspective, human capital (as reflected in educational attainment, test scores, noncognitive skills, and health) might be viewed as the key factor in determining intergenerational income mobility. In principle, well-designed policies that can equalize human capital differences would be the natural starting point for policymakers.

Social scientists in other disciplines tend to focus on other forces that can impede intergenerational mobility including family structure, institutional factors, and characteristics of communities. For example, inadequate social and cultural capital have sometimes been advanced by scholars as important factors in explaining why some places experience persistent poverty. More recently, there is a growing interest in the role of human biology in shaping socioeconomic outcomes and trajectories, particularly at the earliest ages of life. Innovative research has shown how our genes, the environment, and the interactions of the two affect many aspects of human capital development, such as cognitive skills, noncognitive skills, and health. Of course, these theories arising from different disciplinary perspectives are not mutually exclusive and likely work in concert. For example, violent crime in a poor neighborhood can both lead to poor social capital as well as induce a stress response that leaves a biological imprint on a child. Such conditions may also lead to low parental investments in children as well as low levels of public investment.

Policies That Improve Early Life Experiences

A strong case can be made that the "low-hanging fruit" for policymakers is to improve the early life environment. An emerging interdisciplinary literature has shown that exposure to "shocks" from the *in utero* period through early childhood has long-lasting impacts on human capital development and later life success. Neurological development is especially rapid in the first few years of life. The neural groove is formed at three weeks of gestation, and about 90 percent of adult brain weight is achieved by age five.[10] The vast complexity of neural connections that are formed early in life implies that children are highly susceptible to environmental influences. A wide range of prenatal exposures have now been linked to worse later life outcomes, including restricted nutrition, disease, radioactive fallout, stress, violence, alcohol, smoking, lead, earthquakes, hurricanes, extreme weather, pollution, and maternal bereavement.[11] Many of these influences also affect children when experienced postnatally.

These kinds of exposures are typically most damaging for low-income families, perhaps best exemplified by the research on poverty-induced stress. Therefore, efforts to improve early life conditions will, in turn, improve upward mobility prospects for poor families. Such policies may also be the most cost-effective ways to improve economic mobility because of the cumulative nature of human capital development, in which early investments make later investments more productive.[12]

So what exactly does that mean for policy? One of the most obvious first steps would be to ensure adequate nutrition for pregnant mothers. This would imply, for example, that we make sure that every effort is made to enroll mothers in WIC and maintain adequate program funding. A recent study by Hoynes, Schanzenbach, and Almond has shown that the introduction of the Food Stamp Program in the 1960s had important long-run effects on high school graduation rates, adult health, and women's economic self-sufficiency.[13] Maintaining and expanding SNAP, the modern federal food assistance program, should therefore also be a priority. Growing research has also shown that home-visitation programs after childbirth by nurses and other child development professionals can have meaningful effects.[14]

It is also increasingly clear that improvements in access to health care early in life have long-run benefits. For example, Kenneth Chay, Jon Guryan, and I have shown that much of the narrowing of black-white gaps in test scores, college attendance, and earnings that occurred over the last two decades of the 20th century can be traced to the desegregation of hospitals in the South during the mid-1960s.[15] In this context, access to hospitals during the postnatal period was found to be critical. In other work, Miller and Wherry found that access to Medicaid, particularly during the prenatal period, led to greater educational attainment and higher income later in life.[16] These studies and others suggest that further efforts to ensure that all children have access to health care through the CHIP program may be warranted.

Environmental pollutants of various kinds have also been clearly linked to short- and long-term outcomes. Research by Isen, Rossin-Slater, and Walker has found that individuals who were exposed to reduced air pollution due to the Clean Air Act experienced improved labor market success.[17] Currie et al. demonstrate a connection between water pollution and measures of fetal health.[18] In the wake of the crisis in Flint, Michigan, over contaminated water, there is a growing recognition that water quality in many communities may be vulnerable. One of the most well-established links between an environmental pollutant and cognitive skill development is exposure to lead, either through paint chips in older houses or through water pipes. Lead exposure is also associated with attention deficiencies and aggressive behavior, and studies in both the US and Sweden have demonstrated that reductions in lead have been associated with significant reductions in crime.[19]

There are two additional points worth highlighting. First, all of the studies cited in this section use quasi-experimental research designs and do not rely on purely observational data, so their conclusions are likely to be more credible. Second, policymakers already have many programs in place that can easily be expanded or improved to help increase early life success and enhance mobility.

Intergenerational Mobility and Educational Policy

A second fundamental way for policymakers to foster greater intergenerational mobility is through improvements in education. One of the most well-established empirical findings in labor economics is that earnings in the labor market increase nearly linearly with educational attainment. Intergenerational associations tend to be significantly reduced when controlling for measures of education. I find, for example, that a large fraction of black-white differences in upward and downward mobility can be accounted for by differences in test scores by adolescence.[20] Although education clearly matters for mobility, it is less clear which particular policies matter.

Here, I consider a few policy ideas beginning with early childhood programs and extending through college. In a recent review of the literature on early childhood programs, Duncan and Magnusson conclude that there is growing evidence that attending good-quality preschool for one or two years results in long-term improvements in educational attainment and earnings and is an important vehicle for improving economic opportunity.[21] Although the research on this topic is more contentious, at a minimum, policymakers should continue to examine the feasibility and design of large-scale preschool programs that can achieve the experience of the many successful small-scale programs.

Turning to traditional K–12 schooling, I consider two broad ideas in which new and better research may have changed the terms of the debate. First, new research by Jackson, Johnson, and Persico suggests that low-income students in schools that obtained sizable gains in funding due to court- or legislature-induced financing reforms later experienced significant gains in educational attainment and income and are now less likely to live in poverty.[22] This suggests that greater school spending on the variety of inputs that may improve school quality may, in turn, improve the prospects for upward mobility for poor children. Second, there is now emerging evidence using both experimental and non-experimental methods that the quality of teachers matters for long-run earnings.[23] This suggests that to improve mobility we need to find ways to expand, rather than contract, school spending and to develop strategies to hire and retain high-quality teachers.

Finally, for higher education, research suggests that there is potential to expand opportunity by simplifying overly complex financial aid application forms that prevent some students from applying.[24] An important area for future research is how to keep students on track while they are in college, as many who start college are unable to graduate.

The Importance of Place

In a series of recent papers, Raj Chetty and Nathaniel Hendren with various coauthors have emphasized geographic location when thinking about intergenerational mobility.[25] They show that there are substantial differences in rates of intergenerational mobility across the United States and also find strong evidence that there are causal impacts of place on mobility. These findings provide support for housing vouchers and other policies that help residents leave bad neighborhoods, but thus far, they offer much less guidance about policies that can improve the communities that they leave behind. Much more detailed research is likely needed before convincing policy recommendations to help such communities can be identified. This new research is suggestive, however, of a potential need for policy to focus particularly intently on areas of especially low intergenerational mobility where multiple interventions may be necessary.

Summary and Concluding Thoughts

The literature on intergenerational mobility strongly suggests that opportunity in America is not as plentiful as it should be. However, statistics on intergenerational mobility do not perfectly map to equality of opportunity, and there is no one clear notion of an optimal rate of mobility. It is also challenging to measure intergenerational mobility in real time. Policymakers need to be aware of these limitations and consider an array of measures. These should include "early warning indicators" of mobility that assess gaps in measures of success by parental socioeconomic status. It would also be useful to consider measures of absolute mobility in addition to the relative mobility measures that have driven most research.

The "low-hanging fruit" for policymakers seeking to improve upward mobility prospects for low-income families is to improve early life conditions beginning with *in utero*. There is now a vast amount of high-quality evidence demonstrating causal connections between early life conditions (e.g., nutrition, health, and stress exposure) and later life outcomes. In many cases, the effects of poor conditions are largest for low-income families. In other cases, policies might be targeted toward this group. An important first step would be to fully fund and expand the set of programs that already have been proven to improve long-term outcomes. Taking that step would demonstrate that policymakers are serious about using an evidence-based approach to improving mobility.

Notes

1. In fact, the statistical method of regression was developed by the Victorian-era social scientist Sir Francis Galton, who was interested in, among other things, the association between parent and offspring height.

2. Janny Scott and David Leonhardt, "Shadowy Lines That Still Divide," *New York Times,* May 15, 2005, http://www.nytimes.com/learning/teachers/featured_articles/20050516monday.html; and David Wessel, "Escalator Ride: As Rich-Poor Gap Widens in the US, Class Mobility Stalls," *Wall Street Journal,* May 13, 2005.

3. See the discussion of the literature in Bhashkar Mazumder, "Estimating the Intergenerational Elasticity and Rank Association in the United States: Overcoming the Current Limitations of Tax Data," in *Research in Labor Economics*, vol. 43, ed. Lorenzo Cappellari, Solomon W. Polachek, and Konstantinos Tatsiramos (Bingley, UK: Emerald Publishing Group, 2016), 87–133, http://www.emeraldinsight.com/doi/abs/10.1108/S0147-912120160000043012.

4. For example, the results in Chetty et al. highlight striking differences between Pennsylvania and Ohio. See Raj Chetty et al., "Where Is the Land of Opportunity? The Geography of Intergenerational Mobility in the United States," *Quarterly Journal of Economics* 129, no. 4 (May 2014): 1553–623, http://www.nber.org/papers/w19844. Aaronson and Mazumder document large differences in intergenerational mobility during the 20th century. Daniel Aaronson and Bhashkar Mazumder, "Intergenerational Economic Mobility in the US: 1940 to 2000," *Journal of Human Resources* 43, no. 1 (2008): 139–72, http://eric.ed.gov/?id=EJ782759.

5. See J. E. Roemer, *Equality of Opportunity* (New York: Harvard University Press, 1998).

6. See Espen Bratberg et al., "A Comparison of Intergenerational Mobility Curves in Germany, Norway, Sweden, and the US," *Scandinavian*

Journal of Economics, forthcoming, http://econpapers.repec.org/paper/hhsbergec/2015_5f001.htm.

7. Sean F. Reardon, "The Widening Academic Achievement Gap Between the Rich and the Poor: New Evidence and Possible Explanations," in *Whither Opportunity: Rising Inequality, Schools, and Children's Life Chances,* ed. Greg Duncan and Richard Murnane (New York: Russell Sage Foundation and Spencer Foundation, 2011).

8. Martha Bailey and Susan Dynarski, "Gains and Gaps: Changing Inequality in US College Entry and Completion," in *Whither Opportunity.*

9. See Gary Solon, "A Model of Intergenerational Mobility Variation over Time and Place," in *Generational Income Mobility in North America and Europe,* ed. Miles Corak (Cambridge: Cambridge University Press, 2004).

10. See Donald F. Huelke, "An Overview of Anatomical Considerations of Infants and Children in the Adult World of Automobile Safety Design," *Annual Proceedings, Association for the Advancement of Automotive Medicine* 42 (1998): 93–113, http://europepmc.org/articles/PMC3400202/. See also Peter Gluckman and Mark Hanson, *The Fetal Matrix: Evolution, Development and Disease* (Cambridge, UK: Cambridge University Press, 2005).

11. Douglas Almond and Janet Currie, "Human Capital Development Before Age Five," in *Handbook of Labor Economics,* vol. 4b, ed. O. Ashenfelter and D. Card (Amsterdam: Elsevier, 2011): 1315–486; and Anna Aizer and Janet Currie, "The Intergenerational Transmission of Inequality: Maternal Disadvantage and Health at Birth," *Science* 344 (May 23, 2014): 856–61, http://www.princeton.edu/~jcurrie/publications/Science-2014-Aizer-856-61.pdf.

12. For a cost-benefit analysis of early versus later interventions, see Orla Doyle et al., "Investing in Early Human Development: Timing and Economic Efficiency," *Economics and Human Biology* 7, no. 1 (2009): 1–6, http://www.sciencedirect.com/science/article/pii/S1570677X09000045.

13. Hilary Hoynes, Diane Whitmore Schanzenbach, and Douglas Almond, "Long-Run Impacts of Childhood Access to the Safety Net," *American Economic Review* 106, no. 4 (2016): 903–34, https://www.aeaweb.org/articles?id=10.1257/aer.20130375.

14. See citations in Tim Smeeding, "Gates, Gaps, and Intergenerational Mobility: The Importance of an Even Start in the Dynamics of Opportunity in America," in *The Dynamics of Opportunity in America: Evidence and*

Perspectives, ed. I. Kirsch and H. Braun (Cham, Switzerland: Springer International Publishing, 2016), 255–95.

15. Kenneth Y. Chay, Jonathan Guryan, and Bhashkar Mazumder, "Birth Cohort and the Black-White Achievement Gap: The Roles of Access and Health Soon After Birth" (working paper, National Bureau of Economic Research, 2009), http://eric.ed.gov/?id=ED505758; and Kenneth Y. Chay, Jonathan Guryan, and Bhashkar Mazumder, "Early Life Environment and Racial Inequality in Education and Earnings in the United States" (working paper, Federal Reserve Bank of Chicago, 2014), http://papers.ssrn.com/sol3/papers.cfm?abstract_id=2540309.

16. Sarah Miller and Laura Wherry, "The Long-Term Effects of Early Life Medicaid Coverage" (working paper, Social Science Research Network, 2016), http://papers.ssrn.com/sol3/papers.cfm?abstract_id=2466691.

17. Adam Isen, Maya Rossin-Slater, and Reed Walker, "Every Breath You Take—Every Dollar You'll Make: The Long-Term Consequences of the Clean Air Act of 1970" (working paper, University of California at Santa Barbara, 2015).

18. Janet Currie et al., "Something in the Water: Contaminated Drinking Water and Infant Health," *Canadian Journal of Economics* 46, no. 3 (2013): 791–810.

19. Jessica W. Reyes, "Environmental Policy as Social Policy? The Impact of Childhood Lead Exposure on Crime," *B. E. Journal of Economic Analysis & Policy* 7, no. 1 (2007), http://www.nber.org/papers/w13097; Jessica W. Reyes, "Lead Exposure and Behavior: Effects on Antisocial and Risky Behavior Among Children and Adolescents" (working paper, National Bureau of Economic Research, 2014), http://www.nber.org/papers/w20366; and Hans Gronqvist, J. Peter Nilsson, and Per-Olof Robling, "Early Childhood Lead Exposure and Criminal Behavior: Lessons from the Swedish Phase-Out of Leaded Gasoline" (working paper, Swedish Institute for Social Research, Stockholm University, September 2014), http://www.stressforskning.su.se/polopoly_fs/1.207429.1413788630!/menu/standard/file/WP14no9.pdf.

20. Bhashkar Mazumder, "Black-White Differences in Intergenerational Economic Mobility in the United States," Federal Reserve Bank of Chicago *Economic Perspectives* 38, 2014.

21. Greg J. Duncan and Katherine Magnuson, "Early Childhood Interventions for Low-Income Children," *Focus* 31, no. 2 (2015), https://www.

researchgate.net/profile/Katherine_Magnuson/publications.

22. Kirabo C. Jackson, Rucker C. Johnson, and Claudia Persico, "The Effects of School Spending on Educational and Economic Outcomes: Evidence from School Finance Reforms," *Quarterly Journal of Economics* 131, no. 1 (2016): 157–218, http://www.nber.org/papers/w20847.

23. Raj Chetty et al., "How Does Your Kindergarten Classroom Affect Your Earnings? Evidence from Project STAR," *Quarterly Journal of Economics* 126, no. 4 (2011): 1593–660, http://www.nber.org/papers/w16381; Raj Chetty, John N. Friedman, and Jonah E. Rockoff, "Measuring the Impacts of Teachers I: Evaluating Bias in Teacher Value-Added Estimates," *American Economic Review* 104, no. 9 (2014): 2593–632, http://www.nber.org/papers/w19423; and Raj Chetty, John N. Friedman, and Jonah E. Rockoff, "Measuring the Impacts of Teachers II: Teacher Value-Added and Student Outcomes in Adulthood," *American Economic Review* 104, no. 9 (2014): 2633–79, https://www.aeaweb.org/articles?id=10.1257/aer.104.9.2633.

24. Eric Bettinger et al., "The Role of Application Assistance and Information in College Decisions: Results from the H&R Block FAFSA Experiment" *Quarterly Journal of Economics* 127, no. 3 (2012): 1205–42, http://isites.harvard.edu/icb/icb.do?keyword=bridget_long&pageid=icb.page547524.

25. Chetty et al., "Where Is the Land of Opportunity?," 1553–623; Raj Chetty and Nathaniel Hendren, "The Impacts of Neighborhoods on Intergenerational Mobility: Childhood Exposure Effects and County-Level Estimates" (working paper, Stanford University, 2015); and Raj Chetty, Nathaniel Hendren, and Lawrence F. Katz, "The Effects of Exposure to Better Neighborhoods on Children: New Evidence from the Moving to Opportunity Experiment," *American Economic Review* 106, no. 4 (2016): 855–902, http://scholar.harvard.edu/hendren/publications/effects-exposure-better-neighborhoods-children-new-evidence-moving-opportunity.

II

Is Productivity the Most Important Determinant of Compensation?

Marginally True: The Connection of Pay to Productivity

DEAN BAKER
Center for Economic and Policy Research

The notion that workers' pay is linked to their marginal productivity has enormous appeal to economists. Much of the reason is for the simple logic of the proposition. Why would an employer ever pay a worker more than the value of what she produced? And conversely, if a worker were paid less than her marginal product, why wouldn't she seek out an employer who was willing to pay a wage equal or close to the value of her marginal product?

There is also a clear moral logic to the tie between pay and productivity. If workers are getting paid their marginal product, then the market has decided how much they should make. This is not an arbitrary decision by an employer or a moral judgment by a government official. The market has settled the question of income distribution for us.

However comforting this view of the labor market may be, there are good reasons for believing it does not apply in important ways to those at both the top and bottom of the distribution. Furthermore, even in the sectors of the labor market where the equation of pay and marginal productivity may be largely true, government policies still play a huge role. The idea that the free market is determining incomes simply does not fit the facts.

The Pay of CEOs

The best place to start this discussion is at the top. The pay of CEOs relative to ordinary workers has soared over the last four decades.

In the 1970s the ratio of the pay of CEOs at large corporations to that of the median worker was close to 30 to 1. In recent years it has averaged between 200 and 300 to 1. If pay corresponds to productivity then we should expect that today's CEOs are hugely more productive than the people who were running major corporations in the fifties, sixties, and seventies.

On its face, that claim doesn't seem to fit the data. Certainly there is no evidence that our corporations have been better at raising productivity economy-wide in the era of very highly paid CEOs. Productivity growth has averaged less than 1.9 percent in the 35 years since 1980 compared with 2.4 percent in the 33 years from 1947 (the first year for which we have reliable data) to 1980. It is also striking that the United States is an outlier in the pay received by its CEOs, measured either absolutely or relative to ordinary workers. CEOs are well paid everywhere, but in Europe and Asia successful CEOs typically earn annual paychecks (including bonuses and options) in the low millions, not the tens of millions pocketed by CEOs in the United States.[1] And, there is no shortage of large, highly successful companies on these continents.

More specifically, there have been numerous studies finding little or no correlation between the pay of CEOs and their performance, as measured by returns to shareholders.[2] For example, one study found a strong relationship between CEO pay and random events beyond their control, such as a link between an unexpected rise in the price of oil and the pay of top executives at oil companies. Another study found that "superstar" CEOs, defined as those who were given awards or were featured on the covers of business magazines, saw a sharp rise in pay even though their subsequent performance lagged that of their peers. A recent study examined the impact of the unexpected death of a CEO, for example in a plane crash, on a company's stock price.[3] In almost half of the cases it examined since 1990 (44.3 percent), the price of the company's stock actually rose following the death of the CEO. If incumbent CEOs are uniquely talented individuals who cannot be easily replaced, then their loss should be unambiguously bad news for the company's shareholders.

Perhaps the most damning study on this topic was a recent analysis of stock options grants in the 1990s.[4] This analysis found that corporate boards failed to recognize that the value of an option was rising hugely over the course of the decade. Since they did not want to appear to be cutting the pay of their CEOs, they felt the need to give them the same number or more option grants, even though this implied a substantially larger pay package that was not warranted by their performance.

The structure of corporate governance provides a simple explanation for an explosion in CEO pay that is unrelated to performance. In the same way that democratically elected governments can have problems with insider deals and patronage jobs for the well-connected, the structure of corporate governance cannot ensure that corporations are run in the best interest of their shareholders.[5]

The shareholders' interests are ostensibly protected from top management by the corporate board. However, the board itself is likely to owe more allegiance to top management than the diverse groups of shareholders it is supposed to represent. Top management typically plays a large role in selecting board members. Furthermore, it is very difficult for shareholders to organize effectively to displace board members who are not seen as acting in their interests. The process for electing and re-electing board members is overwhelmingly tilted toward insiders. It is generally far easier for unhappy shareholders to sell their stock than to organize a challenge to incumbent board members.

The incentives for an individual board member typically push them toward going along with ever higher CEO pay. Board members generally get paid several hundred thousand dollars annually for a position that requires relatively little time. It is not uncommon for a board member to serve on three or four boards of major corporations, even while holding down a highly paid full-time job.[6] Since there is virtually no risk of losing a cushy job and stipend from going along with higher CEO pay, whereas raising a challenge can mean an unpleasant confrontation that could eventually lead to being removed as a director, it is not surprising that most directors are content to see CEO pay go ever higher.[7]

The disconnect between CEO pay and productivity not only matters for the CEOs and top management of major corporations, but also affects pay patterns for top management at hospitals, universities, and even private charities. It is now common for the presidents of these institutions to earn salaries of over $1 million, with their top underlings also earning paychecks that are vastly higher than their counterparts would have received four decades earlier. The president of a major university can rightly point out that they would get far higher compensation at a private company of the same size. In short, the failure of the corporate governance process leads to a serious disconnect between pay and productivity for a relatively small share of the labor market, but one that comprises many of its top earners. The basic story here is that the market mechanism that should bring pay and productivity into line simply does not operate given the incentives of the individuals directly involved in setting pay scales.

Pay at the Bottom: The Minimum Wage

If the incentive structure in the system of corporate governance has the effect of breaking the link between pay and productivity for those at the top of the pay ladder, there are also good reasons for questioning the link for those at the bottom. In the case of minimum-wage workers it is not so much a story of pay being out of line with productivity, but rather a situation in which productivity itself may be a function of pay. That means that it is possible for the same worker to get higher pay and still not have his or her pay exceed his or her level of productivity.

There are two basic stories that can explain this situation. The first is a relatively simple story of monopsony, where the wage the employer pays all of his or her workers is affected in part by the wage he or she pays the lowest paid worker. In this story, if the lowest paid employee were to get a raise, the marginal cost to the employer is not just the higher pay to this worker, but also the increment that she must add to other workers' pay as well.

While the story of monopsony is usually applied only to cases like small towns with a single major employer, it is reasonable to think that most employers face a monopsonistic market to at least a limited extent. To get a divergence of pay from marginal product, all that is necessary is some interdependence in the wage structure. If employers feel a need to keep some gradation between workers based on seniority, skills, or other considerations, then a raise to the least-paid worker implies higher wages to other workers as well. In such situations, we would expect the worker's marginal product to exceed his or her pay. A rise in the minimum wage breaks the link in pay from the standpoint of the employer, because the pay to other workers does not depend on whether or not he or she chooses to hire a worker at the new, higher minimum wage. The higher minimum wage puts the impact of this decision outside of the employer's control.

The other reason why productivity might depend in part on pay for low-wage workers is that workers will be better workers if they get a higher wage. This can take a variety of forms, but the basic story is that they would be more committed to their job. The most easily measured aspect of this relationship is turnover, and it can be shown that higher minimum wages are associated with a lower rate of turnover. Since turnover carries substantial costs for employers, even in the least-skilled jobs, workers are effectively increasing their productivity from the standpoint of the employer if they stay at their job longer.

These two effects can go far toward explaining why modest increases in the minimum wage have generally been associated with little or no job loss.[8] The implication of these arguments is that the pay of workers at the bottom end of the pay scale can often be raised while still keeping wages in line with productivity. This means that there is no meaningful link between pay and productivity for these workers as well.

Returns to Rents: The Monkey Wrench in Pay Scales at the Middle

While a failed corporate governance structure removes the link between pay and productivity for workers at the top end of the wage ladder, and complications around monopsony and the endogenous determination of productivity can affect the link for those at the bottom, there are also important factors that matter a great deal in the middle of the wage distribution.

In recent decades the wages of manufacturing workers have fallen sharply relative to the pay of other workers. A major part of this story is the increasing openness of the United States to trade. Both Democratic and Republican administrations have worked to remove trade barriers so that it would be as easy as possible for US corporations to manufacture goods abroad and then import them back into the United States. This policy had the effect of putting manufacturing workers in the United States with low-paid workers in the developing world who may be paid less than one-tenth as much as their US counterparts. This low-cost competition reduces the marginal productivity of US workers, and predictably, it led to lower wages.

However, the structure of trade agreements was not simply a natural event. While there was a clear focus on facilitating foreign investment in manufacturing, there was little or no effort to bring down the barriers that protect doctors, dentists, and other highly paid professionals from their counterparts in other countries. For the most part these barriers were left in place or even strengthened while other barriers were being eliminated. This has allowed the real wages of these professionals to rise compared with most of the rest of the labor force.

In this case there is not necessarily a divergence between pay and productivity; it is rather a case where government imposed supply restrictions causes the marginal productivity, and therefore the pay, of these professionals to be far higher than would be the case if we had free trade more broadly.[9] In effect, the government has adopted trade policies that lower the marginal product of large segments of the workforce (manufacturing workers and workers in the sectors that attract displaced manufacturing workers), while keeping in place policies that ensure a high marginal product for a group of highly educated professionals who sit near the top of the pay ladder.

Government policy also leads to large rents in other ways. Patent and copyright protection cause the protected items to sell for prices that are often several thousand percent above the free market price. This is clearest in the case of prescription drugs. Drugs that can be safely manufactured and distributed for a few hundred dollars per treatment can instead be sold for hundreds of thousands of dollars due to patent monopolies. This form of protection creates many jobs with very high marginal products, but this is due to the government's grant of monopoly, not any intrinsic feature of the jobs.

There are other ways to finance the research and development of new drugs that do not require patent monopolies.[10] This can allow researchers to be compensated for their labor, but without the patent monopoly they would have a far lower marginal product and therefore considerably lower pay than under the current system. (We also wouldn't have the absurd problem of debating whether the government or private insurers should pay tens or hundreds of thousands of dollars for drugs that could be profitably manufactured for a few hundred dollars in a free market.)

While patents are arguably more appropriate as a mechanism to finance innovation in sectors other than pharmaceuticals, the system has almost certainly gone too far in extending protection. In 1998, a company succeeded in getting a patent on a peanut butter and jelly sandwich.[11] Excessive issuances of patents lead to rents not only for the patent holders, but also for lawyers and for those marketing the product at its patent-protected price.

The tax system also creates enormous opportunities for rents. Those capable of developing innovative tax schemes have extremely high marginal products, since they are saving large amounts of money for their employer. This is much of the story of the private equity (PE) industry, which has produced many of the richest people in the country. While some of the success of PE companies is due to their ability to turn around poorly managed firms or to supply capital to allow for the expansion of innovative companies, much of it is attributable to the PE firms being better able to manipulate the tax code than the companies they buy. Insofar as this is true, the marginal product and pay in the PE industry would fall sharply if we had a better conceived tax system.

The Financial Industry

The financial industry is another major source of rents in the US economy. While the industry serves an enormously important purpose in allocating capital from savers to those who want to invest, there is good reason to believe that it has become increasingly inefficient over the last four decades. The narrowly defined financial sector, investment banking and securities and commodities trading, has increased in size by a factor of five relative to the larger economy over the last four decades.[12] This explosive growth stemmed from an unwinding of the depression-era regulation designed to contain the industry and the enormous growth in computing power. The former removed legal barriers, and the latter allowed for a vast increase in the amount of trading that could take place and the type of financial instruments that could be traded.

The financial industry is the home of many of the highest earners in the economy. A recent analysis of high-income taxpayers found that 18.4 percent of those in the top 0.1 percent were employed in finance.[13] These people are likely paid in accordance with their marginal product, but that has little relationship to their contribution to the economy. An algorithm that allows a hedge fund to effectively front-run trades by being a fraction of second quicker than other traders can be enormously profitable to the hedge fund, but it does not make the economy more productive. Recent research provides evidence that a bloated financial sector, like the one we have in the United States, can be a drag on growth.[14] The implication of this research is that policies that make the financial industry smaller will lead to more rapid economic growth. In short, the highly paid people in the financial sector may be earning their marginal product, but it reflects their ability to appropriate income from other actors in the economy, not their productive contribution to the economy.

Aggregate Demand and Marginal Product

There is another important way in which government policy affects productivity. As we have seen since the collapse of the housing bubble in 2007, the economy can be stuck below full employment for long periods of time. In an economy that is below full employment there are many workers who see their marginal product fall sharply simply because there is less demand for what they produce. To take a simple example, the marginal productivity of autoworkers in Michigan fell sharply in 2009 when the demand for US-made cars was down 50 percent from its pre-recession level.

In the context of an economy that is far below its potential level of output, the marginal product of millions of workers is determined by the willingness of Congress and the Fed to pursue stimulatory fiscal and monetary policies. In the absence of stimulatory policies to restore full employment, these workers will have very low productivity not because of their own failings, but the failings of policymakers in Washington.

Conclusion: The Link Between Pay and Productivity Is Not What It's Cracked Up to Be

For much of the labor market there is clearly a link between pay and marginal productivity, but it is not one that should provide much comfort to economists or the public in general. In vast sectors of the labor market, policy determines who is in a position to earn rents and who is not. Policy also determines levels of aggregate demand in the economy, which has an enormous impact on productivity and therefore pay. In addition, in determining the pay for those at the top, corporate CEOs and other high-level executives in both the corporate and nonprofit sectors, market discipline doesn't work since the proper incentives do not exist.

The net result is that we should recognize that there is considerable room to alter the pay scales in the economy, not by making pay unequal to productivity but by altering the factors that determine productivity. And in the case of the top-level executives, the key change will be to get pay back in line with productivity, which in most cases is likely to mean a substantial cut in earnings for those at the top.

Notes

1. Nuno Fernandes et al., "Are US CEOs Paid More? New International Evidence," paper presented at the European Finance Association, Bergen, Norway, 2009, http://papers.ssrn.com/sol3/papers.cfm?abstract_id=1341639.

2. Bebchuk and Fried compile much of this evidence, in addition to presenting some of their own work on the topic. See Lucian Bebchuk and Jesse Fried, *Pay Without Performance: The Unfulfilled Promise of Executive Compensation* (Cambridge, MA: Harvard University Press, 2004).

3. Timothy J. Quigley, Craig Crossland, and Robert J. Campbell, "Shareholder Perceptions of the Changing Impact of CEOs: Market Reactions to Unexpected CEO Deaths, 1950–2009," *Strategic Management Journal*, March 29, 2016, http://onlinelibrary.wiley.com/doi/10.1002/smj.2504/abstract.

4. Kelly Shue and Richard Townsend, "Growth Through Rigidity: An Explanation for the Rise in CEO Pay," *Journal of Financial Economics*, forthcoming, http://www.lse.ac.uk/fmg/events/GrowthThroughRigidity2.pdf.

5. There is a separate argument as to whether corporations should serve a broader group of stakeholders, including workers and the communities in which they operate, but I will leave that one aside for this discussion.

6. Erskine Bowles may hold the record in this respect, sitting on the boards of Morgan Stanley, General Motors, and Cousins Properties even as he served as president of the University of North Carolina.

7. There is a literature that reaches the opposite conclusion, arguing that CEO pay is closely related to firm performance. Perhaps the most widely cited argument along these lines is research showing that the pay of CEOs in companies controlled by private equity firms is comparable with or higher than the pay of CEOs in publicly held companies. For example, see Henrik Cronqvist and Rudiger Fahlenbrach, "CEO Contract Design: How Do Strong Principals Do It?" *Journal of Financial Economics*, forthcoming, http://papers.ssrn.com/sol3/papers.cfm?abstract_id=1786132. This result is interesting because there is no problem of diffuse ownership at companies controlled by PE firms. This finding can be explained in two ways. First, in a context where patterns of CEO pay have been set by publicly traded companies that cannot effectively put a check on excessive pay, PE companies would be risking getting especially inept CEOs if they were to offer

pay that was substantially below prevailing levels. The other explanation is that PE companies are generally looking to conduct major transitions in the portfolio companies under their control. They hope to do a major overhaul that will substantially increase corporate profitability in a relatively short time horizon. In principle this would be a far more demanding task than what is expected of most CEOs, who typically continue a well-established pattern of operation. Under these circumstances it would be reasonable to expect that CEOs of the companies held by PE firms would command a higher salary.

8. For a fuller discussion of these issues, see John Schmitt, *Why Does the Minimum Wage Have No Discernible Effect on Employment?* Center for Economic and Policy Research, February 2013, http://cepr.net/documents/publications/min-wage-2013-02.pdf.

9. Kleiner et al. and Winston and Crandall argue that the pay of these professionals is also supported by government licensing requirements. These requirements prevent less highly paid professionals, such as nurse practitioners in the case of doctors, from doing work for which they are fully qualified. This helps to sustain the demand for the services of the more highly paid profession. See Morris M. Kleiner et al., "Relaxing Occupational Licensing Requirements: Analyzing Wages and Prices for a Medical Service" (working paper, National Bureau of Economic Research, February 2014), http://www.nber.org/papers/w19906; and Clifford Winston and Robert W. Crandall, *First Thing We Do, Let's Deregulate the Lawyers* (Washington, DC: Brookings Institution Press, 2011).

10. Dean Baker, "Publicly Funded Clinical Trials: A Route to Sustained Innovation with Affordable Drugs," Center for Economic and Policy Research, March 2016, http://cepr.net/publications/reports/publicly-funded-clinical-trials-a-route-to-sustained-innovation-with-affordable-drugs-working-paper.

11. See US Patent and Trademark Office, "Sealed Crustless Sandwich," December 21, 1999, http://www.google.com/patents/US6004596.

12. These data are taken from 2016 Bureau of Economic Analysis National Income and Product Accounts, Table 6.2B, line 55 plus line 59 divided by line 1, and Table 6.2D, line 59 divided by line 1. See US Department of Commerce, Bureau of Economic Analysis, National Income and Product Accounts Tables, Tables 6.2B and 6.2D, August 6, 2015, http://bea.

gov/iTable/iTable.cfm?ReqID=9&step=1#reqid=9&step=1&isuri=1.

13. Jon Bakija, Adam Cole, and Bradley T. Heim, "Jobs and Income Growth of Top Earners and the Causes of Changing Income Inequality: Evidence from U.S. Tax Return Data," Williams College, April 2012, https://web.williams.edu/Economics/wp/BakijaColeHeimJobsIncomeGrowthTopEarners.pdf.

14. Stephen G. Cecchetti and Enisse Kharroubi, "Reassessing the Impact of Finance on Growth" (working paper, Bank for International Settlements, July 2012), http://www.bis.org/publ/work381.pdf.

Does Productivity Still Determine Worker Compensation? Domestic and International Evidence

ROBERT Z. LAWRENCE
Harvard University

The American dream is that each generation should live twice as well as the previous one, and this requires that incomes rise at an annual rate of around 2 percent per year. At this pace, incomes will double every 35 years. Between 1947 and 1970, average real compensation in the US increased at annual rate of 2.6 percent—a pace that was actually faster than required to achieve the dream. But since 1970, the average real compensation of US workers has grown at less than 1 percent per year, and at that pace it would take almost a lifetime to see incomes double.

In principle, living standards should reflect productivity, and as shown in Figure 1, for the first three decades of the postwar period, there was a remarkably close relationship between the growth in worker pay and the growth of labor productivity. Between 1947 and 1970, the time series for hourly output per worker in the nonfarm business sector and the real average hourly compensation paid to those working in that sector moved closely together (see Figure 1). Since the late 1960s, however, these series have grown apart. Between 1970 and 2011, for example, while output per hour in nonfarm business averaged an annual increase of about 2 percent per year, average real hourly compensation grew at only half that rate. The result was that over the four decades the rise in output per worker exceeded average real compensation by 48 percent.

Figure 1. The Productivity-Compensation Gap

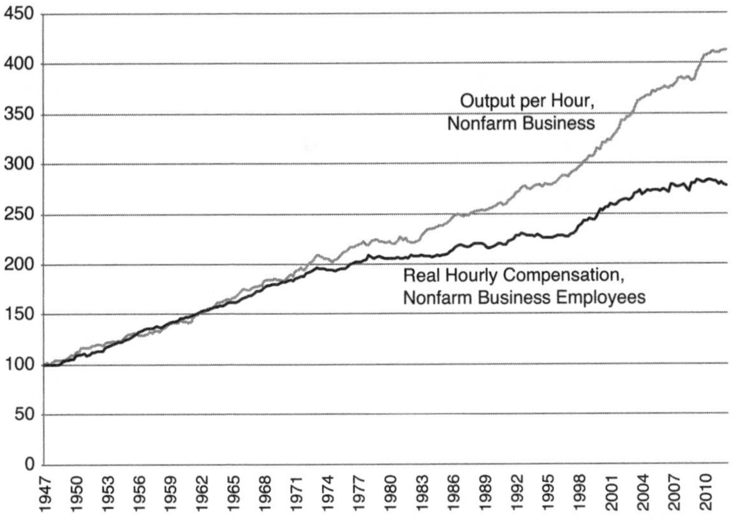

450
400
350
300
250
200
150
100
50
0
1947 1950 1953 1956 1959 1962 1965 1968 1971 1974 1977 1980 1983 1986 1989 1992 1995 1998 2001 2004 2007 2010
Output per Hour, Nonfarm Business
Real Hourly Compensation, Nonfarm Business Employees

Source: Susan Fleck, John Glaser, and Shawn Sprague, "The Compensation-Productivity Gap: A Visual Essay," *Monthly Labor Review* 134, no. 1 (2011): 57.

Although average real compensation earned by workers in the aggregate has at least shown some growth since 1970, the picture is even bleaker when we consider the real hourly wage rates of production and nonsupervisory workers—a category that accounted for more than two-thirds of overall US employment and 80 percent of private employment. As illustrated in Figure 2, between 1970 and 2012 when deflated by the Consumer Price Index (CPI), the wages of these workers showed almost no growth despite an increase in output per hour in the business sector of 124 percent. Indeed, in 1982–84 dollars, the average real hourly US wage in 2014 of $8.96 was barely above the $8.70 earned in 1970.

Given these data, it is not surprising that many believe that the link between productivity growth and worker pay that was so strong prior to 1970 has now been broken, with dire implications for most American workers. One of the premises supporting the US economic

Figure 2. Hourly Wages and Output per Hour, 1970–2013

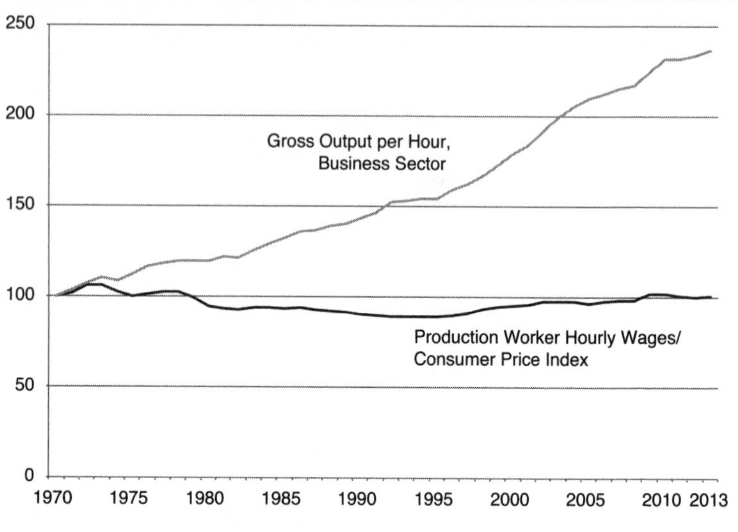

Note: 1970 = 100
Source: US Bureau of Economic Analysis; and US Bureau of Labor Statistics.

system is that "a rising tide will lift all boats" and the gains from economic growth will tend to be widely shared. The strong impression given by Figure 1, however, is that most workers are being left behind for reasons unrelated to their productivity performance. This has led some to question the basic idea that pay reflects workers' social contributions (marginal product) and instead to point to weak wage growth as resulting from a decline in worker bargaining power.[1] These data have also been used to support government policies that more directly determine pay (such as higher minimum wages) and new overtime pay regulations.[2]

The idea that wages are unrelated to productivity also provides support for international trade skeptics. If developing countries such as Mexico and China can maintain low wages in the face of rising productivity growth, it is surely unwise to expose US workers to foreign competition.[3]

Outline

In this paper, I will dispute the use of Figure 2 to support the contention that changes in power rather than marginal productivity are required to explain wage growth. In Section 1, I will argue that the proposition that US wages and productivity tend to move in tandem has actually continued to be valid in the United States, at least prior to the financial crisis in 2008. I will present evidence that 63.2 percent of the gap between the growth in average real hourly wages and output per hour that took place between 1970 and 2014 that is illustrated in Figure 2 can actually be explained by reasons that have nothing to do with income inequality. Moreover, the evidence that growing income inequality accounts for some of the gap does not mean that the competitive model of wage determination should be abandoned. Even if average wages do reflect worker (marginal) productivity, there is no guarantee that the wages of all workers will rise proportionately, or that the distribution of income between labor and capital will remain unchanged. And there is certainly no guarantee that the resulting distribution of income should necessarily be considered as just.

Indeed, I find that (1) about 30 percent of the gap in Figure 2 is due to increased wage inequality, i.e., the failure of the growth in real compensation of production and nonsupervisory workers to keep pace with the average compensation of all US workers; and (2) 6.8 percent of the gap reflects an increase in the income share of profits that occurred primarily over the past decade. In Section 2, I analyze this wage inequality in greater depth; in Section 3, I demonstrate that internationally average wage differences move in line with average levels of labor productivity; and in the conclusion I briefly draw some policy implications.

Section 1: The Gap Between US Productivity and Pay: What Is It Really?

A number of implicit assumptions are made when productivity and wages are contrasted in the manner depicted in Figures 1 and 2.

Prior to 1970, given the close association between compensation and productivity growth shown in Figure 1, most of these assumptions were not particularly consequential. But since that time several have played an important role in accounting for the gap. I will show, by analyzing the gap that has emerged in Figure 2, that once these factors are taken into account, contrary to the impression left by these figures, overall average US labor compensation has actually tracked average US labor productivity fairly well since 1970.

The first issue concerns the measurement of output per worker. The use of *gross* output in the nonfarm business sector has two problems. First, it fails to take account of capital depreciation, and second, it neglects the labor-productivity growth that occurs outside the nonfarm business sector. Capital depreciation, which is included in gross output, does not represent a source of additional income, and thus a *net output* measure that takes depreciation into account is more appropriate. In recent years, the share of depreciation in output has increased as the role of short-lived equipment has become more prominent in the capital stock.[4] In addition, the growth in output produced outside the nonfarm business sector by workers in the government and nonprofit sectors and by the self-employed should also be taken into account. A more appropriate and inclusive measure of output is net domestic product (NDP; i.e., GDP minus depreciation of capital) and a more inclusive measure of labor input is full-time equivalent (FTE) employment, which takes account of both full- and part-time workers. I find that taking depreciation into account and measuring labor productivity as the ratio of NDP to FTE employment explains about 20 percent of the 2013 gap in Figure 2.

A second issue relates to the use of wages to measure worker earnings. The full cost of employing workers includes benefits as well as wages. Thus, compensation rather than take-home pay is a more appropriate measure of worker marginal product. This is especially important since with rising costs for health care and Social Security, benefits have become an increasingly important component of compensation. In 1970, for example, aggregate benefits were equal to 13 percent of aggregate wages, but by 2014 they amounted to 25 percent.[5] Thus, between 1970 and 2014, the series for total compensation rises 10.6 percent more rapidly than the series for wages. This means that the series for wages alone, illustrated in Figure 2, understates the increase in worker earnings, and taking compensation rather than only wages into account explains 8.2 percent of the 2013 gap.

A third issue concerns which workers and what types of pay are included in the wage measure. The average hourly earnings series reflects only the wages of production and nonsupervisory workers. But overall worker compensation should include the wages of other workers such as those in managerial and professional occupations. It should also include performance-based pay such as commissions and bonuses. More arguably, but important in the data, is the fact that aggregate compensation also includes qualified stock options that often make up a substantial part of the earnings of the most highly paid executives. These workers have enjoyed much more rapid wage growth than those represented in Figure 2, and their exclusion explains about 30 percent of the 2013 gap.

A fourth issue relates to the manner in which the nominal variables such as compensation and output are deflated. In Figures 1 and 2, the output measures have been deflated using the implicit price indexes for GDP in the nonfarm business sector, whereas the compensation or wage measures have been deflated by the CPI. In theory, under competitive conditions, workers will be paid their marginal product, i.e., their marginal product in terms of the goods and services they produce, not the goods and services they consume.

For example, if productivity in the production of computers doubles,[6] absent productivity growth elsewhere, we would expect the relative price of computers to halve.[7] Since the marginal product of a worker producing computers would have doubled, wages of workers in the computer industry and indeed wages of all workers would have *doubled in terms of computers they could buy*. But if other prices and wages remain constant, workers' buying power with respect to other products would not change. Thus, all workers would experience real wage growth far less than 100 percent. Notice that this theory tells us that wages of similar workers throughout the economy will all rise to reflect productivity in individual sectors—i.e., there is no link in general between productivity growth in one industry and the general buying power of workers in that industry—but only between productivity growth in an industry and the buying power of workers purchasing the products of that industry.

Thus, to track the consistency of productivity and wage growth in general, nominal wages should be deflated by an output price index—to obtain a measure known as the real product wage—rather than by a measure of the cost of consumption, which would indicate general buying power and include the prices of goods and services such as imports and housing, which domestic workers do not produce. It is the product wage, the wage deflated by the output price index, rather than the real or consumption wage that should be compared with output per worker to determine labor's share in income. Since 1970, the prices of the goods and services that workers produce have increased slower than the prices of the goods and services that are measured by the CPI. Between 1970 and 2012, for example, the CPI increased by 34 percent more than the nonfarm business-sector deflator. Thus, an important reason for the gap illustrated in Figure 1 is the declining terms of trade between the product and the consumption wage. This difference accounts for 35 percent of the gap.

Moreover, the CPI is in any case a questionable measure of the cost of living.[8] The deflator for personal consumption expenditures (PCE) in the national income accounts is a better measure of the cost of consumption. The CPI depends on households surveys that rely on individuals' faulty recall. The PCE uses establishment data that are regarded as more reliable. In addition, the CPI measures the changing costs of a fixed market basket of goods (a Laspeyres formula), whereas the PCE takes account of the fact that consumers respond to price changes by altering the shares of the goods they purchase (a Fisher-Ideal formula). The PCE is more comprehensive. The CPI only includes the goods and services purchased by households. The PCE also takes account of purchases that are made for consumers by firms and institutions and the government—for example, health care. Between 1970 and 2013, the PCE suggests that real compensation has grown more 13.5 percent more rapidly than the CPI.

Figure 3. Net Domestic Product and Real Product Compensation per Full-Time Equivalent Employee

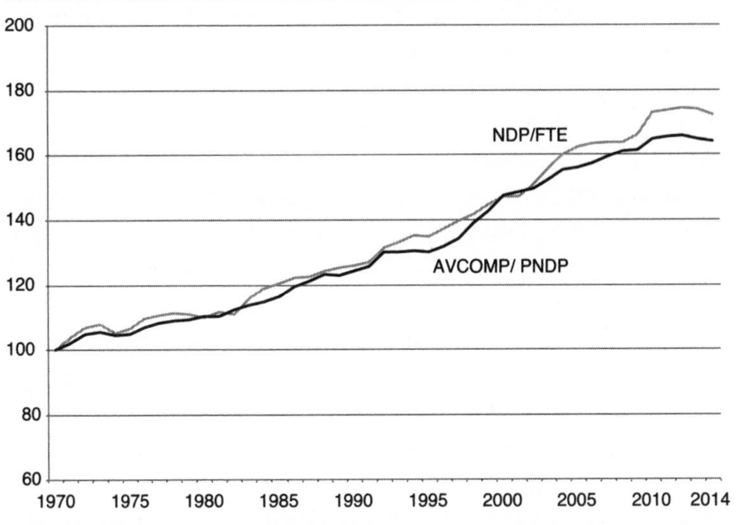

Source: US Bureau of Economic Analysis, National Income and Product Accounts Tables, http://www.bea.gov/iTable/iTable.cfm?ReqID=9#reqid=9&step=1&isuri=1.

Figure 3 makes all the adjustments suggested by these considerations. As depicted by the lighter line, labor productivity is measured comprehensively as the ratio of net domestic product (in 2009 dollars) to full-time equivalent employment. As depicted by the darker line, real product compensation is measured as average nominal aggregate compensation per full-time equivalent employee from the national income accounts deflated by the price deflator for net domestic product, which actually mirrors the PCE very closely. This juxtaposition provides a very different picture of the relationship between labor productivity and real compensation since 1970. *Between 1970 and 2001 properly measured, there was no difference between the growth of real output per full-time equivalent worker and the growth in real (product) compensation paid to workers.*[9] This also implies there was no increase in the share of income going to profits over these three decades.

As can be seen in Figure 3, the relationship between these variables tends to fluctuate over the business cycle. Wages tend to rise relative to output toward the end of expansions and during recessions—look at recession years such as 1981–82, 1991–92, and 2001—whereas wages tend to lag behind productivity growth during the initial phases of expansions.

Although real product compensation grew after 2000, it did not fully catch up to net output per worker by the 2008–09 recession, and in the years following the recession, the gap between wages and net output widened. As shown in Figure 3, between 2000 and 2014, real compensation per full-time employee increased by 11.1 percent—or an annual rate of just under 0.75 percent. Real output per worker increased by 17.2 percent. Had compensation kept pace with labor productivity between 2000 and 2014, real product compensation would have grown at an annual rate of 1.1 percent—still a slow rate—and by 2014 would have been 5.0 percent higher than it was. Thus, since 2000 the relationship between the growth in output per worker and real compensation has diverged, but the magnitude is far less than might be imagined from taking the data in Figure 1 or Figure 2 at face value. Moreover, if wages follow their normal cyclical pattern as this current expansion matures, this gap should be expected to close.[10]

Figure 4 provides a visual summary of the various factors that explain the gap illustrated in Figure 2 in 2013.[11] The darker bars show the role of three major factors: price adjustments, other technical adjustments, and increased inequality. The components of each of these factors are shown in lighter gray. As can be seen, the price effects reflect the large difference in the behavior of the CPI and the nonfarm business deflator (PBUS). Part of the difference is captured by the difference between the CPI and the PCE, part by the PCE and the PBUS, and part by PBUS and the deflator for net domestic product. A second set of technical factors includes the use of wages rather than compensation, gross rather than net output, and the focus on the nonfarm business sector rather than the economy as whole. Finally, the contribution of wage inequality dominates the contribution of increased income inequality—a topic I now consider in greater depth.

Figure 4. Percentage Contributions to Gap Between Output per Hour and Real Hourly Wages in Figure 2, 1970–2013

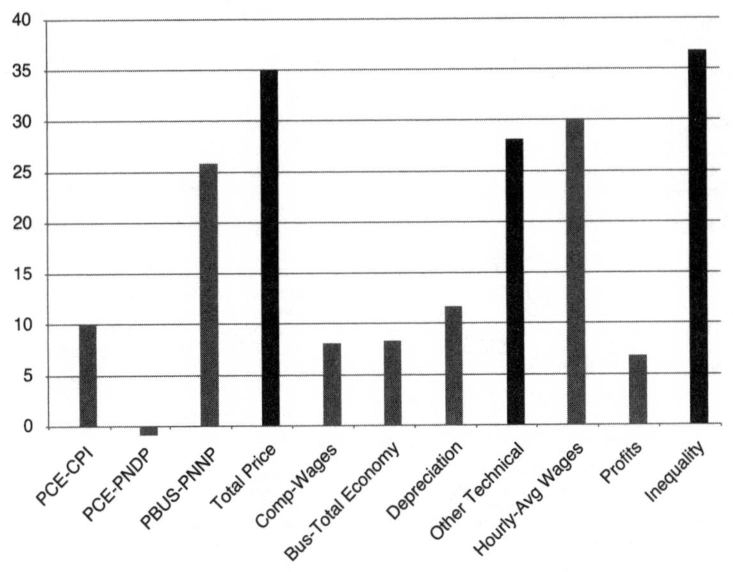

Source: US Bureau of Economic Analysis; and US Bureau of Labor Statistics.

Section 2: Growing Wage Inequality

While Figure 3 shows that in the aggregate real worker compensation has basically kept pace with the rise in real output per worker, the role of growing wage inequality that is implied by the different wage trajectories of production and nonsupervisory workers and those with high-paying occupations should not be ignored. Emmanuel Saez has used tax and Social Security data to provide time series for the shares of wage earnings earned by workers at different levels of the wage distribution.[12] I have used these shares data to allocate annual aggregate nominal wage income measures in the national accounts to workers at different levels of the wage distribution.[13] I then adjust these measures to estimate compensation by applying the ratio of aggregate compensation to aggregate wages in the national income accounts. I use the data on full-time equivalent employment

Figure 5. Average Real Compensation Growth per FTE at Different Percentiles Using PCE Deflator, 1970–2011

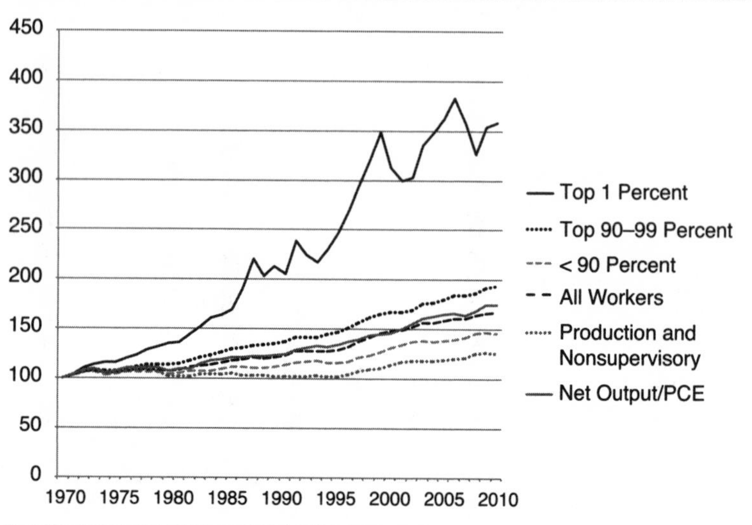

Note: 1970 = 100
Source: US Bureau of Economic Analysis; and Emmanuel Saez, tax and Social Security data, http://eml.berkeley.edu/~saez/.

to estimate average per worker compensation in current dollars and the consumption price deflator to convert compensation into 2009 dollars. The results are shown in Figure 5.

Figure 5 replicates the results for total compensation and net output per FTE deflated by the PCE deflator shown in Figure 3. It shows that these series track each other fairly closely, having grown at annual average rates of 1.25 and 1.37 percent, respectively, between 1970 and 2011. However, the average real compensation growth disguises large differences in the growth of worker earnings at different wage levels. As we move up the wage distribution, earnings have grown increasingly rapidly. Making corrections by using a different deflator and accounting for benefits in addition to wages does raise the estimated real earnings growth of production and nonsupervisory workers, but their real compensation growth has nonetheless been extremely slow. Instead of remaining static as in Figure 2, between 1970 and 2011, this estimate of the real compensation of production and nonsupervisory workers averages an annual growth rate of just 0.55 percent per year and increased by 25.3 percent over the whole period.

Average real compensation of workers in the bottom 90 percent of the wage distribution averages 0.92 percent annual growth and increased by 46 percent over the period. By contrast compensation of workers between the 90th and 99th percentiles increased at a pace of 1.6 percent per year and grew 93.5 percent between 1970 and 2011; thus, even these elite workers saw their compensation grow at a rate slightly slower than that required for the American dream. The top 1 percent experienced growth averaging 3.1 percent annually and increased by 258 percent. All told, average real compensation growth since 1970 has been much weaker than earlier. Indeed, the growth in the annual real compensation of the top 1 percent of 3.1 percent is not all that much faster than the 2.7 percent annual average growth in the average compensation of all workers between 1947 and 1970. Had the pace of productivity growth during those years been maintained and shared, the earnings of all US workers would have risen like those for the top 1 percent!

As a result of this divergent growth, between 1970 and 2011, according to Saez, the share of wages going to the top 1 percent of wage earners increased from 5.13 to 11.03 percent (i.e., 5.98 percentage points), and the share of those between the 90th and 99th percentile from 20.45 to 23.85 (i.e., 3.4 percentage points). Had the top 1 percent retained their share at 5.13 percent, with the rest of their earnings accruing to the lower 99 percent in proportion to their original earnings, the remaining 99 percent of workers would have experienced an additional increase of 6.7 percent, and the top 1 percent would have seen their real wages rise by the average wage growth of 67 percent, rather than 257 percent. Had there been no change in the overall shares in compensation between the top 10 percent of workers and workers below the 90th percentile, the average compensation of workers in the bottom 90th percentile would have been higher by 14 percent. For production and nonsupervisory workers this would have meant real compensation growth of

42.5 percent rather than 25 percent over the 41-year period. Even if there had been no increase in income inequality, real compensation per worker would have grown at 1.37 percent per year, a rate that is only half the annual average increase between 1947 and 1970. Clearly, the US has been plagued not only by increased inequality but also slower productivity growth.

It is beyond the scope of this paper to provide a complete explanation for the growing wage inequality that accounts for some of the gap in Figure 2, but I will simply note that there are numerous explanations for rising inequality that are consistent with the assumption that labor is paid its marginal product. One such explanation emphasizes forms of skill-biased technical change.[14] Other explanations point to the impact of immigration and international trade using the Stolper-Samuelson theory.[15] Similarly, explanations for the high returns earned by superstars explain how the most well-paid workers could experience increased marginal products and thus higher wages and indeed rents when the market for their services expands.[16] There are also several accounts of the rising share of profits that use a framework in which factors of production earn their marginal products.[17] As I have shown,[18] it is quite possible for labor's marginal product to rise and for labor's share and wages to fall.[19] Of course, the fact that some theories *could* explain what has happened in terms of changes in marginal productivity does not imply that institutional factors such as reduced union power, weak corporate governance,[20] and politically granted rents[21] might not have played a role. But it is not sufficient to point to the growing gap that is illustrated in Figures 1 and 2 to argue that they have.

Section 3: Productivity and International Competition

Ultimately, firms from different countries compete on costs, and unit labor costs will reflect both output per worker and wages. Thus, the fact that wages reflect average productivity helps explain how countries at different levels of economic development can gain from international trade.

It is common in the US debate, for example, to hear the arguments that ignore the role of productivity differences and claim that highly paid US workers cannot compete with workers in poor countries that earn much lower wages. Ross Perot famously predicted that if the North America Free Trade Agreement was passed, there would be "a giant sucking sound," which would be the jobs on their way to Mexico. Senator Bernie Sanders has similarly opposed the Trans-Pacific Partnership on the grounds that workers in the United States should not have to compete with workers in Vietnam, where the minimum wage is equivalent to 56 cents an hour.

These positions on trade are troubling. Taken to an extreme, the US would only trade with countries with wage rates similar to (or higher than) its own. This would prevent countries from following in the footsteps of countries such as Japan, South Korea, and China, which have used trade as the lynchpin of their economic development strategies and raised billions out of poverty.

But those making such arguments fail to understand why American wages are so much higher than those in poor countries in the first place. It is not that US workers have somehow managed to extract levels of pay in excess of their levels of productivity. Instead, they have higher wages because on average US workers are more productive because of the advantages conferred by US economic institutions and endowments. Because their workers have higher skills, are better educated, work with more plant and equipment, have access to superior technologies, and operate in a system with better institutions and social capital, firms that are based in the United States *can* on average afford to pay their workers higher wages and still remain cost competitive. By contrast, average wages are low in poor countries because of poor skills, inadequate plant and equipment, inferior technologies, and often weak institutions. Given these disadvantages, only by paying low wages are firms in poor countries able to compete.

The strong relationship between average productivity and average wages is illustrated in Figure 6. I show data for average dollar hourly labor compensation in manufacturing reported by the Bureau of Labor Statistics and use per capita GDP measured in dollars to represent average output per worker in 32 countries reported by the World Bank. While the match between these two measures is not perfect, since hours worked per capita differ by country, the correlation between them is very high (–0.93). Visually, the strength of the relationship is clear. Indeed if we plot the two measures against each other and fit a regression line to the data, we find the slope is almost equal to a 45-degree line showing that each 1 percent increase in relative productivity is associated with a 1 percent increase in relative wages, and the regression can explain 87 percent of the variance.

Mexico provides a good example. Mexican manufacturing wages are about a sixth of those in the US—the same relationship as Mexican labor productivity. In 2012 average hourly compensation in Mexican manufacturing was $6.36 (17.8 percent of the average hourly compensation of US manufacturing workers of $35.67). Similarly, per capita income in Mexico was $9,560 (18.2 percent of US per capita income of $52,530).

It might also come as a shock that judged by the average productivity of the Vietnamese economy, the minimum wage of 56 cents an hour that Senator Sanders seems to consider outrageously low and a reflection of their lack of labor rights is actually higher than the $15 an hour minimum wage that Senator Sanders has ambitiously advocated for the US. In 2012, average GDP per capita in Vietnam was just 3 percent of average GDP in the US. This means that the minimum US wage that would bear the same relationship to output per worker as the Vietnamese minimum wage would actually be 33 * 56 cents, or $18.85 an hour.

There is however an element of truth in these claims, but it will only apply to some US industries. Given the level of US wages, as anyone familiar with David Ricardo's principle of comparative advantage will recognize, there will indeed be some industries in which the US advantages in technology and productivity are insufficient to offset high US wages, and in these industries the US has a comparative disadvantage and *will* find it hard to compete; but there are also many other US industries that do have the necessary productivity advantages to more than offset America's higher pay, and in these industries the comparative advantage lies with the US firms. Thus,

Figure 6. 2012 GDP per Capita and Average Hourly Compensation in Manufacturing

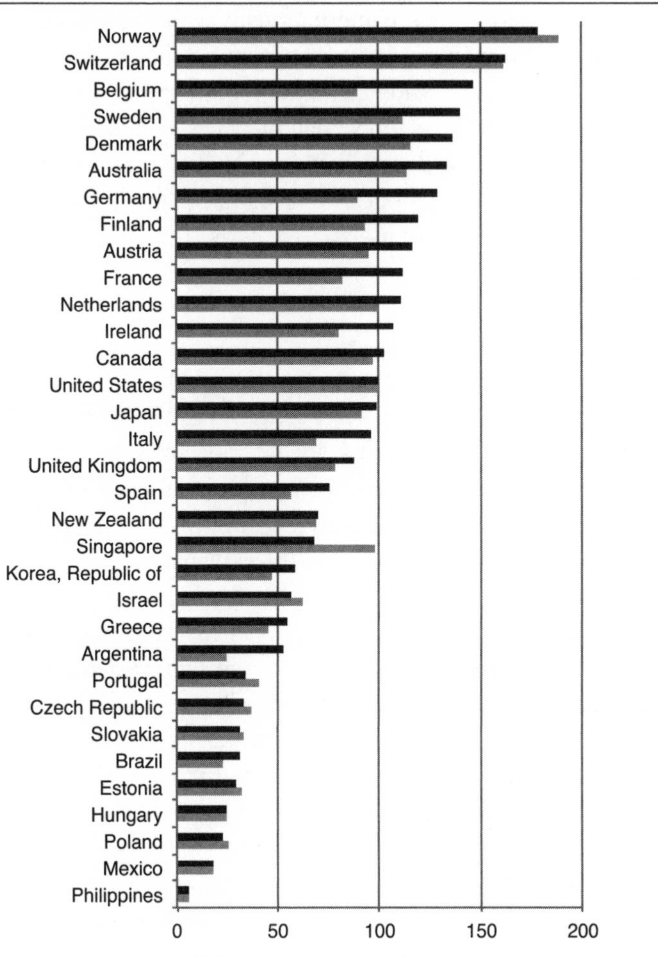

Note: US = 100
Source: US Bureau of Labor Statistics and World Bank.

despite Mexico's lower average wages and America's superior average productivity, for example, both countries gain when each specializes in producing the products made by the industries in which they have a comparative advantage.

In sum, those who oppose free trade with low-wage countries are shortchanging the competitiveness of US workers when they claim Americans cannot compete internationally with firms based in these countries. There are many industries in which they can, and they do. Indeed, if wage costs are all that matter for international competition, it is hard to explain how almost half of all US-manufactured exports valued at almost a trillion dollars in 2015 were sold in low-wage developing countries. Yet once we recognize that in these industries, productivity more than offsets labor costs, the explanation is not hard to find.

Concluding Comments

There is a view that figures such as the first two presented in this paper demonstrate that wages do not reflect productivity growth and thus highlight the failure of conventional economic theories to explain developments in the US economy. Some argue this evidence points to the need not only for explanations that emphasize institutional factors but also for policies that raise the average worker's share in output through institutional measures such as raising the minimum wage, reregulation, stronger antitrust measures, the strengthening of unions, and trade protection.

I have shown that, when the data are presented in an appropriate way, they actually show that with the exception of a growing profit share since 2000, average economy-wide wages in the US have tended to reflect aggregate productivity growth. This has not meant that these wage gains have been equally or proportionately shared. The failure of the wages of some workers to match aggregate productivity growth, however, should not necessarily be interpreted as a failure of the ability of conventional economics to explain these developments. Indeed, many of the explanations of the role played by globalization and technology in generating increased inequality rely on models in which workers are nonetheless paid their marginal products, i.e., in which wages reflect productivity. The same is true of explanations for the more recent increase in profit shares.

This paper has highlighted that the core reason for the slow growth in average US compensation has been slow productivity growth, and policies that boost productivity such as investments in human, physical, public, and intellectual capital should surely be prioritized. However, some of the measures that enhance productivity could further increase income inequality, and in any case over the past four decades numerous forces in the economy have led to increased income inequality. In my view however, it is far better to respond by adopting measures that enhance market resource allocation by promoting competition and trade rather than thwarting them, and to redistribute income directly through more progressive taxes and transfer programs.

Notes

1. See Joseph Stiglitz, *Monopoly's New Era*, Project Syndicate, May 13, 2016.

2. According to James Sherk, Labor Secretary Tom Perez has advocated new overtime regulations on the basis that firms no longer pay workers according to their productivity. James Sherk, "Workers' Compensation: Growing Along with Productivity," Heritage Foundation, May 31, 2016, 3.

3. Jeronim Capaldo, Alex Izurieta, and Jomo Kwame Sundaram, "Trading Down: Unemployment, Inequality and Other Risks of the Trans-Pacific Partnership Agreement" (working paper, Global Development and Environment Institute, Tufts University, January 2016).

4. Robert Z. Lawrence, "Recent Declines in Labor's Share in US Income: A Preliminary Neoclassical Account" (working paper, National Bureau of Economic Research, June 2015).

5. US Bureau of Economic Analysis, National Income and Product Accounts Tables, Tables 6.2b–d, http://www.bea.gov/iTable/iTable.cfm?ReqID=9#reqid=9&step=1&isuri=1.

6. I implicitly assume here that the industry is competitive, and productivity growth is Hicks-neutral, i.e., that it augments labor and capital equally. R. G. D. Allen, *1968 Macro-Economic Theory: A Mathematical Treatment* (London: MacMillan, 1968), chap. 13.

7. William D. Nordhaus, "The Sources of the Productivity Rebound and

the Manufacturing Employment Puzzle" (working paper, National Bureau of Economic Research, 2005). Nordhaus presents evidence that industry productivity growth is fully passed through into industry product prices.

8. See Sherk, "Workers' Compensation," 8–10.

9. Since the changes in the NNP and PCE deflators were very similar, there is no difference between the changes in real product and real consumption compensation.

10. Indeed, the gap closed slightly between 2014 and 2015. Had labor compensation maintained its 2000 share in net domestic product in 2015, compensation would have been 4.4 percent higher.

11. For a similar analysis, see Lawrence Mishel, *The Wedges Between Productivity and Median Compensation Growth*, Economic Policy Institute, April 26, 2012; and Sherk, "Workers' Compensation."

12. Emmanuel Saez, tax and Social Security data, http://eml.berkeley.edu/~saez/.

13. US Bureau of Economic Analysis, National Income and Product Accounts Tables.

14. David Autor, *The Polarization of Job Opportunities in the U.S. Labor Market: Implications for Employment and Earnings*, Center for American Progress and The Hamilton Project, April 2010; David Card and John E. DiNardo, "Skill-Biased Technological Change and Rising Wage Inequality: Some Problems and Puzzles," *Journal of Labor Economics* 20, no. 4 (2002): 733–83; and Claudia Goldin and Lawrence F. Katz, *The Race Between Education and Technology* (Cambridge, MA: Harvard University Press, 2008).

15. Wolfgang Stolper and Paul Samuelson, "Protection and Real Wages," *Review of Economic Studies* 9, no. 1 (1941): 58–73. For a survey of trade and wages, see William R. Cline, *Trade and Income Distribution* (Washington, DC: Peterson Institute for International Economics, 1997). For a skeptical view of the explanation based on skill-biased technical change, see Lawrence Mishel, Heidi Shierholz, and John Schmitt, "Don't Blame the Robots: Assessing the Job Polarization Explanation of Growing Wage Inequality" (working paper, Economic Policy Institute, November 2013).

16. Sherwin Rosen, "The Economics of Superstars," *American Economic Review* 71, no. 5 (1981): 845–58; and Xavier Gabaix and Augustin Landier, "Why Has CEO Pay Increased So Much?" *Quarterly Journal of Economics* 123, no. 1 (2008), 49–100. For more on these theories, see Robert Z.

Lawrence, *Blue-Collar Blues: Is Trade to Blame for Rising US Income Inequality* (Washington, DC: Peterson Institute for International Economics, 2008).

17. Michael Elsby, Bart Hobjin, and Aysegul Sahin, "The Decline of the U.S. Labor Share," Brookings Institution, September 2013; and Loukas Karabarbounis and Brent Neiman, "The Global Decline of the Labor Share," *Quarterly Journal of Economics* 129, no. 1 (2014), 61–103.

18. Lawrence, "Recent Declines in Labor's Share in US Income."

19. Ibid. Labor augmenting technical change will increase the effective supply of labor as well as the marginal product of labor, but if the elasticity of substitution between capital and labor is less than one, this could reduce wages in the same way as an increase in the labor supply.

20. See Lucian Arye Bebchuk and Jeffe M. Fried, "Executive Compensation as an Agency Problem," *Journal of Economic Perspectives* 17, no. 3 (Summer 2003): 71–92.

21. Joseph Stiglitz, *The Price of Inequality* (New York: Norton, 2012).

III

How Can We Build Workers' Skills?

Is "Skill" a Topic for Policy?

PETER CAPPELLI
University of Pennsylvania

The notion that the US has big problems with workforce skills that demand public policy attention is a relatively new idea that was ramped up with "man bites dog" stories during the Great Recession, in which some employers said that they couldn't find candidates to do their jobs, typically low-paid, physically demanding tasks. The stories grew from there with reports, especially from consulting companies and vendors, saying that employers had difficulty finding appropriate candidates for their positions even in the face of high unemployment rates.

Although the question as to what they were looking for was almost never asked, the assumption in those stories and reports was that employers were looking for young people right out of school. What employers couldn't find was almost never asked, either, but the assumption was usually that school leavers didn't learn enough in school to be able to perform the jobs in question. IT employers in particular complained that there was a shortfall of college graduates in that field. These arguments tied employer complaints and their concerns about competitiveness to education practices. The link to policy was born, played out in seemingly endless reports including several associated with the National Academy of Sciences.[1]

Employers Provided Skills

Those of us who are older can remember a time when the topic of the skills available in the workforce was a very sleepy thing, something that employers took on themselves.[2] Industrial engineers designed blue-collar jobs; personnel psychologists identified the skills that were required for them and set up training programs to teach new hires those skills. More advanced skills came about through experience, and that happened naturally through lifetime employment, internal promotion ladders, and simple seniority-based systems. Vocational education tracks in high school prepared some students for some of the entry-level positions, although the amount of hiring into blue-collar jobs vastly overshadowed the number of students with any vocational education experience. On the craft side, union and joint union-employer apprentice programs were the mainstay of building skills.

Arrangements on the white-collar side were even more internal in their focus. After WWII, organizational development specialists within the human resource function helped design organizational charts and the career paths that moved candidates up and across them. Elaborate talent management systems began with multiyear workforce plans followed by schedules for internal promotion to meet those plans. New candidate hiring was accompanied by a year or more of classroom training and then a lifetime of investments in stretch assignments, coaching, management training, and so forth, all designed to produce a uniquely skilled and prepared team of executives. This was also the case for engineering roles, in which new hires would be slotted immediately into training and development experiences that would also last for years.

The notion that employers paid for skills was enshrined in employment law via the Fair Labor Standards Act, which says that employers have to pay for any training (including the wages of the workers being trained) that the employer requires them to have.[3]

There was an effort in the early 1990s to make a public policy case for skills, defined broadly. In an era when we saw countries with apparently highly skilled workforces such as Japan and Germany doing so well, the thought was that we could change the way businesses operated, moving us to higher-value products especially in manufacturing, by upskilling the workforce. Supply could create its own demand. That notion expanded into a grand vision of identifying the skills that each job required and how any job seeker could get those skills.[4]

What happened to the model in which employers handled their skill needs internally? It started to unravel with changes in the economy in the 1970s that made long-term economic forecasts and the planning-based systems of companies that rested on those forecasts unreliable. It accelerated with "reengineering" and corporate restructuring programs that broke up predictable job ladders and career paths. Widespread layoffs of white-collar workers and managers beginning in 1981 were perhaps the bellwether event.

Since then, the corporate mantra has been "flexibility": get skills just when you need them and get rid of them when you don't, an approach that is anathema to the long-term orientation of the earlier planning approach. The demand for skills has become much more "just in time." That has contributed to continued growth of temporary help, something that historically tapers off as the economy recovers from recessions. Most important, it shifts hiring from something that takes in entry-level workers to the primary way to fill all jobs. A generation ago, roughly 10 percent of vacancies in corporations were filled from the outside, through "entry-level" jobs. Now that figure hovers between 60 and 70 percent. To illustrate the consequences, the investment firm Blackstone recently calculated that US companies spend about $30 billion per year on human resource vendors, and $27 billion of that went to "talent acquisition," which is hiring.

One obvious consequence of this change has been declining attachments between employers and employees. Although tenure with employers rose during the Great Recession because no one was quitting, the long-term trends show much greater turnover across employers than in previous generations, especially in larger corporations. Data on the extent of training in the US is sorely lacking, but the most recent evidence shows sharp declines through the 2000s.[5] Presumably there is no need to train if we are bringing skills in from the outside.

The shift to outside hiring is dramatic and may explain employer complaints about inadequate candidates even in the face of extensive unemployment: most of the jobs they are filling require considerable experience. It's hard to find candidates with, e.g., 10 years of experience using their machine tools and dealing with their clients, a role that in the past would have been filled internally. The decline of systematic skill building and the shift to outside hiring in large companies has spillover effects on smaller employers who often used the modest turnover from their larger peers to fill their own needs.

The New Model

The argument that US employers are now in a bind with respect to skills may well be true, given the dramatic change in their business model and the goal of trying to hire in candidates who need no training. This has nothing to do with student achievement in school. There is no evidence that it has declined over time. In fact, compared with earlier generations, there isn't much interest among employers in hiring at the entry level, and therefore in hiring school leavers. Nor does it have anything to do with changing skill requirements. There is no evidence of significant increases here, either.

To the extent that they hire talent from each other, employers also create turnover problems for each other. (The topic of employee retention, now a central concern in business, did not exist for practical purposes until the 1990s.) That means they need to hire much more often, which makes hiring an even bigger challenge. To the extent that they believe their own employees won't stay, they don't want to invest in those employees, and that further increases the need to hire from the outside to meet skill needs. How do school leavers get a first job when fewer employers have "entry-level" positions for those without prior experience? That problem has received a fraction of the attention of the employer problem, yet it is considerably more important from a policy perspective.

One simple response to this new model, and one that has received little airing, is to say that this is not a policy issue at all. Skills are an employer problem. In the language of business, it is a sourcing problem: it is the job of employers to get the workforce they need, and employers will work it out themselves. If the pain of trying to fill vacancies by hiring gets high enough, employers will reengage with training and develop their own candidates.

There are some difficulties with the "do nothing" position that start with the fact that it may be complicated for employers to go back to providing and paying for entry-level skills, what economists call "general" skills that are useful elsewhere, because other employers will simply wait and hire those individuals away as soon as they are trained. No one wants to be the first one back into that model. There clearly are ways to retain trained individuals, but they require practices like reducing layoffs and promotion-from-within that most companies now play down. Short of all employers instantaneously reverting to something like the earlier model (and binding themselves to not hire each other's trainees is likely illegal), it does take some effort for individual employers on their own to address this problem.

Given those constraints, there are essentially two policy responses to this new employer model. The first one, aimed at what we might think of as high school jobs, basically plays out the traditional planning approach that companies used in the past but in the public realm. The largest single program in terms of budget, the federal government's Workforce Innovation and Opportunity Act (administered by the states), is the latest in a decades-long attempt to anticipate what jobs will be in demand and prepare candidates for those jobs. Over time, there have been many improvements in the approach, especially devolving much more responsibility to local levels, but thinking that it still involves asking employers what they will want in the future and then trying to deliver it to them would not be far from wrong, albeit with a nationwide set of interest groups weighing in and a bureaucracy to match.[6]

There has been a consensus for decades as to what would help those entering the job market right out of high school make a smoother transition into jobs. It involves bridging the school-to-work gap by getting employers to provide structured experiences in the workplace for young people that include everything from simple job shadowing (showing students what a day at work is like in different fields) to part-time work to more sophisticated co-op programs that integrate classroom and work experiences.

Apprenticeships are arguably the best known and possibly the best way to prepare young people for work. Registered apprenticeship programs—the kind that teach craft skills like plumbing—are the most rigorous of these experiences, and they have been in decline for decades. The number of apprentices fell almost by half just in the 2000s. There continue to be efforts to develop "youth apprenticeships," which provide work experience sometimes with classroom-based training, but so far, the number of employers willing to participate in these programs is a drop in the bucket compared to the need.

Schools could do more to help prepare students for work by giving greater priority to some of the basic skills that employers care about, such as the ability to communicate and get along with others. To be clear, though, the complaints that employers have about school leavers have been the same for generations, and they mainly focus on maturity—the ability to show up on time, to take responsibility for one's actions, and so forth. There has never been a magic bullet for turning teenagers into adults, and expecting schools to do that at the same time as they are trying to teach academic skills is a lot to ask.

Arguably the biggest controversy in the high school track to jobs concerns vocational education, programs that in the past taught specific job skills—auto mechanics, basic craft work, and so forth. Coursework in Career and Technical Education (CTE), as it is now known, by high school students declined substantially over the past generation, especially since the 2000s, in large part because of the concern that vocationally oriented tracks in high school represented dead-ends as opposed to more academic tracks that could lead to college. There have been many innovation programs in delivering skills training in high school, but they lack scale and, as the numbers above suggest, seem to be declining in influence.

The second track—and this is where things are new—aims at postsecondary education.[7] The idea, articulated in some places and hinted at in others, is that college can provide the job training that employers do not want to do any longer. One part of this approach attempts to deal with the vacuum created by the withdrawal of vocational education and apprenticeship by pushing the skill-building task onto community and two-year colleges. For high school students who want to be an electrician now, the most obvious path is to wait until they graduate and then pursue that training in the community college. The caveat is they have to pay for it out-of-pocket and wait longer than they would have through the vocational education path.

The demands on community colleges to provide training now are staggering in scale, given the flood of older individuals trying to secure new skills combined with recent immigrants and school leavers trying to get any skills. Some estimates suggest that as many as one-quarter of students in community colleges already have four-year degrees. Although community colleges are paid for and operated by local and to some extent state governments, the federal government now has a huge investment in providing job skills: half of the $30 billion per year spent on Pell grants, the main source of funding for college students in the US, now goes to mature students over age 24. Most of them are there seeking job skills, and most commonly they are doing that at community colleges. The federal government didn't make that investment in job training intentionally, nor is it doing much of anything to oversee the results.

Even bigger changes may be underway in bachelor degree programs. Contrary to the views of some pundits that students are not trying to major in fields where the jobs are, the evidence is overwhelming that students are chasing the job market, albeit often not getting good results. The most popular major by far is business, and the second is teacher training/education, both degrees that lead directly to specific jobs. Beyond that is the explosion of new majors that sound like job titles—health care administration, casino management, fashion merchandising, and so forth. About 12 percent of students in college now attend for-profit schools, which are almost completely dedicated to the mantra of college as preparation for a specific job. By some measures, a quarter or more of the budgets of such colleges goes to marketing to persuade students and their parents that a degree from this college or that one is the gateway to a great career in hospital records administration or some other field.

Whether college as job training actually leads to good jobs is another question about which we have little information. When employers are asked what is important to them about job candidates who just left high school or college, academic coursework hardly figures at all, especially for college.

Workforce skills enter policy at the four-year-degree level explicitly through the choices that state officials make as to which programs to support and how much to fund them. Perhaps the most explicit example of this is that officials in at least 15 states have new programs in place to steer students toward particular majors where they believe employers want to hire.[8] Similar conversations are no doubt underway in every state. Those officials are somehow sure they know where jobs will be. Usually that is in STEM fields: science, technology, engineering, and math.

The first thing to note about STEM is that the different fields underneath it don't have much in common with each other. There has never been much demand for undergraduate science or math majors, and there isn't much now. A recent Texas study, for example, found that sociology grads there earned slightly more than biology grads.

The good job market in STEM has really only been in engineering, but that is also a notoriously cyclical field that doesn't always have jobs for grads. Just ask students in petroleum engineering, which had been the hottest job in the US when freshmen poured into those programs a few years ago. By the time they graduated, years later, that market collapsed, not just because of the oil glut but also because of the surge in supply from all the students who took the advice to go to where the jobs are.

Engineering, of course, is actually a series of fields, each with its own labor market. IT engineers can't switch and do civil engineering work, and petroleum engineers can't do nuclear engineering. You are picking an occupation in engineering in ways that you are not with many other majors, and you pick it years before you actually enter. It is also important to note that a good first job out of college isn't the same thing as a good career, and many fields offer more attractive long-term careers than engineering.

Even if we could predict where the jobs will be in the future, the assumption that well-paying jobs will stay that way even when lots more graduates move into them is simply wrong. Nor is it the case that we can simply mold a student interested in literature into a good engineer. If graduates with science and math degrees do better than those with communication degrees, how much of that is due to the fact that the former were more able before starting their programs is impossible to say.

The current approach of seeing college education as job training also pushes the costs of acquiring such skills onto students and their families, and there are limits as to how much more students can pay. The average US college student and their family pays up to seven times more for college than in other countries. The US also sends a very high percentage of high school grads onto college—70 percent, the majority of whom go to bachelor degree programs—but we have the second worst graduation rate of any of our peer countries: only 40 percent of full-time students graduate in four years, only 60 percent in six years. Going to college is no guarantee of graduating from college. Those who go to college and don't graduate have made a disastrous financial decision.

Where Does All This Leave Policy?

A very strong argument could have been made that, except for helping those who are disadvantaged in seeking jobs, securing the employees an employer needs is the most basic task of business and employers, and government has no business trying to take that over. Why public funds should be spent providing something that businesses have long done for themselves is an important question, especially for those who believe in more limited government.

As a practical matter, state and local governments often find themselves competing for the affections of employers by offering up skilled workforces or by paying what would have been the costs of training workforces to entice employers to move to their location or stay there. One could make a strong argument that such an approach is at least better than just giving employers tax cuts, which had been the common approach, but it seems persuasive that society and taxpayers would be better off if we did not have any such competition for taxpayer funds.

Public policy is inadvertently pulled into the skills question on the higher education side by the fact that so many college students have responded to the difficulty in getting a first job by pursuing vocationally oriented college programs and that so much federal money goes into subsidizing those decisions. Except for addressing outright fraud in the for-profit world, which has mainly been done by state attorneys general, little has been done in the policy world to address these fundamental changes that have taken place in postsecondary education.

Specifically, if colleges are enticing students with the promise of jobs and spending taxpayer subsidies to colleges and to students in the process, why is no information required as to whether graduates even get jobs, let alone what kind of jobs they get? At the state level, who decided that the mission of public education—which historically focused on producing a more informed citizenry—could be served just as well through programs in tourism management as through traditional, academic degrees? Why is the apparent focus getting students their first job as opposed to something broader, such as helping them prepare for a longer-term career?

It is perfectly reasonable to argue that public colleges should not have gotten into the business of job training at all. Given that we have expanded access to public colleges to many students through borrowing that makes them very dependent on securing higher-wage jobs to pay off their debt and that students and their families want to pursue coursework that can lead them to a good job, it is hard for the public college system not to take the issue of job training seriously. Here are some simple ideas to do it better.

The first goes back to high school, and that is to rethink the decision about backing away from vocational education. States such as Massachusetts have developed sophisticated programs of technical training that do not preclude their students from pursuing a college degree at some point. Making students who might benefit from that kind of training wait until college to get it—where they often have to borrow money to pay for it—now seems like a dated idea.

The second has to do with marketing vocationally oriented college degrees. We should make such marketing be more like the requirements for financial marketing—after all, it is the biggest financial investment most people will ever make—that requires schools to explain the risks associated with using debt to pay for college and makes them provide credible evidence on how student investments in those degrees in the past have paid off.

The third recommendation is to find ways to get employers back in the business of providing training for entry-level workers just out of school. Moral arguments are rarely sufficient to make changes of this magnitude, but it would help to knock down explicitly the idea floating around that it is somehow the responsibility of government to provide trained workers for business.

Another battlefront of ideas is where employers can aim their lobbying cannons on state officials to steer students toward learning the skills that those employers would like to hire. The reason that is unconscionable is because such steering means using tax dollars to get students and their families to spend their own money developing those skills while the employers invest nothing themselves and make no commitments to hire any of those graduates.

It is difficult to see how any serious effort to develop work skills can function without employer involvement, and that has to mean more than having associations issue reports from Washington. The UK has had some success basically bribing employers to participate in youth apprenticeship programs in which skill training is provided by independent, accredited organizations one day per week. In a country as big and diverse as the US, maybe a national policy makes no sense. Maybe the best we can do is return to the School-to-Work movement of the mid-1990s and the at least modestly successful School-to-Work Opportunities Act, which offered some support for individual employers to engage with local high schools and colleges to develop programs to smooth the transition of students out of school and into jobs. A big proportion of the employers who engaged in such programs did it out of a sense of social responsibility, but others did it as a way to find better workers faster. Any reasons for helping school leavers again get the work skills needed to begin a career would be a good thing.

Notes

1. A review of these studies and the public dialogue concerning them is in Peter Cappelli, "Skill Gaps, Skill Shortages, and Skill Mismatches: Evidence and Arguments for the United States," *ILR Review* 68, no. 2 (2015).

2. This topic area in business is now known as talent management, and a review of the historical developments concerning talent management as well as the changes in it is in Peter Cappelli, *Talent on Demand: Managing Talent in an Age of Uncertainty* (Boston: Harvard Business Review Press, 2008), chaps. 2–3.

3. The caveat is that the act covers only hourly or production workers, and employers can obviously require that job candidates have any set of skills before they are hired.

4. The argument about redesigning the economy by upskilling the workforce was put forth most famously in National Center on Education and the Economy, *America's Choice: High Skills or Low Wages! The Report of the Commission on the Skills of the American Workforce*, 1990, http://eric.ed.gov/?id=ED323297. The extension into defining skill requirements on a national level was the Secretary's Commission on Achieving Necessary Skills managed by the US Department of Labor. The National Skills Standard Act of 1994 created a board designed to establish standards for skill requirements organized initially around industries. That effort was sinking under its own bureaucratic weight even before the incoming Bush administration had the opportunity to pull the plug.

5. The decline of internal labor markets and the rising power of the outside market has been discussed at some length, arguably first in Peter Cappelli, *The New Deal at Work: Managing the Market-Driven Workforce* (Boston: Harvard Business Review Press, 1999). Results for training include C. Jeffrey Waddoups, "Did Employers in the United States Back Away from Skills Training During the Early 2000s?" *ILR Review* 69, vol. 2 (2016): 405–34. There are many studies of changes in tenure; one that emphasizes the special decline in the largest companies is Matthew J. Bidwell, "What Happened to Long-Term Employment? The Role of Worker Power and Environmental Turbulence in Explaining Declines in Worker Tenure," *Organization Science* 24, no. 4 (2013): 1061–82. Tenure has increased since the Great Recession, but there is every indication that this is temporary and

simply because there were no other jobs to take.

6. This summary ignores special programs targeted to virtually every group that is perceived as having disadvantages in seeking employment. Those programs offer a variety of help, including support for training and job-hunting skills.

7. References to the material in this section can be found in Peter Cappelli, *Will College Pay Off? A Guide to the Most Important Financial Decision You'll Ever Make* (New York: PublicAffairs, 2015).

8. Patricia Cohen, "A Rising Call to Promote STEM Education and Cut Liberal Arts Funding," *New York Times*, February 21, 2016.

Worker Skills and the US Labor Market: What Role Should Policy Play?

HARRY J. HOLZER
Georgetown University

The rewards to higher education and related measures of skill in the US labor market have risen dramatically over time. In particular, the value of a postsecondary degree—in terms of the earnings gain it generates compared with only a high school diploma—has roughly doubled since 1980. For instance, those with bachelor's (BA) or higher degrees earned less than 40 percent more than high school graduates in 1980, while today they earn nearly 80 percent more on average.

The market rewards associate (AA) degrees to some extent, and BA and especially graduate degrees even more, with the value of graduate degrees continuing to grow over time; it also rewards non-academic postsecondary credentials, such as certificates.[1] But there is a lot of variation in pay across fields of study, with credentials in STEM (science, technology, engineering, and math) offering a strong market premium, especially in high-demand fields such as health care or advanced manufacturing.[2] While the returns to liberal arts degrees at the BA level are lower, the communication, analytical, and critical thinking skills that they sharpen often generate payoffs in jobs and especially for those who enter and complete graduate school programs. And there also appear (in most studies) to be labor market rewards for attending high-quality institutions, such as the elite private colleges and flagship public universities.

Because of the high labor market rewards to postsecondary education, the earnings gaps between those who have more such education versus those with less contribute strongly to earnings inequality in the US and its increase over time (although mostly within the bottom 99 percent of earners). And, if anything, higher educational attainment gaps between high- and low-income students have been rising over time. Thus, if more lower- and middle-income students could obtain postsecondary credentials, opportunity would rise, and inequality would fall in the US.

Why have the returns to higher education grown over time? Economists continue to debate how much of this is due to market forces, such as "skill-biased" technical change and various kinds of globalization,[3] and how much comes from deliberate policies that weaken important labor market institutions, such as collective bargaining and minimum wage laws, which help equalize earnings between the more- and less-skilled.

No doubt, both market and policy forces have been important, but most mainstream economists tend to put greater weight on the market forces. Indeed, some weakening of institutions is likely driven by market forces, since it is harder for these institutions to effectively raise wages without reducing employment if product and labor markets grow more competitive; and this, in turn, seems to have occurred, since both consumers and employers now have many more choices and ways of avoiding high-priced products and labor as a result of digital technologies and global forces.[4]

What Problems Limit Higher Education Attainment?

In such a labor market, and with the rewards to education so high, young Americans now have strong economic incentives to invest in higher education, and as a result, college enrollments have risen substantially in the past three decades. In fact, over two-thirds of high school graduates now enter some kind of postsecondary program after high school.

But there are a range of market "failures" that might cause too few students to obtain their degrees, despite rising enrollments. For example, some students might have very imperfect information about the choices available to them regarding where to attend and what to study, or imperfect capital markets might make it hard for students to obtain loans for such investments, and therefore force them to rely too heavily on their parents' liquid assets to finance their higher education. And, even when these markets work reasonably well, low-income students might experience strong disadvantages in the process, creating "equity" as well as "efficiency" problems with the market outcomes.

How are these problems manifested in education outcomes? For one thing, completion rates among those who enroll have fallen in recent years; only about 50–60 percent of those enrolling in four-year colleges and universities graduate within six years, and only about 20 percent of those enrolling in two-year programs do so. Completion rates are especially low for disadvantaged students, even when their high school achievement was fairly good.

And, among those who finish, many obtain credentials that the labor market doesn't reward. For students getting their BAs and ultimately enrolling in graduate programs, this is mostly not a problem. But for those in associate degree programs, especially if they do not transfer to a four-year college and complete a BA, the value of AA degrees in the liberal arts is quite low. Yet, at least in some states, nearly half of those receiving AA degrees get them in "general studies" or "liberal studies" and obtain virtually no labor market reward for them, even while applied science (AS) degrees and certificates in high-demand fields are more highly rewarded.

What accounts for the low completion rates of so many students, and for their failure to earn degrees with market value? The data show that too many students enter college with poor academic preparation from the K–12 years, and have trouble completing college-level material; indeed, as many as 60 percent of community college students require remediation (called "developmental" education) before they can take courses for credit, and many students never complete the remediation. Other problems include the high and rising costs of college in the US, which strain the liquid assets of students and their families, and the poor information that first-generation college-goers from poor or immigrant families have about where to apply, where to attend, and how to do well once they get there. Both of these problems reflect the "market failures" we described above, and hurt low-income students especially hard. And low-income students must frequently work to support families while they attend college, often part-time, and that also inhibits their ability to perform well in their studies.

Besides the many problems that students bring to higher education, the institutions they attend often compound their problems. On average, disadvantaged students attend weaker institutions—as measured by the average grades and test scores of students there—even when they had high achievement in high school. And these weaker institutions contribute to the low completion rates of disadvantaged students, over and above the problems caused by their personal characteristics. In particular, many of the lower-tier four-year and public two-year colleges have much lower resources per student, which generates crowding and scheduling difficulties for important classes and constrains support services.

Students fail to enter high-paying fields for a variety of reasons. In the STEM fields, it might be because they don't like math or science or are not good at it. But students get little counseling along the way about what the labor market rewards, so they might fail to choose more rewarding paths. Also, even when students choose to enter high-demand fields—such as nursing and health technician jobs—many public institutions have little incentive to expand teaching capacity in them. These institutions receive the same tuition dollars (and the same subsidies from the state, which we discuss below) regardless of whether students complete their courses of study or what they earn afterwards.

In addition, the high-demand technical fields can be more expensive, with high costs of maintaining equipment and instructor salaries (especially if they are from the private sector and teaching part-time). With the same revenue but higher costs, colleges that are constrained by tight resources have little incentive to provide more classes in these fields, and as a result, many students have great difficulty getting into the classes they need. And, given the fairly unstructured nature of community colleges, many students simply get lost in the shuffle and fail to make important choices and transitions in a timely way.[5]

Finally, many low-income students now attend for-profit colleges, where costs are much higher and completion rates are sometimes lower than in the nonprofit schools. Students often pile up considerable debt attending these colleges, which is especially problematic for those who do not complete their programs or whose credentials lack market value.

Overall, rising labor market rewards to higher education, and especially high-demand fields, should generate large numbers of students enrolling in and completing credentials in those fields. But a range of market failures and other disadvantages facing low-income or immigrant students reduce their ability to complete college credentials and to choose rewarding fields of study.

Skill Investments Outside College

But what about other skills and training in which workers might invest, besides those they obtain in higher education? Traditionally there have been a number of ways for workers to get them: (1) career and technical (vocational) education in high school; (2) on-the-job training; or (3) work-based learning models, like apprenticeships, which effectively combine the two.

Career and technical education (CTE) should provide an alternative path to skills for students who do not necessarily want to attend college right away. Historically, vocational education in the US has generated modest improvements in the earnings of students who did not attend college, and some evidence suggests that it improved high school graduation rates among such students. But it has usually been fairly low in quality, and was widely seen as a weaker (and somewhat stigmatized) alternative to "college prep." Furthermore, low-income and minority students were "tracked" into vocational education and away from college preparatory studies, thereby limiting their chances for upward mobility and reinforcing historical patterns of inequality and limited opportunity. As a result, fewer students over time enrolled in vocational education, while attending college right away became a fairly universal goal.

But the failure of so many students to complete college has reignited interest in alternative "pathways" for students that begin in high school and continue afterward in community colleges and/or the job market. In addition, the quality of CTE has been growing over time, with students taking more challenging math, science, and English classes. Newer models of CTE do not preclude college prep classes or college-going; indeed, in some cases, they eliminate the separation of CTE from college preparatory work. Instead, the stated goal now is for students to be both "college and career ready" and to be able to choose from a range of pathways that directly enter college, the labor market, or various paths between the two.

The best of the newer models—such as Career Academies, Linked Learning in California, and High Schools That Work—provide project-based learning, with much math and science instruction "contextualized" into applied settings.[6] Students obtain both general academic instruction and courses in a particular "career cluster" or program of study, along with related work experience in a high-demand sector. These models also generate paths into two-year or four-year colleges, as well as the labor market. But the transition away from old-fashioned vocational education occurs slowly, with the stigmas of the past continuing to limit the willingness of academically strong students to take CTE classes; and institutions in the field also change slowly, as instructors and staff cling to older, lower-quality models of instruction and organization.[7]

In contrast, on-the-job training historically has been mostly provided by the employer at the worksite, through both "formal" training programs and "informal" on-the-job learning. Although employers might provide the training, workers pay for it (through lower wages) at least partly or fully; the share paid for by employers should decline as the training becomes more general and less "specific" to a firm or sector, since employees can leave the firm at any time and take their training with them when it becomes quite general.

Of course, if employers are dissatisfied with the quality of the workers they hire, or they believe they are at risk for high turnover, they might also choose to invest fairly little in them. Additional market failures—such as imperfect employer information about worker quality or training options, rigid wages, and capital market problems for the firm—might once again limit the amount of training provided, especially by smaller employers.

Indeed, some data sources suggest that on-the-job training by employers has been declining over time, although there is some disagreement about this fact, and at least some employers seem to be expanding their training efforts.[8] But, even if true, there are different interpretations of what drives the decline. For instance, rising skill demands among employers likely mean they must substitute externally provided (by institutions of higher education) training in place of providing it internally; it does not necessarily prove a lack of interest in or need for skilled workers by these employers.

To overcome some of the problems associated with on-the-job training and its difficulties, work-based learning models like apprenticeship are starting to make a comeback. Apprenticeships are a way of ensuring that workers get substantial training that is very relevant to a firm's needs. Workers pay some or all of the costs of training through lower wages, although their earnings are usually still quite substantial. They also obtain a certification at the end of the process, which ensures the portability of the training. And, increasingly, the on-the-job component is complemented by classes at a community college and a certificate or associate's degree. But because the market failures described above might cause employers to provide less than a socially optimal amount of apprenticeships, policy measures might be needed to encourage or assist employers to provide more of them.[9]

A few more broad points merit some discussion here. For one thing, many US employers complain about their inability to hire or retain sufficiently skilled employees, even at the sub-BA level. Perhaps they have always done so, but the frequency and volume of complaints seem to be rising. Particularly, employers in health care, advanced manufacturing, information technology, transportation and logistics, and some services tend to frequently complain about this.[10]

The typical economist response to this problem—that they should simply raise wages to attract more workers—is of dubious value in an internationally competitive industry (such as manufacturing) or one where there is pressure to limit costs (such as health care); and higher wages do not guarantee that a skilled supply of labor will be forthcoming, as some employers have learned after raising wages in very technical occupations (such as machine-tooling or precision welding).

Does any of this suggest a skills "mismatch" in the labor market between employer needs and worker skills? If shortages in worker skills persist in particular sectors or in the labor market overall, then some case for the existence of a "mismatch" might be made. As noted above, there must be some reason for why the usual market mechanisms do not cause it to clear, by allowing more workers to obtain the needed skills; the range of market failures that we have noted above might provide these reasons, while additional "frictions" in the market might also prevent the skilled workers from "matching" to the employers with jobs for them.[11]

But does the available evidence actually support the notion of mismatch, at either the aggregate level or in specific sectors? The most recent aggregate data do not imply a rising "mismatch" between the skills of unemployed workers and those needed in vacant jobs. Though the ratio of vacancies to unemployed workers has been rising in recent years, there are apparently other explanations than "mismatch" for why this is occurring.[12]

But, in specific sectors like health care, information technology, and advanced manufacturing, a stronger case can be made for ongoing mismatches, which might be exacerbated by the imminent retirement of skilled baby-boom workers.[13] Employers really do not suffer lost production or profits for very long in these sectors, since they have a wide range of strategies available for meeting their skill needs—such as outsourcing or offshoring work, or increasing recruiting as well as more training.[14] On the other hand, if these production needs could be met through the creation of more skilled workers, it would generate higher earnings and lower inequality for US workers, which may be a socially preferable strategy.

This raises one final point. If employers are skeptical about their ability to meet skill needs cost-effectively—or if technology and globalization give them options for making high profits by using only low-wage, low-skill labor—they will often choose to do so, even though "higher-road" strategies to profits that also benefit workers might be available, too.[15] These developments might help explain the ongoing shrinking of the middle-skill and middle-wage jobs in the labor market, with rising polarization of workers into high-wage or low-wage jobs occurring.[16]

But employers might still underinvest (relative to what is socially optimal) in the creation of high-productivity jobs, and this underinvestment might be rising over time. In other words, there is a "public good" aspect to skill investment and high wages that many firms might not be internalizing. Indeed, a combination of high profits but low productivity and earnings growth in the US could result from such a situation, which is what the aggregate data indicate right now and over most of the past few decades.[17]

All of these considerations create a strong case for public investment in education and training, to deal with the underinvestment in such skills generated by inefficiency and market failures as well as the inequities created by the problems of disadvantaged students and workers. Efforts to help match workers with the firms that need their particular skills could be important as well.

Education and Training Policies in the US

The public sector in the US has long subsidized higher education, especially at the state level, and there have been major federal efforts to help disadvantaged workers get more job training and other labor market services for several decades now.

In higher education, state governments heavily subsidize their public two-year and four-year colleges and universities, thus generating lower tuition costs as a result.[18] Subsidies per student tend to be higher for the flagship four-year universities than for the lower-tier colleges, and for four-year rather than two-year colleges, and higher-income students more frequently attend the flagship schools, thus creating a regressive component to aid for public education. "Hope" scholarships in some states that give students tuition-free educations, especially at the flagship universities, can be regressive for the same reason.

On the other hand, other components of financial aid, especially at the federal level, are more progressive. For instance, Pell grants provide scholarships to low-income college students—at a cost of about $35 billion per year—although dropout rates are very high, and evidence that they raise college completion among the poor is very limited. Other forms of financial aid, such as loans and work-study, are financed by Title IV of the federal Higher Education Act and benefit lower-income students as well. And the Carl T. Perkins Act provides roughly an additional $1 billion to states and localities to enhance their CTE offerings, although over 90 percent of CTE funding remains state and local.

Federal funding has also been provided for other forms of job market training and services for disadvantaged workers (and those displaced by technology and globalization) since the early 1970s. This effort began with the Comprehensive Employment and Training Act (CETA) in 1973. CETA was ultimately replaced by a series of other training programs, culminating in the Workforce Opportunity and Innovation Act (WIOA) in 2014.[19] While funding for federal higher education programs has risen over time, funding for WIOA and its predecessor programs has fallen very steadily since 1980. At the moment, federal funding for WIOA—including for the American Job (or One-Stop) centers at which workers get job search assistance and skills counseling in addition to very limited amounts of training—totals about $5 billion.[20] Federal funding for workforce services can also be found in a large number of other programs, such as Temporary Assistance for Needy Families (TANF) and Supplemental Nutrition Assistance Program (SNAP), although the amounts spent are usually much smaller in magnitude.[21]

With resources having grown over time in higher education while they declined in workforce services, and with a labor market that rewards many higher education credentials, programs have been developing that attempt to bridge the gaps between higher education and the labor market, especially at the sub-BA level. For instance, "sector partnerships" between employers in high-demand fields and community colleges (plus an intermediary who brings them together) have grown around the country, generating more programs to provide the credentials that the employers seek and reward, and rigorous analysis suggests they can generate strong earnings improvements for low-income students who obtain these credentials. "Career pathway" programs help low-income students get academic training plus related work experience as they try to move through a series of jobs in fields such as health care; "stackable credentials" are being developed for those who can only do so one step at a time, because of family responsibilities.[22]

WIOA encourages more such programs to be developed, and many states are trying to do so as well. But the best of these programs need to be replicated and further scaled while we generate more evidence on exactly which approaches work best for both employers and students. And, since none of these approaches will likely work with students who are "hard to serve" or "hard to employ," other efforts to raise their earnings and employment are needed too.[23]

What Changes Should We Make in Higher Education and Workforce Policy?

In light of the trends over time in the labor market and in policy approaches, I believe three sets of federal and state policy changes are warranted:

- More resources should be made available to community (and perhaps lower-tier four-year) colleges to train students for high-demand fields, along with stronger incentives for these institutions to spend the resources effectively.

- Funding and technical assistance should be provided to help states expand high-quality CTE and work-based learning programs, such as apprenticeships.

- Governments at all levels should be committed to expanding high-skill and high-wage employment practices by financially rewarding employers who build such workplaces and by providing technical assistance to them.

The first goal requires a mix of new funding plus new accountability for higher education institutions. Any new funding should be closely targeted to expanding teaching capacity in high-demand fields and providing services that help low-income students, such as career counseling or child care. These could also fund needed reforms in developmental education or financial aid and efforts to build more structure and guidance for students into community college programs.[24] States are already beginning to impose accountability on their colleges and universities by tying funding to measures of performance, which should include both academic measures for students in college and earnings measures after they leave.[25] The federal government could also provide some additional resources to states that impose such accountability, through a mechanism such as the Race to the Top program used in K–12 education early in the Obama administration.

While I support careful provision of more resources to community colleges, I do not support recent calls for universally free community college. Such a step would lead many students who now attend four-year college right after high school to instead start at community colleges, where their academic outcomes and preparation would likely worsen while lower-income or lower-achieving students would be increasingly squeezed out of limited-capacity programs of study. Providing free higher education even to students from higher-income families does not seem sensible in an era of such constrained public resources.

The second goal is best served by targeted federal support for CTE curriculum design, more support services for students and teachers in the field, and evaluation efforts while states try to expand pathways into higher education and the labor market for CTE students. Getting consortia of employers and educational institutions more involved in these efforts is critical. Using Perkins funds to strengthen incentives for innovation and evaluation in this area would make sense. And providing federal or state support for apprenticeships through grants, tax credits, technical assistance, and marketing make sense, too.[26]

Achieving the third goal requires targeting the demand side of the labor market (i.e., employers) directly in ways that are a bit less clear.

State and local economic development policies often do so already, but in very inefficient ways that create large windfalls for businesses and zero-sum competitions for large employers (even those paying low wages) between states.

Instead, governments at all levels should state a commitment to assisting and incentivizing more employers to take the "high road" of higher productivity and better worker skills to profits. Incentives could include grants, tax credits, preferences in government contracting and procurement, and even using large funding sources (like Medicare and Medicaid) to reward these employers. Technical assistance could come from entities like the Manufacturing Extension Partnership and service-sector versions of it. Political leaders could use the "bully pulpit" to establish commitment to producing better jobs. And any such experimentation must come with much evaluation to develop knowledge of what really works in this area and what doesn't.

Conclusion

The US labor market increasingly rewards some, although not all, postsecondary skills and credentials. Yet labor market failures and other barriers preclude many students and workers, especially those from disadvantaged backgrounds, from obtaining them. And, while some employers have difficulty finding or generating sufficiently skilled workers, others seem to be abandoning production methods that require skills (especially short of a BA) as they pursue profits through cost-minimizing strategies.

The above trends require us to support skill-building efforts involving community colleges and employers and that help disadvantaged students the most. Revitalizing high-quality CTE pathways that begin in high schools and encouraging more apprenticeships seem in order. And encouraging more employers to take the "high road" to profitability, through financial incentives, technical assistance, and public encouragement, seems warranted as well.

These approaches will likely help disadvantaged students with strong basic skills and labor market attachment. For those lacking these attributes—including ex-offenders and the disabled—other efforts are needed to encourage and reward labor market activity, such as moderately higher minimum wages and expansion of the earned income tax credit.[27]

Notes

1. Real earnings among workers with BAs only have been fairly flat since 2000 and have declined modestly among young college graduates. But the ratio of their earnings to those of high school graduates has remain roughly constant. Only workers with graduate degrees have enjoyed real earnings growth since 2000.

2. The STEM premium likely reflects the fact that such education or training requires stronger underlying math and science skills among students, as well as that many US students do not like math or science and choose not to major in it. So demand for STEM skills has risen more rapidly than its supply, causing the STEM premium to rise over time.

3. Skill-biased technical change occurs when new technologies generally substitute for one group of workers, like those with lower education, but complement another, like those with higher education. Globalization can take many forms, such as the imports of goods produced abroad, offshoring services abroad, or immigration to the US.

4. The greater choices available to consumers (because of Internet shopping or product market deregulation) and to employers (due to digital technologies and globalization) would both make labor demand curves more *elastic*, which implies greater risk of job loss when wages are set above market levels.

5. See Judith Scott-Clayton, "The Shapeless River: Does a Lack of Structure Inhibit Student Progress at Community Colleges?" (working paper, Center for Community College Research, Columbia University, 2011).

6. Career Academies have been rigorously evaluated and show substantial long-term impacts on the earnings of students, especially at-risk young men. The other models are promising as well but have not been similarly evaluated.

7. See David Stern, "Pathways or Pipelines: Keeping High School Students' Future Options Open While Developing Technical Skills and

Knowledge" (unpublished paper, University of California, Berkeley, 2015).

8. For evidence of declining employer investment in on-the-job training, see Peter Cappelli, "Skill Gaps, Skill Shortages, Skill Mismatches" (working paper, National Bureau of Economic Research, 2014). For an interpretation of Cappelli's evidence and an analysis that questions it, see Robert Lerman, "Are Employers Providing Enough Training? Theory, Evidence and Policy Implications" (unpublished paper, Urban Institute, 2015).

9. Currently there are roughly 400,000 registered apprenticeships in the United States, which is much smaller as a fraction of the total workforce (about 158 million) than is found in most EU countries.

10. See, for example, Deloitte and Manufacturing Institute, "The Skills Gap in Manufacturing, 2015 and Beyond," 2015.

11. Mismatches can occur if the trained workers are concentrated in different states or regions than the jobs that need them, or if the training is not for the specific or updated skills that employers seek.

12. For instance, Davis et al. argue that the rising vacancy rate reflects longer vacancy durations, as employers seem less hurried to fill positions. See Steven Davis, Jason Faberman, and John Haltiwanger, "The Establishment-Level Behavior of Vacancies and Hiring," *Quarterly Journal of Economics* 128, no. 2 (2013): 581–622.

13. See the National Academy of Sciences, *The Supply Chain for Middle-Skill Jobs: Education, Training, and Certification Pathways*, National Academy Press, 2016.

14. For a critique of the claims made by the Manufacturing Institute on shortages of skilled workers, see Paul Osterman and Andrew Weaver, "Why Claims of Skill Shortages in Manufacturing Are Overblown," Economic Policy Institute, March 26, 2014. For evidence that firms in the same industry can choose to pay above- or below-market wages, see Fredrik Andersson, Harry Holzer, and Julia Lane, *Moving Up or Moving On: Who Advances in the Low-Wage Labor Market* (New York: Russell Sage Foundation, 2006).

15. See Zeynep Ton, *The Good Jobs Strategy* (New Harvest, 2014); and Beth Shulman and Paul Osterman, *Good Jobs America* (New York: Russell Sage Foundation, 2011).

16. My own calculations suggest that the shrinking middle is mostly occurring in old-fashioned production and clerical jobs, which required virtually no postsecondary education but paid fairly good wages; demand is

actually rising in the newer middle where such credentials are increasingly needed, as in health care and other fields. See Harry J. Holzer, "Job Market Polarization and US Worker Skills: A Tale of Two Middles," Brookings Institution, 2015.

17. See Robert J. Gordon, *The Rise and Fall of American Growth: The U.S. Living Standards Since the Civil War* (Princeton, NJ: Princeton University Press, 2016). See also Martin Baily and Barry Bosworth, "Productivity Trends: Why Is Growth So Slow?" Brookings Institution, 2015.

18. In the past decade or so, the share of state budgets devoted to subsidizing higher education has declined a bit, although it has risen over the past several decades. See Sandy Baum, Charles Kurose, and Michael McPherson, "An Overview of American Higher Education," *The Future of Children* 23, no. 1 (2013).

19. CETA was replaced by the Job Training Partnership Act (JTPA) in 1982, which in turn was replaced by the Workforce Innovation Act (WIA) in 2000 and by the WIOA in 2014.

20. The 3,000 or so One Stop offices also provide worker access to other Labor Department programs and benefits like unemployment insurance. Any training provided by WIOA today comes in the form of Individual Training Accounts, which are vouchers that can be used for training at any approved local provider, including community colleges. But funding for these vouchers is very modest and mostly spent for very short-term training.

21. See the US Government Accountability Office, *Multiple Employment and Training Programs*, 2011. At the time, the GAO report listed a total of 46 different federal workforce development programs and suggested much overlap between them. But the vast majority are very small and target very specific populations. When WIOA was authorized in 2014, about a third of these programs were consolidated.

22. See David Fein, "Career Pathways as a Framework for Program Design and Evaluation" (working paper, US Department of Health and Human Services, Office of Program Research and Evaluation, 2012); and Sheila Maguire et al., *Tuning In to Local Labor Markets*, Public/Private Ventures, 2010.

23. The "hard-to-serve" are often defined as individuals with very low cognitive skills, physical or emotional disabilities, or other barriers to work

(such as having criminal records), which can also make them difficult to train, particularly in the STEM fields where strong basic reading and math skills are often required.

24. See Bridget Terry Long, "Addressing the Academic Barriers to Higher Education," in Melissa S. Kearney and Benjamin H. Harris, eds., *Policies to Address Poverty in America*, Hamilton Project and Brookings Institution, 2014; and Thomas Bailey et al., "Redesigning America's Community Colleges" (Cambridge, MA: Harvard University Press, 2015).

25. See National Conference of State Legislatures, "Performance-Based Funding for Higher Education," www.ncls.org.

26. The Department of Labor has recently begun providing funding to encourage more apprenticeships through its American Apprenticeship Grants program.

27. I believe that moderate increases in federal or state minimum wage levels (i.e., up to $10 or so) will raise incomes for a wide range of workers and families without jeopardizing many jobs, although I mostly oppose increases above that level. See the Congressional Budget Office, *The Effects of a Minimum Wage Increase on Employment and Family Income*, 2014. I also endorse efforts to increase the earned income tax credit (EITC) for childless adults to incentivize the hard-to-serve to accept low-wage employment. An effort to do so in New York City, called Paycheck Plus, is now under evaluation by MDRC.

IV

How Can We Make Work Pay?

Supporting Work, Inclusion, and Mass Prosperity

GLENN HUBBARD
Columbia University

Support for an economic system—and its political legitimacy—depends in no small part on its ability to generate benefits that are both substantial and broadly shared. While it goes without saying (or should) that policies that advance overall economic growth are beneficial, such policies may not be sufficient to raise incomes of low-wage individuals. Cross-sectional differences in labor force participation and earnings prospects highlight this concern. In this essay, I focus on inclusion, through policies to support *work* for low-wage individuals as opposed to incomes *per se* (through welfare programs, for example).

The present political climate in the United States and other major industrial economies reflects a suspicion of existing economic institutions' ability to generate work opportunities broadly and of politicians' interest in doing so. Indeed, frustration with mainstream political leaders on this point has led to calls to undermine the liberal order (in the classic sense) underpinning our economic spending or to increase welfare spending to take the place of lost opportunities for work and earnings.

Two framing problems have led us down this path that is healthy neither for the economy as a whole nor for low-wage workers in particular. The first relates to labor market policies dating back to the 1930s emphasizing temporary spells of unemployment, putting aside support for entry into the labor force and reemployment after long-term job loss. While federal retraining programs exist, labor market policy has not emphasized inclusion in the sense of continuous support for work by low-wage individuals. Indeed, though beyond the scope of this essay, existing policies underemphasize this objective by not being centered on work support *per se* and by raising implicit marginal tax rates on earnings, as in the phaseout of the earned income tax credit (EITC) or the phaseout of subsidies for health insurance in the Patient Protection and Affordable Care Act.

The second part of the problem in framing policies to support work—policies I think of as advancing *inclusion*—is that policy discussion is often narrow, about individual interventions, rather than about an agenda for inclusion. Framing such an agenda requires a look back at the importance of inclusion in the economic model on which the West's prosperity is founded.

By "model," I mean the 18th-century Enlightenment foundation of Adam Smith, David Hume, and others that ushered in mass prosperity by releasing individuals' enterprising spirits. This core Enlightenment idea embraced individual freedom to start a business without state approval and the ability to increase or decrease the business' scale. Smith particularly understood that such freedom would enhance innovation, productivity, and employment better than state-sanctioned monopolies. This conception centered on inclusion in the sense of open markets. But there was also a view that the free enterprise system would lack broad legitimacy if many were left out of its opportunities and rewards. The Scottish Enlightenment philosophers championed broad opportunity and the removal of state favoritism and bailouts of the connected (a lesson worth remembering today!). And the Scots advocated government interventions to support inclusion.[1]

Seen through this lens of foundations of mass prosperity, the failure of policymakers to advance inclusion has led to threats to that prosperity. The 2016 presidential campaign is replete with proposals from both Democrat and Republican candidates for regulation and protectionism that would retard innovation and productivity. As a lack of inclusion animates this flirtation with potentially ruinous economic policies, an alternative of low-wage subsidies for work is as obvious as it is too lightly addressed.

Bolder interventions for inclusion have faced opposition from many politicians on both the left and right. On the left, devotion to welfare assistance or public training programs fits poorly with the idea that private enterprise best advances prosperity. The right's view that low-wage employment subsidies are a budget cost to be avoided as interfering with market forces is also counter to the Enlightenment view. Many conservatives have traded off support for social insurance programs for support in limiting regulations and taxes. But such a trade-off misses the centrality of low-wage workers' need to participate in work and the advancement and satisfaction it brings.

To evaluate a policy pivot toward inclusion, I explore below reforms of the existing EITC to promote work and alternative subsidies to benefit the employment earnings of low-wage workers. I then place such reforms in the context of a broader policy agenda for inclusion and mass prosperity.

Supporting Work by Expanding the Earned Income Tax Credit

The EITC, introduced in 1975, offers a good place to start a discussion of polices to support work, as it is already a part of the federal tax system. The EITC is essentially a tax credit available to lower-income households with earned income. Because the tax credit is refundable, it is available to those with incomes too low to owe much, if any, federal income tax. Indeed, the bulk of EITC expenditure is via tax refunds (though some reforms have suggested advancing the credit).

That the EITC is an important part of the safety net is clear, with recent data showing that almost one-fifth of all tax filers and more than two-fifths of filers with children receive the credit.[2] Whether it supports work sufficiently is a more open question, as variation in EITC payments across households depends more on the number of children than the filer's work.[3]

Mechanically, the value of the credit is determined according to a benefit schedule with income regions: a phase-in of the credit, followed by a plateau and then a phaseout of the credit. That is, as the credit phases in, its value rises with each additional dollar earned, supporting work. Once the credit value is at its maximum, its value achieves a plateau, wherein incremental earnings do not raise the credit value. In the phaseout, the credit declines with earnings, raising the effective marginal tax rate on earnings (a potentially costly disincentive for work and advancement), until its value is zero. While amounts vary across taxpayers with no, one, two, or three or more children, this basic structure holds. Since its introduction, the credit has been expanded in 1987, 1993, and 2009 (this most recent change being set to expire in 2017). As of 2015, the maximum credit ranged from $503 for filers with no children to a more than fourfold increase of $6,242 for filers with three or more children.

Understanding Incentive Effects of the EITC

The EITC supports work by changing incentives on the extensive margin (whether to work) and the intensive margin (how much to work). Because the phase-in wage subsidies (negative marginal tax rates) are significant for households with children, the net-of-tax wage from starting work is boosted substantially for those households. The net effect as a work support of the EITC when the recipient is already working is more ambiguous. The phase-in region generates a positive substitution effect (from negative marginal tax rate) and a negative income effect (from the money transfer) on work. In the plateau and phaseout regions, negative incentives to increase work are present (as the phaseout generates a higher marginal tax rate on earnings). Incentives can be more complicated for married households. For example, to the extent the primary wage earner earns enough on his or her own to be in the credit phaseout range, the secondary earner can only decrease the couple's credit by working.

These economic effects have been explored empirically by economists.[4] The most significant effect found is the positive effect of the EITC on the labor force participation of single mothers with children, with extensive margin elasticities (with estimates between 0.30 and 0.45).[5]

Finally, economic intuition suggests that, to the extent the EITC increases labor force participation and hours worked, it could reduce pre-tax wages for low-skilled workers. That is, employers could capture a portion of the credit. Some evidence suggests this effect is present,[6] but statistical bounds suggest the need for additional research.

Refocusing the EITC on Support for Work

Returning to the general interest in work-support policies to stimulate initial attachment to work, a key area for reform is to extend the EITC's reach to childless workers. The EITC's origin in large part as an alternative to cash welfare for households with children shaped its early design toward households with children. If the objective is to support work in general and to compensate for eroding wages of low-income workers in particular, more support of childless workers is important. Such expansions have been put forth across the political spectrum by President Barack Obama, Speaker Paul Ryan, Governor Jeb Bush, and others. While moving in the direction of increasing the EITC available to childless workers, none of these proposals bring the value to childless workers close to that for workers with children.

One version toward that end, analyzed by Hoynes and Rothstein, would set the maximum credit for a single childless adult equal to the current level for a single adult with one child and keep the phase-in rate the same as for households with one child.[7] Hoynes and Rothstein set an income width for the plateau of $5,000 and a phaseout rate of 15.98 percent to equal that of the current one-child schedule. Such an expansion would cost $18.3 billion per year (in addition to the current $68.5 billion annual cost of the EITC),[8] nearly quintupling the average credit for childless workers.

Proposals to increase the generosity of the EITC must still confront links between the design of the credit and labor supply. For example, while the EITC has significant positive effects on labor force participation of single parents, it reduces the labor supply of married women as secondary earners.[9] Such an effect could be mitigated by a secondary earner deduction to lessen the penalty on the second worker[10] or a shift to a British-style tax system based on individuals, not households, to reduce tax rates on secondary earners (as proposed by Governor Jeb Bush in the 2016 presidential campaign).

To summarize, refocusing the EITC on support for work requires a significant expansion of the credit's generosity to childless workers. Such an expansion would promote incentives to participate in work, particularly for single individuals. If the EITC is to be the vehicle to promote inclusion, consideration could be given to design changes (within the EITC narrowly or the income tax system broadly) that reduce marginal tax rates on earnings in the credit's phaseout range and on earnings of secondary earners.

Considering a Broader Set of Policies to Advance Inclusion

Discussion of policy changes to advance inclusion often centers on EITC expansion and/or reform, given the program's experience and codification in both law and political acceptability. A more thoroughgoing rethinking of policy away from the short-term unemployment framing to which I referred in the introduction leads to other proposals to bolster wages to encourage entry into and ongoing participation in the labor force and to encourage reemployment of individuals who have lost their jobs. As with the EITC, there are promising policy ideas to consider.

The first relates to wage subsidies to boost labor demand. As my Columbia colleague and Nobel laureate Edmund Phelps has observed, the loss of opportunities for work implies more than just lost wages for directly affected individuals.[11] Such loss leads to negative externalities in crime, drug use, high tax rates to fund social assistance, and other ills. Phelps argues that funds to support work could be drawn from amounts saved by reducing negative externalities through low-wage subsidies for employment.

Conceptually, one simple such subsidy would be a lump-sum employment subsidy paid to firms that would be the same for all individuals. In this form, the wage support benefits low-skill, low-paid workers relatively more and all else equal reduces unemployment relatively more for these individuals. These effects are not offset if lump-sum taxes or decreases in government spending are used to fund the wage support. Alternatively, one could fund the wage subsidy with a proportional wage tax. The resulting subsidy to low-wage workers would remain relatively large. Higher-wage workers would face a higher net marginal tax rate on earnings. A graduated subsidy—akin to the structure of the EITC—further concentrates benefits on low-wage workers at a lower cost than a flat subsidy, but with the cost of elevated marginal tax rates on work in the phaseout income range of the subsidy.

Seen in this way, wage subsidies dominate the call for a much higher minimum wage in two respects (both applying to the EITC as well). The first basis is philosophical: what ethical benchmark countenances the loss of some job to boost the pay of those (needy or not) fortunate enough to keep their jobs? The second reflects economic efficiency, as the wage subsidy bolsters incomes without the decline in employment.

Wage subsidies for the able (for firms or the EITC) also dominate the call for greater welfare assistance or a guaranteed basic income. The alternatives that fail to support work not only deprive individuals of noneconomic benefits associated with work today (e.g., self-esteem and social connection), but also future such benefits and economic benefits of advancement and higher earnings made possible by continuous engagement in the labor force.[12] It is also ironic that prominent technology industry executives advancing a guaranteed basic income no doubt consider their own attachment to work as important—why not inclusion for all?

The second focuses on *reemployment*, with two additional alternatives as opposed to supplementing wages of those currently employed or encouraging labor force participation. The first alternative, *Personal Reemployment Accounts*, would combine for individuals likely to encounter a long spell of unemployment a fund to support income and retraining while unemployed with a reemployment bonus if a new job is found within a given period of time. President George W. Bush proposed the accounts in 2003,[13] and demonstration studies were conducted, although the proposal never became federal law. (Governor Mitt Romney proposed a similar idea in the 2012 presidential campaign.) The demonstrations revealed little take-up of training services (one policy goal), but significant success of the reemployment bonus in encouraging reemployment.

A second alternative to promote reemployment is *wage insurance*, paying a supplement to make up part of the gap between earnings from a new job and earnings from a better-paying job lost. Discussed for many years, wage insurance addresses the problem of diminished income after reemployment (as opposed to making up part of lost income during a spell of unemployment, as in traditional unemployment insurance).[14] Such assistance is quite limited in practice. Trade adjustment assistance, to supplement incomes of those who lost jobs because of trade, has been on the books since 1962, and was increased significantly as part of the Trade Act of 2002. Funding has been modest, though, and displaced workers include many more individuals than those whose job loss is attributable to trade per se.

As with the reemployment bonus[15] feature of Personal Reemployment Accounts, meaningful wage insurance can accelerate reentry to work, keeping the path of skill enhancement through employment. Absent wage insurance, income losses from reemployment can be large, especially for middle-aged workers for whom the period of loss is long. Wage insurance could be financed by increasing unemployment insurance taxes or by redirecting funds spent on federal training programs.

Conclusion

The policy options I have described are ambitious and, in some cases, a substantial incremental budget requirement for federal expenditure. Four observations are in order on this point. The first relates to the counterfactual: as I noted above, political support for pro-growth policy (a strong economic and budget gain) requires inclusion, and work supports may also diminish the need for social welfare spending on the same individuals. These trade-offs deserve serious policy and budget attention. Second, an evaluation of labor market policies and proposals and sources of funds from existing programs (including unemployment insurance and federal retraining programs) should be conducted, led within the Executive Office of the President by the Office of Management and Budget and the Council of Economic Advisers. Third, though beyond the scope of this essay, more attention needs to be paid to preparation for work for many individuals—education, yes, but also vocational training and retraining. Finally, and most important, budget decisions are about choices. Our economic system has a moral and political imperative for inclusion. Advancing that inclusion should require us to reduce tax expenditures and social spending on more well-to-do individuals. The current political *Sturm und Drang* notwithstanding, an agenda for inclusion is within our grasp.

Notes

1. In the American historical setting, such mass prosperity and inclusion themes can be most clearly seen in Abraham Lincoln's ambitious agenda for opportunity and inclusion—emphasizing emancipation, of course, but also the Homestead Act, land-grant colleges, and the transcontinental railroad.

2. Hilary W. Hoynes and Jesse Rothstein, "Tax Policy Toward Low-Income Families" (working paper, National Bureau of Economic Research, March 2016), http://www.nber.org/papers/w22080. See Marianne P. Bitler, Hilary Hoynes, and Elira Kuka, "Do In-Work Tax Credits Serve as a Safety Net?" *Journal of Human Resources* (March 8, 2016).

3. I will return later to supporting work via increases in labor force participation versus increases in hours worked conditional on participation.

4. Joseph V. Hotz and John Karl Scholz, "The Earned Income Tax Credit," in *Means-Tested Transfer Programs in the United States*, ed. Robert A. Moffitt (Chicago: University of Chicago Press, 2003), 141–97; and Austin Nichols and Jesse Rothstein, "The Earned Income Tax Credit" (working paper, University of California, Berkeley, March 2015), http://eml.berkeley.edu/~jrothst/workingpapers/nichols-rothstein-draft_Mar2015.pdf.

5. Raj Chetty et al., "Does Indivisible Labor Explain the Difference Between Micro and Macro Elasticities? A Meta-Analysis of Extensive-Margin Elasticities," *NBER Macroeconomics Annual* 27, no. 1 (2012): 1–56; and Hilary W. Hoynes and Ankur Patel, "Effective Policy for Reducing Inequality? The Earned Income Tax Credit and the Distribution of Income" (working paper, University of California, Berkeley, July 2015).

6. Jesse Rothstein, "Is the EITC as Good as an NIT?: Conditional Cash Transfers and Tax Incidence," *American Economic Journal: Economic Policy* 2, no. 1 (2010): 177–208.

7. Hoynes and Rothstein, "Tax Policy Toward Low-Income Families."

8. The Obama administration's proposal to increase the childless EITC is less generous and less costly, but would still more than double the average credit for childless workers relative to current law.

9. Nada Eissa and Hilary W. Hoynes, "Taxes and the Labor Market Participation of Married Couples: The Earned Income Tax Credit," *Journal of Public Economics* 88, nos. 9–10 (2004): 1931–58.

10. See Melissa S. Kearney and Lesley Turner, "Giving Secondary Earners a Tax Break: A Proposal to Help Low- and Middle-Income Families," Brookings Institution, December 4, 2013, http://www.brookings.edu/research/papers/2013/12/03-proposal-help-low-income-families-kearney.

11. Edmund S. Phelps, *Rewarding Work: How to Restore Participation and Self-Support to Free Enterprise* (Cambridge, MA: Harvard University Press, 1997).

12. Some proponents of a guaranteed basic income focus on its potential simplifying advantage of combining various targeted means of support for low-income individuals. As my focus here is on supporting work, I do not evaluate this admittedly promising feature of such proposals.

13. See Council of Economic Advisers, *Economic Report of the President*, US Government Printing Office, Washington, DC, 2003.

14. Design of a successful wage insurance program is complicated, owing in part to the potential for moral hazard, but unlike other labor market reforms it addresses lost income upon reemployment. Analysis can consider costs and effectiveness given different degrees of insurance and eligibility by income and age. See Robert J. La Londe, "The Case for Wage Insurance," Council on Foreign Relations, September 2007.

15. A lump-sum reemployment bonus can provide enhanced incentives for search for work before and after job loss. There is, however, need for more study of how the lump-sum bonuses affect the speed with which individuals return to work.

What Do We Really Know About the Employment Effects of the Minimum Wage?

JUSTIN WOLFERS
University of Michigan

A Google search for "Why not raise the minimum wage to $100 an hour" yields 601,000 results.[1] While undoubtedly popular—both on Google and with the general public—it's not actually a serious policy proposal to make work pay. Instead, it's a glib response too often offered by those opposed to raising the minimum wage whenever they are confronted with research showing that past minimum wage rises have not had unduly large disemployment effects.

There's a good reason not to raise the minimum wage to $100 per hour. It's the same reason why it can make sense to eat a few apples without eating a hundred. Eating one apple makes me better off because the marginal benefit of that first apple exceeds the marginal cost. And eating a second apple is also a good idea if the marginal benefit still exceeds the marginal cost. But at some point, the marginal cost exceeds the marginal benefit, and I'll stop buying apples. Buying one apple doesn't condemn me to buying a hundred. Instead, the best choice comes from comparing marginal benefits and marginal costs each step of the way.

The same logic should underlie any rational debate about the minimum wage.

But there's a chasm between this very simple logic and the minimum-wage debate today. The debate now centers on whether raising the minimum wage causes any job losses. But this isn't the relevant question for policy. Instead, each time you think about adjusting the minimum wage by a nickel, you should ask the same question you would ask when deciding whether to eat another apple: will the marginal benefit exceed the marginal cost? In this essay, I plan to highlight three fundamental problems in how existing evidence is typically used in the policy debate.

First, most research on the minimum wage answers a narrower question than the policy debate demands. Most studies measure how employment changed following an increase in the minimum wage. They tend to show that at relatively low levels, the disemployment effects of raising the minimum wage are quite small. I think of this as making the case that an effective social policy should include a minimum wage. But how high should that minimum wage be? A useful answer must be based on some sense of how the balance of marginal benefits and marginal costs changes as the minimum wage changes. Policymakers need to know how the employment effect varies at different minimum-wage levels.

Second, existing empirical studies have focused almost exclusively on the short-run effects of raising the minimum wage—the effects that are evident in the year of the change or, in the best cases, over the next few years. But useful policy emphasizes the long-run effects instead. Recent research has shown that the short run is not very informative about the long run.

Third, the minimum wage has been adjusted in a seemingly arbitrary fashion, with each wage hike proving to be effectively temporary, as inflation has eroded the real value of each wage hike. The half-life of a typical minimum-wage rise is only a handful of years. As a result, studies of these wage hikes accurately measure the consequences of temporary wage shocks. But temporary shocks likely yield different responses than permanent changes, and so existing studies say little about the likely consequences of more lasting changes in minimum wages.

Taken together, these three points suggest that we know far less about the optimal minimum wage than you might otherwise infer from the existence of hundreds of minimum-wage studies. Indeed, my reading is that there is profound uncertainty about the optimal minimum-wage level.

This ignorance does not undercut the argument that we should raise the minimum wage any more than it undercuts the argument that we should lower it. In medicine, the principle, "First, do no harm," might create a small-c conservative bias, leading surgeons not to tinker with poorly understood mechanisms. But there's no parallel principle in economics, and even if there were, it's not clear what it would entail. Inflation has reduced the real value of the minimum wage by a third since 1968.[2] Is allowing the minimum wage to wither in real terms really doing nothing? What does it mean to not change the policy in the face of changes in the economy—including ongoing productivity growth, changes in family finances, the skill level of minimum-wage workers, and the declining number of students working minimum-wage jobs?

This essay surveys what we know and don't know about the minimum wage, with an eye to broadening it beyond the question of whether disemployment effects exist. My goal is to provide guidance that will help policymakers better scrutinize the claims made about the consequences of alternative minimum-wage policies. A secondary purpose of this essay is to outline a research program for empirical labor economists to get closer to understanding the optimal level of the minimum wage.

Some Background and a Framework

The minimum-wage debate has reached a rather stale and fruitless standoff. Several high-profile quasi-experimental case studies in the early 1990s suggested that under some circumstances, raising the minimum wage might increase employment or perhaps leave it roughly unchanged. These findings dismantled the previous consensus that the minimum wage had large disemployment effects.

It also shifted the policy debate. Instead of debating how large or small the disemployment effects of the minimum wage were, the new debate became whether there was a disemployment effect at all. It may be true that over some range the minimum wage has no impact on employment. But unfortunately, the debate has become overly focused on the number zero, with the left insisting that raising the minimum wage leads to zero job cuts, and the right countering that the number is larger than zero.

This debate leaves us unprepared for the harder questions. It's easy to say that we should raise the minimum wage for as long as it continues to reduce inequality without causing job losses. But once we've reached the point where we face real trade-offs, a richer framework is required.

The minimum wage is a redistributional policy, and it should be evaluated as such. The marginal benefit of raising the minimum wage is the value of the redistribution that follows, putting money in the hands of low-wage workers, at the expense of capital owners, who get lower profits, and/or consumers, who pay higher prices. The marginal cost of raising the minimum wage is jobs that are lost when labor costs rise. The optimal policy involves raising the minimum wage until the point at which the marginal benefits no longer exceed the marginal costs.

This is where the empirical literature becomes important. The redistributional benefits of the minimum wage are relatively easy to measure. Exhaustive household surveys detail which families are most likely to gain from a higher minimum wage, as well as the extent to which different families are likely to bear the burden of higher prices or lower profits. As the minimum wage rises, the marginal beneficiary is less likely to be poor, suggesting that the higher the minimum wage, the lower this redistributional marginal benefit. These declining marginal benefits need to be compared with marginal costs of a higher minimum wage, which are the jobs lost. This framework points to the importance of measuring how many jobs would be lost at each level of the minimum wage.

Are the Estimates Policy-Relevant?

Minimum-wage studies evaluate disemployment effects of particular increases in the minimum wage, estimating the minimum-wage elasticity of labor demand. In mathematical terms, they're measuring *dlog (employment)/dlog (minimum wage)*—the change in employment resulting from a change in the minimum wage.

The problem is that there's not just one constant employment elasticity. Rather, it varies depending on the minimum-wage level. It's likely that raising the minimum wage from a high level yields larger job losses than when raising it by an equivalent amount from a lower level. This is both because a higher minimum wage affects more workers, and because a higher minimum shifts workers' wages more.

Empirical studies estimate a weighted average of this elasticity over the range of variation that is in the data—the average treatment effect. If this average treatment effect is small, it suggests that the jurisdictions being studied have typically had minimum wages that are too low. And if it's high, it suggests that the minimum wage was too high. But the average treatment effect says nothing about how much higher or lower the minimum wage should be.

Answering that question requires estimates of how the elasticity varies with the level of the minimum wage. It would be best if analysts could estimate the marginal treatment effect at each level of the minimum wage. Given data limitations, that is perhaps too much to hope for. But it may be feasible to estimate the rate at which the employment effects change. By this view, it would be more useful if future studies focus on measuring $d^2 \log(\text{employment}) / d\log(\text{minimum wage})^2$. It's a point that Alan Manning recently made, arguing: "Of course there is some level of the minimum wage at which employment will decline significantly. The literature should reorient itself towards trying to find that point."[3]

Such a reorientation is particularly pressing now, when proposed reforms would raise minimum wages to levels that lie outside of our historical experience. For instance, since 1979, the real value of the federal minimum wage—after adjusting for inflation—has varied between a low of $5.86 in June 2007 and a high of $9.29 per hour way back in January 1979. And even though the range of state minimum wages is wider, it is still limited. Over the same time period, the highest inflation-adjusted state minimum wage was only $10.35 (Alaska, in 1979!), and among the contiguous states, the maximum was $9.45 (the state of Washington, in 2009). These are the experiences that inform the empirical literature.

Figure 1. Real Minimum Wage, by State

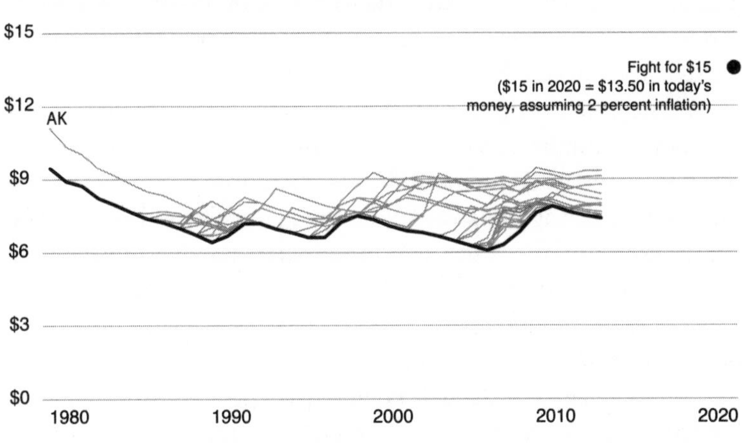

Note: Maximum of state and federal minimum wage in 2015 dollars, adjusted using the CPI-U-RS.

Source: Ben Zipperer and David Evans, "Where Does Your State's Minimum Wage Rank Against the Median Wage?," Washington Center for Equitable Growth, November 5, 2014, http://equitablegrowth.org/minimum-versus-median-wage-by-state/.

By contrast, the "Fight for $15" has already succeeded in getting the states of New York and California to commit to a $15 per hour minimum (by 2021 and 2022, respectively; roughly $13.50 in today's dollars).[4] Several cities—including Los Angeles, New York City, San Francisco, and Seattle—have also committed to phasing in similar increases.[5] There are also active campaigns in many other jurisdictions to raise the minimum wage to a similar level.

How then should we assess these proposals for a $15 minimum wage—or even a $10 or $12 minimum—which lie outside the range of domestic historical experience? As Figure 1 shows, most past adjustments lie in the $5 to $9 per hour range.

Historical experience alone can't predict the consequences of unprecedentedly high minimum wages. Thoughtful extrapolation must rely on other information. For example, it may be helpful to use calibrated models that rely more heavily on economic theory and an understanding of the behavior of workers and firms estimated from other contexts. Isaac Sorkin's recent paper, for example, yields a lot of insight.[6]

Another promising line of inquiry comes from noting that the effect of the minimum wage likely depends on its bite, relative to the rest of the wage distribution. As such, it is worth evaluating the minimum wage relative to the median wage and other measures describing the wage distribution. The median hourly wage of full-time employees in the United States in 2015 was $19.46. If it grows at a rate of 3.5 percent per year (reflecting roughly 2 percent inflation and 1.5 percent productivity growth), then a $15 minimum wage in 2022 will be about 61 percent of the median hourly wage. While this is fairly high by historical standards, it's not unprecedented. Indeed, from 1979 to 1981, the federal minimum wage was at least 60 percent of the median hourly wage in at least half a dozen (mostly poor) states.

One subtle issue arises when analyzing the ratio of the minimum wage to the median wage: the denominator of this ratio is itself a measure of the strength of the local labor market. Thus, even if the minimum wage has no effect on employment, a strong local labor market would both raise employment and lower this ratio. This negative correlation may make it look like there are large disemployment effects even where none exists. This problem arises when comparing the minimum wage with the current median wage. However, no such problem arises if comparing the minimum with a historical average or some other indicator.

The minimum wage is often higher in other countries, as Figure 2 illustrates. This highlights the value of cross-national comparisons. Most leading industrialized nations have a higher minimum wage than the US. For instance, the national minimum wage in Australia is close to $15 (USD) per hour, and the unemployment rate in Australia is 5.7 percent. Further study of the minimum wage in foreign countries would help us better understand the effects of the minimum-wage levels currently being debated in the United States.

Figure 2. Real Hourly Minimum Wage

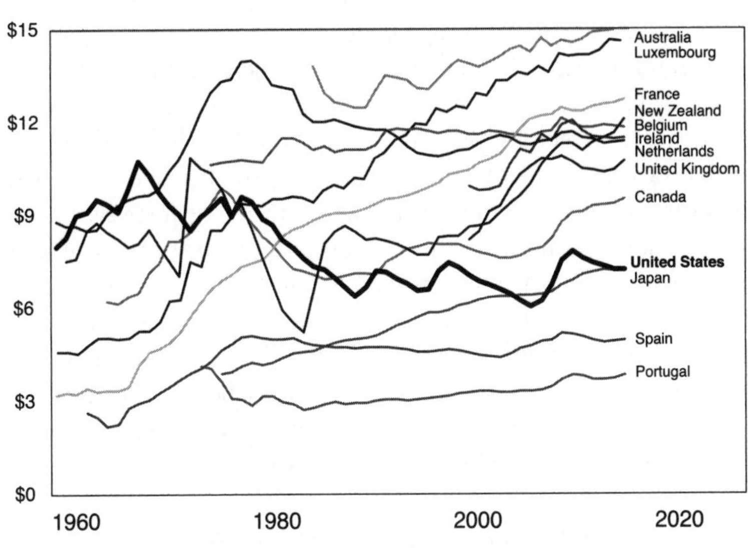

Note: Measured in 2014 prices, at 2014 exchange rates.
Source: Organisation for Economic Co-operation and Development, OECD.Stat, "Real Minimum Wages," https://stats.oecd.org/Index.aspx?DataSetCode=RMW.

Are We Analyzing the Right Outcomes?

The minimum-wage literature focuses on short-run effects. Perhaps the most famous study in the "new economics of the minimum wage"—the comparison by Card and Krueger of fast food restaurants in New Jersey and Pennsylvania—analyzed changes in employment roughly eight months after New Jersey raised its minimum wage.[7] Much of the literature follows in their footsteps, estimating either the contemporaneous relationship between the minimum wage and employment, or effects lagged by a quarter or perhaps a year.

But it's likely that adjustment to a higher minimum wage may take much longer. Standard analyses of labor demand point to two separate forces linking minimum wages and employment. The first is the "scale effect," where higher costs lead firms to raise prices, which leads consumers to buy less, causing the firm to scale back its production. This ultimately leads to less employment. It is likely that this response occurs relatively rapidly.

Second, there's a "substitution effect," where raising the relative price of labor leads firms to substitute toward alternative inputs instead. Most commonly, this takes the form of capital-labor substitution, where businesses invest in labor-saving machines. But such investments take time and may not be seen with the first year or two of a minimum-wage increase. For instance, high wages may lead supermarkets to install self-checkout scanners, but these need to be programmed and customized for each store, and then installed, and both staff and customers need to be trained. Higher minimum wages may also lead to substitution toward foreign labor as work gets offshored. Again, reorganizing the workplace so that some tasks remain and others are offshored is likely to take years.

Long-run effects may take even longer, when firms are reluctant to substitute toward new machines while their existing machines are still functioning well. A familiar analogy makes this point: higher gas prices won't lead you to immediately junk your SUV, but when your SUV finally reaches the end of its life span, you might replace it with a hybrid. And in the very long run, higher labor prices might spur research into new machines that replace low-skill workers, a process known as directed technical change.

The long-run adjustments discussed so far point to a higher minimum wage yielding larger job losses in the long run than in the short run. However, this need not be the case. In the short run, there's nothing that workers can do to adjust to the higher minimum wage, but in the longer run, they can invest in acquiring skills that make them more employable at higher wages. Moreover, a higher minimum wage provides more incentives for firms to invest in training, so that their workers have the skills needed to make their wages cost-effective.

Not only might these effects play out over a few years after a change in the minimum wage; some might occur in anticipation of a change. To minimize disruption, it may make sense to begin making adjustments as soon as it becomes clear that they will eventually be needed. And forward-looking investment decisions should reflect not only the current level of the minimum wage, but also announced future changes, as well as expectations of future changes.

The point is simply that adjustments to employment that occur contemporaneously with a minimum-wage hike likely don't represent the true long-term effect. Sorkin provides a calibrated model—an educated guess as to how the labor market works—which illustrates a rather striking finding.[8] He shows that both models in which the long-run elasticity is large and those in which it is small would lead to the sorts of small short-run employment elasticities typically found in most empirical studies. The point he makes—compellingly—is that existing studies are not very informative about long-run effects.

Are We Analyzing the Right Experiments?

The empirical literature typically focuses on policy "experiments," in which minimum wages are raised in some jurisdictions and outcomes are tracked and compared with those in comparable jurisdictions. The problem is that these experiments typically involve only temporary adjustments to the minimum wage, often with a half-life of only a few years. For instance, Card examined the increase in the minimum wage that was passed by Congress in November 1989, raising it over a year and a half from $3.35 to $4.25.[9] By September 1996, inflation had completely eroded the value of that 27 percent increase.

As Sorkin describes it, "the variation in the real value of the Federal minimum wage follows a 'sawtooth' pattern of regular nominal increases that are temporary because they are eroded by inflation."[10] The same pattern is also evident in state minimum wages for most of the period analyzed in the existing literature.

Since most of these reforms are temporary, the existing literature largely estimates the effect of a *temporary* increase in the minimum wage. This distinction is key, because employers likely respond differently to temporary rather than permanent wage changes. For instance, a permanent increase in the minimum wage might lead a store to invest in self-checkout machines. However, this investment might no longer be economical if it is only expecting to pay higher wages for a few years. Effectively, the more lasting the increase in the minimum wage, the longer the period over which labor-saving investments yield large wage-saving dividends.

Again, returning to an earlier analogy: the prospect of paying higher gas prices forever might lead you to replace your worn-out SUV with a hybrid. But if gas prices are going to be higher for only a few years, then buying a hybrid makes less sense because the future savings from buying less gas may no longer outweigh the higher purchase price up front. So too, a permanent change in labor costs may lead firms to invest in labor-saving machines, but a temporary blip will yield a more muted response.

A temporary minimum-wage shock also yields different dynamics than a permanent one. With a permanent shock, the firm's response likely builds through time, gradually approaching the long-run effect. An empirical study that pays careful attention to these long-run effects might plausibly capture the entire adjustment to this new long run. But with a temporary shock, the response is more muted relative to the effect of a permanent shock, because it has less of an effect on the net present value of future wage costs. Importantly, the effect likely becomes even more muted over time, as the wage increase is inflated away. As such, the dynamic response of employment to a temporary shock is entirely different than that in response to a permanent shock. The employment consequences of permanent shock likely grow through time, while those following a temporary shock may get smaller.

In turn, this may help explain why existing studies have failed to find substantial long-run employment effects following minimum-wage hikes. One might conclude that the long-term employment consequences of raising the minimum wage are small. But an alternative interpretation is that these studies are finding that the long-term employment consequences of *temporary* minimum-wage hikes are small.

The intuition for why temporary shocks don't yield substantial lasting effects on employment is straightforward: minimum-wage hikes typically don't yield large lasting effects on the *minimum wage*, and so their effects on employment are also likely to be passing.

This argument—that a temporary wage change won't yield much of a lasting employment effect because it doesn't have a lasting wage effect—holds true both in models in which a permanent wage change might have a small or large effect on employment. The point here—which, again, I owe to Sorkin—is that temporary shocks do little to sort out how sensitive employment would be to a lasting change in the minimum wage.[11] This suggests we should be even more cautious in interpreting the existing evidence.

One counterargument is that if most policy experiments are temporary, that it is sufficient to study the effects of temporary wage hikes. It is true that many reforms are temporary. But the more important policy choices are long-lasting. Policymakers in California, Oregon, Washington, and Washington, DC, have adopted higher minimum wages than in the rest of the country—this has been a lasting policy difference—even as their own adjustments have followed a sawtooth pattern. And over a period of decades, the US has adopted a low minimum wage relative to other industrialized nations. These are also persistent policy choices.

These persistent policy differences point to a need for research that is focused on estimating the lasting effects of lasting reforms. I see several ways forward. A number of states have passed reforms that yield more lasting minimum-wage hikes, with rates linked to automatic inflation adjustments. Brummund and Strain analyze 10 of these reforms, and as more data accumulate following these reforms, this approach should receive far more attention.[12]

The literature has also become overly focused on natural experiments. These experiments have the advantage of reducing the likelihood that the estimated effects are confounded by the effects of other factors. However, the cost is that nearly all of them estimate parameters that are of limited policy relevance—the short-run response of employment to a temporary wage shock. There is surely much to be learned from evaluating the effects of persistent differences, particularly because they are more likely to reveal the long-run effect of a lasting change in minimum-wage policy. The clear disadvantage is that it can be hard to be sure that these differences don't reflect other factors. Rather than controlling for these differences—as difference-in-difference analyses do—it might be worth analyzing them more carefully. In the absence of an ideal long-run natural experiment, there is a trade-off between analyzing minimum-wage changes that most closely approximate an experiment, and those that are most similar to the policy reforms under consideration. It's a trade-off between experiments that yield less biased estimates of less interesting parameters and cross-sectional differences that are more likely to yield more biased estimates of more policy-relevant parameters.

Concluding Thoughts

If you are interested in understanding the short-run effect of a temporary increase in the minimum wage, then the existing literature is tremendously helpful. Researchers have explored a number of plausible research designs and an array of useful datasets, and there is an emerging consensus—best summarized in Congressional Budget Office report—that the disemployment effects are likely very small.[13]

But if you are interested in what level to set the minimum wage, the existing literature is nearly hopeless. Plausible reforms lie far outside the bounds of historical experience. We don't have useful estimates of the extent to which employment effects vary with the minimum wage. Since policymakers tend to implement short-run fixes, we know a lot about the effects of temporary reforms, but very little about the consequences of lasting reform. And our existing estimates of the short-run consequences are consistent with there being small long-run effects as large.

Available estimates of the consequences of a $15-per-hour minimum wage are almost pure guesswork. Dylan Matthews, a journalist, recently wrote of a "really fascinating phenomenon: left-wing economists saying off the record that $15/hr is super-dangerous, but not saying that publicly."[14] I think that the economists he's speaking to are wrong. It's not that we know that the consequences of a high minimum wage are likely to be bad; it's that we have very little idea of what those consequences will be. The existing empirical literature gives very little useful guidance about the likely effects of a $15 minimum wage, leaving me profoundly uncertain. Research that helps fill this enormous void in our knowledge will be incredibly valuable to the policy debate.

Notes

1. Google, https://www.google.com/webhp?sourceid=chrome-instant&ion=1&espv=2&ie=UTF-8#safe=off&q=Why+not+raise+the+minimum+wage+to+%24100+an+hour%3F.

2. Council of Economic Advisers, "The Economic Case for Raising the Minimum Wage," February 12, 2014, https://www.whitehouse.gov/sites/default/files/docs/final_min_wage_slides_-_no_embargo.pdf.

3. Alan Manning, *The Elusive Employment Effect of the Minimum Wage*, Center for Economic Performance, 2016, 16, https://ideas.repec.org/p/cep/cepdps/dp1428.html.

4. New York State, "Governor Cuomo Signs $15 Minimum Wage Plan and 12 Week Paid Family Leave Policy into Law," April 4, 2016, https://www.governor.ny.gov/news/governor-cuomo-signs-15-minimum-wage-plan-and-12-week-paid-family-leave-policy-law; and Michele Haydel Gehrke, "California Passes Legislation to Phase-In $15 Minimum Wage by 2022," *National Law Review*, June 18, 2016, http://www.natlawreview.com/article/california-passes-legislation-to-phase-15-minimum-wage-2022.

5. Victor Luckerson, "Here's Every City in America Getting a $15 Minimum Wage," *Time*, July 23, 2015, http://time.com/3969977/minimum-wage/.

6. Isaac Sorkin, "Are There Long-Run Effects of the Minimum Wage?" *Review of Economic Dynamics* 18, no. 2 (April 2015): 306–33, http://www.sciencedirect.com/science/article/pii/S1094202514000283.

7. David Card and Alan B. Krueger, "Minimum Wages and Employment: A Case Study of the Fast-Food Industry in New Jersey and Pennsylvania," *American Economic Review* 84, no. 4 (1994): 772–93, http://davidcard.berkeley.edu/papers/njmin-aer.pdf.

8. Sorkin, "Are There Long-Run Effects of the Minimum Wage?"

9. David Card, "Using Regional Variation in Wages to Measure the Effects of the Federal Minimum Wage," *Industrial and Labor Relations Review*

46, no. 1 (October 1992): 22–37, http://davidcard.berkeley.edu/papers/fed-min-wage-var.pdf.

10. Sorkin, "Are There Long-Run Effects of the Minimum Wage?" 307.

11. Ibid.

12. Peter Brummund and Michael Strain, "Real and Permanent Minimum Wages" (working paper, American Enterprise Institute, February 2016), https://www.aei.org/wp-content/uploads/2016/02/brummund-strain-min-wage.pdf.

13. Congressional Budget Office, *The Effects of a Minimum-Wage Increase on Employment and Family Income*, 2014, https://www.cbo.gov/publication/44995.

14. Dylan Matthews, tweet, April 14, 2016, https://twitter.com/dylanmatt/status/720786520509165568.

V

Do Public Policies That Reduce the Reward to Work Significantly Diminish Labor Supply?

The US Safety Net and Work Incentives: Is There a Problem? What Should Be Done?

ROBERT A. MOFFITT
Johns Hopkins University

Whether the US safety net discourages work is an age-old question that has been debated by policymakers, researchers, and the general public. Despite the many years of discussion, it still is an important topic, no less so today than it has been in the past. However, while this essay is concerned primarily with the issue of whether the country's system of safety net programs discourages work, it should be stated at the outset that this is an overly narrow framing of the issues, for a consideration of work disincentives in safety net programs cannot be isolated from the purposes of those programs themselves and what they intend to accomplish. Most would agree with the broad view that safety net programs are intended to provide assistance to those families, adults, and children who are in particularly dire need and circumstances, and that assistance should be provided in a way that leads to an improvement in the families' situations and that provides a route out of their desperate straits. Simply framing the question as whether safety net programs encourage or discourage work risks losing sight of the overarching goals we should be trying to achieve.

Nevertheless, the place to start is with the narrow question of whether the US system of safety net programs discourages work. The bulk of this essay will be devoted to that question. Only at the end will it turn to the broader issue, and that is where a number of policy changes will be proposed to address that broader issue. But on the narrow question, the essay will demonstrate the following points. First, the work disincentives in most safety net programs, taken individually, are modest and unlikely to have a major impact on work effort. Second, work disincentives are quite a bit higher for families who receive benefits from multiple programs, but the percentage of low-income families who receive multiple benefits is too small to make this an important factor. Third, the availability of tax credits to low-income families has a major impact in reducing work disincentives to families with very low incomes. Fourth, however, work disincentives are considerably greater for families with slightly higher incomes but who are still poor or almost poor. Fifth, work disincentives for families with very low incomes have dramatically fallen over the past 30 years while those for higher-income but still poor families have risen. At least the first of these trends is good news for those concerned about work effects of safety net programs. Sixth, the recent expansion of the Medicaid program and associated creation of health insurance exchanges have a variety of positive and negative work incentives whose net effect is unclear at this time. Seventh, the research evidence on whether financial work disincentives actually have an effect on work behavior shows very modest effects for most programs, with only occasional exceptions.

Despite what may seem to be a sanguine and optimistic view of the work disincentives in the nation's safety net programs, I will conclude that the system is doing very little at the moment to help families help themselves, and this is where policy could be markedly improved.

Work Incentives in US Safety Net Programs

The US system of safety net programs—or what analysts call means-tested programs, those for which eligibility requires that family or individual income or earnings fall below certain levels—is quite complex, and that complexity cannot be completely avoided when discussing the programs and their effects on work incentives. Different programs serve different needy groups and operate differently, and they have different, often complicated, structures of work disincentives that affect some families differently than others.

For a consideration of work incentives, the key traditional concept is that of the benefit-reduction rate, or BRR (sometimes also called the marginal tax rate), which denotes the rate at which benefits are reduced as income rises. A high BRR generally is interpreted as having higher work disincentives, and a low BRR is generally interpreted as having smaller work disincentives. The BRR varies dramatically across different safety net programs. For example, the second-largest program in the country in terms of recipients is the Supplemental Nutrition Assistance Program (SNAP), formerly known as Food Stamps, which provides food assistance to low-income families. It has an approximate 24 percent BRR after taking account of deductions. But the largest program in the country is the Medicaid program, which provides medical assistance to low-income families. Aside from some minor copays, the program has a 0 percent BRR up to the eligibility point—that is, benefits are not reduced as income rises—and then has a BRR in excess of 100 percent at the point at which eligibility is lost. That is, benefits drop to zero for work beyond that point, and the family's effective income not only does not rise, but actually drops. (The Affordable Care Act has an impact on this feature, as described below.) The third-largest program is the National School Lunch Program, which provides free or reduced-price lunches to low-income children. It also has a 0 percent BRR up to a certain income level (130 percent of the poverty line), but beyond that the child can only receive a reduced-price lunch, effectively representing a positive BRR. Then, as in the Medicaid program, subsidies are lost entirely when income goes beyond the income eligibility level. Other important programs are the Women, Infants, and Children program, which provides nutritional education and food purchase support for pregnant women and those with young children, and which has a 0 percent and 100 percent BRR as in the Medicaid program; subsidized housing programs, which have an approximate 30 percent BRR; and the Supplemental Security Income (SSI) program, which provides cash support to low-income disabled and aged individuals and which has a 50 percent BRR. The Temporary Assistance for Needy Families (TANF) program, serving low-income families with children, is smaller than any of these and has a BRR that ranges widely across states but averages about 40 percent.

In a special category are tax credits, particularly the well-known earned income tax credit (EITC) and the child tax credit (CTC), both administrated through the tax system and the IRS. While not ordinarily thought of as safety net programs, they are essentially equivalent because they provide benefits only to families with incomes below certain levels. These tax credit programs have negative BRRs, meaning that additional income actually increases the tax benefit incurred. The EITC BRR can be as high as –45 percent, which is a major subsidy to work, while the CTC has a smaller negative BRR and provides credits much lower in magnitude than those in the EITC. However, both tax credits are phased out eventually, and the BRR in the phaseout region—where additional income lowers the tax credit—can be high, as high as 21 percent for the EITC, for example.

Are these financial penalties large or small? On intuitive grounds and before considering any research evidence, that is a difficult question to answer. However, one criterion is to compare these BRRs to the top marginal tax rate in the federal income tax. That top rate is almost 40 percent, so one criterion to use is to ask whether the BRRs in safety net programs are above the rate paid by the highest-income families in the society. By this criterion, the 100 percent rates in Medicaid and a few food programs for low-income families are obviously high. However, it should be kept in mind that most people don't really look at the effect of earning one more dollar but rather the effect of working full-time instead of part-time, or of working part-time or not at all. The BRR created by the Medicaid program is much less than 100 percent for those choices but could still approach 40 percent. However, the SSI BRR of 50 percent would also seem high when compared to the 40 percent tax criterion as well. But the other programs have BRRs less than 40 percent and, of course, the tax credits have negative BRRs.

While this implies that the individual BRRs in safety net programs are usually not excessive, it misses the fact that many families receive benefits from multiple programs. In that case, increases in income can result in greater total BRRs, as several benefits are phased out at the same time. Take, for example, a family receiving benefits from SNAP and TANF and who is living in subsidized housing. The Congressional Budget Office (CBO) has calculated that BRRs for such a family in 2012 ranged from 17 to 52 percent at very low incomes (e.g., below $10,000 annually) but rose to 66 to 95 percent at somewhat higher ranges (e.g., $10,000 to $20,000).[1] Moreover, these total BRRs include the federal tax credits; in their absence, the BRRs at very low incomes would be even higher. These rates also exclude the Medicaid program, which, as noted above, should add a high 100 percent BRR at the point at which eligibility is lost (typically around $7,000 of income in 2012). By the criterion used above—anything above 40 percent should be regarded as excessive—these BRRs are very high indeed.

However, such calculations greatly overstate the problem because the fraction of families who actually participate in multiple programs is modest. Table 1 shows the fractions of US low-income families participating in multiple programs in 2013 separately by whether their private income is below 50 percent of the official government poverty line or between 50 percent and 100 percent of that line. Among all families in the lower income range, 45 percent—almost half—receive benefits from no programs at all. Another 30–31 percent receive benefits from only one program, with sole receipt of SNAP the most common. Another 17 percent receive benefits from only two programs, and only 1 percent receive all three of the programs used in the CBO example just described. The percentages are even smaller for those with slightly higher income ranges but still in poverty. They are larger for single-parent families, but even for them, only 4 percent of families receive the three programs. There is no other program combination that has more than 1 percent of families participating in it.

However, this table excludes Medicaid, which, as already noted, is the most widely received program. But when Medicaid is added in, CBO calculations show that the largest and most common multiple-benefit receipt combination among low-income families

Table 1. Percent of US Low-Income Families Receiving Multiple Safety Net Benefits, 2013

	All Families		Single-Parent Families	
	Very Low Income	Low Income	Very Low Income	Low Income
No Program	45	58	25	30
One Program Only				
SNAP	23	24	32	41
TANF	<1	0	<1	0
Housing	2	1	2	3
SSI	5	4	2	3
Two Programs Only				
SNAP, TANF	2	1	5	2
SNAP, Housing	7	5	14	13
SNAP, SSI	8	3	6	3
Three Programs				
SNAP, TANF, Housing	1	1	4	4

Notes: Very-Low-Income Families have private income between 0 and 50 percent of the government poverty line. Low-Income Families have private income between 50 percent and 100 percent of the government poverty line.
Source: Author calculations from the Survey of Income and Program Participation.

with children is simply the combination of Medicaid and SNAP, which was received by 10 percent of all families with income below 250 percent of the poverty line and 22 percent of single-parent families in 2012.[2] For families receiving only SNAP without Medicaid, but receiving all federal tax credits and also paying payroll taxes and other state and federal income taxes, the median BRR for families with very low incomes was only 13 percent, and it was only 24 percent for those with incomes just below the poverty line.[3] If Medicaid is lost around $7,000 of income, the latter BRR would not be affected, but the former would be higher, depending on what range of earnings one were to examine, although it would still be modest if a wide range were considered. The CBO estimates these BRRs to be almost identical in 2016, after the implementation of the Affordable

Care Act, with the only difference that Medicaid in some states will not be lost until much higher income levels are reached (see below).[4]

Another approach to the question of what BRRs are for low-income families who receive multiple benefits is to calculate the total amount of benefits received by all families at different levels of income, and to determine how those totals change as family income rises. Column 1 of Table 2 shows those figures for low-income families in 2013. Families with very low private incomes in that year received, on average, $442 in total monthly benefits from the 12 leading programs (excluding Medicaid), including families who received nothing. Table 1 showed that 45 percent of these families were in this category. Families with somewhat higher incomes, but still below the poverty line, received $590, a greater amount because of tax credits from the EITC and CTC, which disproportionately flow to those families with higher incomes. This implies a BRR of −18 percent for a family moving from a very low income to a low income. But for families with income just above the poverty line, only $332 are received per month, implying a BRR of 30 percent when moving from income just below the poverty line to income just above it. For single-parent families, the first BRR is about the same, at −19 percent, but the BRR at the higher income levels is greater, at 42 percent. This is because single-parent families receive more benefits than other families, and hence more benefits are lost as income rises.

These figures show that work incentives are unlikely to be much of a problem for very-low-income families, even if payroll taxes and Medicaid were added, for BRRs are negative without those programs and would be positive but small with them. Work incentives are more of an issue for families with higher incomes who, when working more, face both the loss of traditional safety net benefits as well as a phaseout of the tax credits. However, one cannot have one without the other. If work is subsidized for families with very low incomes, then those subsidies have to be phased out later unless they are continued all the way up to high-income families, which would make the programs no longer means-tested. An important question is whether the larger BRRs for higher-income families induce less work among them, and the answer to that question

Table 2. Total Real Monthly Benefits Received and Benefit-Reduction Rates for US Low-Income Families, 1983 and 2013

	2013	1983
All Families		
Average Monthly Benefits		
Very Low Income	$442	$606
Low Income	590	255
Near Poverty	332	168
Benefit-Reduction Rate (BRR)		
From Very Low to Low Income	–0.18	0.42
From Low Income to Near Poverty	0.30	0.10
Single-Parent Families		
Benefit-Reduction Rate (BRR)		
From Very Low to Low Income	–0.19	0.75
From Low Income to Near Poverty	0.42	0.12

Notes: Nonaged, nondisabled families only. Very Low Income corresponds to private income between 0 and 50 percent of the poverty line, Low Income corresponds to private income between 50 and 100 percent of the poverty line, and Near Poverty corresponds to private income between 100 and 150 percent of the poverty line. Total benefits are the sum of actual benefits, received from SNAP, TANF, subsidized housing, SSI, General Assistance, WIC, veterans benefits, other cash welfare, the EITC and CTC, and social insurance benefits from Unemployment Insurance and Social Security retirement in real 2009 dollars. The BRR is calculated as the change in benefits divided by $833 of monthly private income, which is the change in monthly income from moving from the midpoint of each poverty rate to the midpoint of the next higher range. Payroll and income taxes other than the EITC and CTC are ignored.
Source: Author calculations from the Survey of Income and Program Participation.

should come from a review of the research evidence on the issue, reviewed below.

Table 2 also shows corresponding figures for BRRs in 1983, 30 years prior. In that year, receipt of benefits from the Aid to Families with Dependent Children (AFDC), the precursor to TANF, was high. In addition, the EITC was much smaller in generosity, and the CTC had not been enacted. As a consequence, BRRs for all very-low-income families was a positive 42 percent and was a very high 75 percent for very-low-income, single-parent families. But the BRR at higher income levels was only 10 to 12 percent. These results show how work disincentives have changed over the last 30 years for US low-income families: they have dramatically fallen for very-low-income families while they have risen for higher-income families. The major source of this change has been the major reduction in receipt of AFDC and TANF benefits for nonworkers, on the one hand, coupled with an increase in tax credits for higher-income families, on the other.

The impact of the Affordable Care Act on these BRRs is an important new consideration when thinking about work incentives among low-income families, for the act changes some of the financial penalties associated with work by low-income families, especially for those receiving Medicaid. For states who adopt the Medicaid plans in the law, the law requires an increase in the upper income limit for eligibility from its past levels, which have often been less than half of the government poverty line, to 138 percent of the poverty line. Such an increase in eligibility will provide greater work incentives to those who might have been dissuaded from work by the 100 percent BRRs at low-income levels existing before the law, for now Medicaid eligibility will only end at a much higher income level. In addition, the provision of health care exchanges means that when Medicaid eligibility ends, health insurance coverage will not end completely but will transition to a government-subsidized plan, thus eliminating the high 100 percent BRRs altogether. In addition, even without any change in the Medicaid program, the introduction of the exchanges will mean that low-income families who were not working or working at low levels will now have a greater incentive to work enough to qualify for exchange coverage, which they may not have had before if they could only find uncovered jobs. This effect will occur even for families in states that do not adopt the new Medicaid program.

As against these positive effects on work, the ACA has negative effects as well. The Medicaid provisions extend coverage to childless adults and some adults with children, and that will induce some increase in work disincentives because such families will now be offered benefits if not working that they did not have before.

(Although, again, this will be ameliorated by the introduction of the exchanges, so there will still be an incentive to work up to 138 percent of the poverty line.) There are also new work disincentives for families at higher income levels, especially above 150 percent or 200 percent of the poverty line, because of the introduction and phase-out of the exchange subsidies. However, while they are important for policy more generally, these effects are not of major importance to the low-income families under discussion here.

There are many other complicated features, and possible effects, of the ACA on work incentives other than these simple ones. However, those will make the net effect of the ACA on work incentives of low-income families even more uncertain than they already are. Actual evidence on how families respond must be obtained to understand the implications of this important new government policy for work among the poor.

What We Know About How Families Respond to Work Incentives

There has been a tremendous amount of research on the work disincentives of safety net programs and the specific effect of changes in the BRRs in those programs. The largest body of research has been conducted on the TANF program, but a significant number of studies have been conducted for the SNAP, Medicaid, and EITC programs as well. A much smaller amount of research has been directed to subsidized housing, SSI, and child food programs. The interesting conclusion one draws from this research is that, despite the obvious financial incentives and disincentives created by the sometimes high BRRs just described, it is actually very difficult to find in this literature much evidence of large effects on work effort for any of these programs.

One important aspect of the question worth noting at the start is that much of the research literature has concerned itself with whether safety net programs have work-disincentive effects because they provide high levels of benefits to nonworkers. That can occur even if the BRR is low. The main issue I am discussing in this essay is the effect of the BRR per se, and it should be stressed that that is not the only issue when discussing the total effects of safety net programs on work.

The large volume of research conducted on the TANF program has mostly concentrated on the effects of the landmark 1996 welfare reform law on levels of work among single mothers. Here the evidence is very strong that that law increased average employment rates and hours of work among that group. Single mothers on the program prior to reform never worked more than 10 percent of the time, yet their employment rates jumped to over 60 percent or more after leaving the welfare rolls.[5] However, most of the positive effects of the law were the result of moving single mothers off welfare, not from increasing work incentives for those on the program. The reductions in the BRR that accompanied the law have not resulted in high levels of work among remaining beneficiaries, among whom only about a third worked in 2013, and that was probably more because of work participation requirements than low BRRs.[6]

The largest program, Medicaid, has also seen a number of studies examining its effects on work effort. Most of these do not directly examine the effect of changing the BRR but rather the overall effects of making families eligible in the first place. Some have studied the major expansions of eligibility that occurred in the 1980s and early 1990s on work levels. Most of those studies have found essentially no statistically significant impact of those expansions. A handful of studies have looked at expansions of eligibility to adult parents and even childless adults, and here there is a considerable range of estimates, ranging from, again, no effects at all to fairly sizable ones.[7] And, as I have already noted, the implementation of the ACA is too recent for much research to have been conducted on it.

One important issue discussed in this research literature is that a program like Medicaid could have smaller effects on work levels than expected because it only subsidizes medical care, not larger needs. Most low-income families would spend very little on medical care themselves in the absence of the program, and hence receiving free medical care from the government does little to free up income to spend on other things. A plainer way to state the problem is: you can't eat Medicaid, or use it to pay the rent or buy clothes for your children. You still have to find income for those items, and that generally means that you have to work.

Studies of the second-largest program, SNAP, have likewise found almost no significant effects on work levels of recipients.[8] There are certain methodological challenges in researching work effects of the program that make it difficult to study, and hence the conclusion that it has almost no work disincentives has to be treated cautiously. In addition, the one study that did find important negative effects was a study of the program in the 1970s, when the program and the general safety net environment were quite different than what they are today. Again, some have suggested that the reason for the lack of an important effect is the noncash nature of the benefit. Unlike with Medicaid, however, most low-income families would spend quite a bit of income on food in the absence of the program, so the program more easily frees up income for spending on other things. But the amount of income freed up is limited because the benefit itself is not large. It is difficult to imagine how a nonworking family could survive on SNAP and Medicaid alone, without other sources of income like earnings.

The EITC is the only other program that has been studied extensively. And here the largest effects have shown positive effects on work levels, not negative ones.[9] Those effects have been most marked for single mothers. The effects of the positive and fairly high BRRs for somewhat-higher-income families during the phaseout of the tax credit may, however, be the cause of the findings from some studies that married women reduce their hours of work by a modest amount because of the program. If their spouses are earning enough to put the family into the phaseout region of the program, additional work by married women reduces the benefit.

The lack of responsiveness to BRRs and other program features in this body of research is most likely for a combination of reasons, including that the BRRs are often not excessive together with the noncash nature of the benefit. It should be emphasized that it does not imply that there might not be significant work disincentives from BRRs that are excessively high. Furthermore, it should also be emphasized that the nature of the research on these programs does not imply that absolutely no recipient works less or earns less because of the program, only that in aggregate, the responses are too small to be detected statistically, and that may be because other determinants of whether a low-income family works swamp the effects of BRRs.

Broadening the Question

Despite the evidence that financial penalties to work are not large for most low-income families and that those penalties that exist do not have major negative impacts on work levels, it is still the case that some BRRs are large for some families and for some programs. Lowering those BRRs would be a reasonable strategy, although its limits need to be understood. Removing the 100 percent BRRs for programs and states that still have them, which result in sudden losses of benefits after a family obtains a single extra dollar of income, could be addressed by a more gradual phaseout achieved by copays tied to income (as in the ACA exchanges). Such a lowering of the BRR would simply spread out the phaseout of the benefit over a wider range of income instead of concentrating it at one income point. It would also increase, not decrease, the caseload of the program and government expenditures. Lowering the BRR in SSI below 50 percent would have the same effect, for example, and lowering some of the high total BRRs in the phaseout region of the EITC would extend eligibility for the program even higher up into the income distribution than it goes already. These are the trade-offs that must be faced when thinking about a strategy of using lower BRRs to encourage more work.

Given the limits on this strategy, others should be considered. One popular strategy is to increase work incentives for the poor by making work pay more than it does now through improving access to child care, transportation, and jobs programs. This would be a meritorious policy reform that would be equivalent to lowering the BRR because it effectively increases the net financial reward to work, and the research evidence on the EITC shows that it could have a positive effect on work levels of the very poor. But it should be kept in mind that the BRRs for very-low-income families are fairly low already. In addition, one has to keep firmly in mind the inevitable trade-off, which is that increasing work supports to the working poor means that BRRs have to be increased for families with slightly higher levels of income, which are already fairly high. Further, this strategy does nothing for the families who struggle to find jobs and cannot find them.

Another strategy would be to increase the human capital and work skills among the poor, either through better funding and more effective job training strategies for adolescents and young adults, improvements in K–12 educational quality, or investments in preschool education. Such policies are very attractive, but they are long-run strategies at best and do not address the problem of what kind of support to provide low-income families in the short run, families with immediate needs.

Another approach would be to follow the TANF strategy, which has increased work levels among single-parent families. However, that strategy has serious drawbacks. While work levels were increased by those reforms, incomes have only increased modestly on average and have decreased for some families. Deep poverty among single-parent families is the same today as it was before 1996 and has increased as a percent of total poverty among such families. The combined effect of work requirements, time limits, and block grants fixed in nominal terms has had the effect of reducing to 3 percent the fraction of single-parent families in deep poverty who receive TANF benefits, which puts downward pressure on their incomes. The work requirements imposed by the 1996 law and later modifications of it are rigid and inflexible, and do little to increase the long-run work skills of the poor and have led many states to simply shed families with poor work skills from the welfare rolls.

While work requirements as implemented in TANF are not achieving all the goals one might want, however, the idea that low-income families have an obligation to perform if they receive benefits is an attractive one. A broader and more flexible conceptualization of those obligations is worthy of serious consideration.

What may be needed are activity requirements, not work requirements, where activity requirements are those which involve some effort among low-income families to improve their situation. It may be through job training, education, or work, for example, which are all beneficial in the long run. For families with special problems like substance abuse or poor health more generally, it may be attending a substance abuse treatment program or visiting health care providers. For families with children, it may mean keeping the children in school or ensuring that they make health care visits on a regular basis. To make these activity requirements effective and not just an excuse to continue receiving benefits without effort, however, programs would have to actually be made available to families and offered to them. They would have to be offered training and education opportunities, supported work environments, substance abuse programs, good health care providers, and adequate child care to enable them to work. Such programs and others of a similar nature deserve further study to address one of the nation's most serious policy challenges.

Acknowledgments

The author would like to thank Gwyn Pauley for assistance with many of the statistics presented in this essay and Eugene Steuerle for comments.

Notes

1. See Congressional Budget Office, *Effective Tax Rates for Low- and Moderate-Income Workers: Data Underlying Figures*, November 15, 2012, Figure 2, https://www.cbo.gov/publication/43709.

2. Ibid., 13, box 1.

3. Ibid., 24, Figure 5.

4. See Congressional Budget Office, *Effective Marginal Tax Rates for Low- and Moderate-Income Workers in 2016: Data Underlying Figures*, November 19, 2015, p. 55, Figure 4, https://www.cbo.gov/publication/50923.

5. James P. Ziliak, "Temporary Assistance for Needy Families," in

Economics of Means-Tested Transfers, ed. Robert A. Moffitt (Chicago: University of Chicago Press, forthcoming).

6. See US Department of Health and Human Services Office of Family Assistance, "Work Participation Rates: Fiscal 2013," Table 1A, http://www.acf.hhs.gov/programs/ofa/resource/wpr2013.

7. Thomas Buchmueller, John C. Ham, and Lara D. Shore-Sheppard, "The Medicaid Program," in *Economics of Means-Tested Transfers*.

8. Janet Currie, "Food and Nutrition Programs," in *Means-Tested Transfer Programs in the United States*, ed. Robert A. Moffitt (Chicago: University of Chicago Press, 2003), 199; and Hilary Hoynes and Diane Whitmore Schanzenbach, "US Food and Nutrition Programs," in *Economics of Means-Tested Transfers*.

9. Austin Nichols and Jesse Rothstein, "The Earned Income Tax Credit," in *Economics of Means-Tested Transfer Programs*.

The Rise of Employment Taxation

CASEY B. MULLIGAN
University of Chicago

Dozens of public policy changes have eroded the reward to work, especially through additional employment taxation. Little, if any, legislation is on the books that would return taxes and subsidies to what they were before the 2008–09 recession. These public policy changes make it likely that, measured in per capita terms, the labor market will remain depressed as compared to what it was.

The Distinction Between Employment and Income Taxes

Earning an income is perhaps the most important reason that people work. By taking away part of the income from work, personal income and payroll taxes remove some of the incentive to work. The same principle applies when government benefits are withheld or "phased out" from families on the basis of their income. The former are explicit taxes because even the politicians refer to them as taxation, whereas the latter are implicit taxes because they are officially labeled as "benefits." Either way, the workers find that they keep only part of what they earn, with the other part helping federal and state treasuries with more revenue received or fewer benefits paid out.

A number of households experience both explicit taxes and income phaseouts, and thereby face especially high disincentives for earning income.[1]

However, in addition to various implicit and explicit taxes on income, there are also implicit and explicit taxes on employment and hours worked that would be discouraging work even if there were not any income taxes, payroll taxes, or means-tested benefits. The employment and hours taxes (hereafter "employment taxes") are revenues paid to, or benefits withheld by, the Treasury on the basis of how many weeks or months that a person is employed, with little regard to the annual income of the worker or her family. The 2010 Affordable Care Act (ACA) features a penalty on large employers who do not offer affordable health insurance to their employees. By 2017, the penalty will be the equivalent of $3,449 per full-time employee-year on the payroll, regardless of how rich or poor the employees are.[2]

There are also benefits that are withheld on the basis of employment. Unemployment benefits, which were enhanced by several pieces of legislation in 2008 and 2009, are an implicit employment tax because they are withheld from individuals during the weeks that they are employed.[3] The American Recovery and Reinvestment Act (ARRA) included a major implicit employment tax because most workers were ineligible for its health insurance assistance as a consequence of their employment status.[4]

In some instances, the work requirements in the SNAP (formerly Food Stamps) and cash assistance programs are a kind of employment subsidy because the benefits are withheld for *not working*. It follows that the *removal* of work requirements has many of the same effects of a new implicit employment tax. Prior to 2009, the removal of SNAP work requirements was linked (at the state level) to federal unemployment benefits. The ARRA waived all states through October 2010. As recently as fiscal year 2015, 36 states remained eligible for statewide waivers.[5]

Disability benefits are an implicit employment tax because they are withheld from persons engaged in gainful employment. I am not aware of statutory changes in disability insurance (DI) eligibility or benefit rules since 2007, but statutory changes are not necessary for DI's effective employment tax rate to increase over time because reductions in worker pay in segments of the economy reduce the opportunity costs of DI participation for those workers.[6] It is also possible that DI application reviewers can become more lenient in a tough economy.[7]

The ACA includes health insurance assistance that is more permanent and ambitious than the ARRA's was, and thereby creates a larger implicit employment tax. In particular, the ACA says that full-time employees and their families cannot receive subsidized health coverage on the ACA's health insurance exchanges unless their employer fails to offer affordable coverage. In other words, employees of a business that offers insurance coverage will only receive the new government subsidies if they work part-time or spend time off the payroll entirely.[8] This is, in effect, an implicit tax on full-time employment.[9] The forgone subsidies include cost-sharing assistance—federal dollars that reduce a family's health insurance deductibles and copayments—as well as premium assistance administered through the federal personal income tax. Altogether, these subsidies can easily be worth more than $10,000 per year.

Much attention has been given to the fact that the new health insurance subsidies are income-tested and thereby create an implicit income tax.[10] I agree that a new income tax has been created, which by itself discourages work among those who are, or would be, employed while they participate in an exchange plan. But for every one of them, there are many more workers for whom the subsidies are an employment tax, because changing their employment status—not their income—is the only way that they can obtain the assistance.

I estimate that almost half of nonelderly household heads and spouses who would have been working full-time without the ACA will directly experience at least one of the ACA's employment taxes. Moreover, the size of the work disincentive can be staggering. A minimum-wage worker, for example, would have to work nine hours per week every week of the year just to create enough value to pay the penalty that his for-profit employer owes because he is on the full-time payroll, and this does not even count the work time needed to create enough value to pay other taxes and to provide for take-home pay for the worker himself.

Of course, most workers earn more than the minimum wage and have various family and employment situations. Figure 1 shows two histograms, reproduced from Mulligan,[11] of the weekly work-hour equivalent of the penalties and subsidies in the amounts that apply in

Figure 1. The Hour-Equivalent Distribution of the ACA's Employment Taxes (based on two hourly wage measures and a 25 percent exchange-features discount)

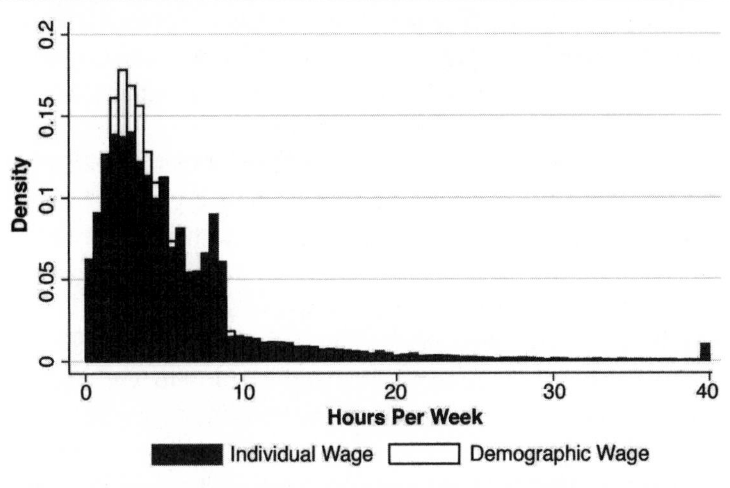

Source: Casey B. Mulligan, "The New Full-Time Employment Taxes," *Tax Policy and the Economy* 29 (2015): 89–132.

calendar year 2016.[12] Neither of the two includes the (slim) majority of workers who do not directly experience an employment tax from the ACA. (They would be represented by a zero-hours equivalent.) The histogram's bump near nine hours per week reflects those aforementioned employees of for-profit employers who are paid minimum wage. Most instances are less than nine hours per week—the average is about five hours per week and the median is about four—but even the central estimates are not trivial because they are a full tenth of a typical weekly work schedule.

Antipoverty Programs as Employment Taxes on Middle-Class Workers

Antipoverty programs such as SNAP and Medicaid are household-income-tested up to a threshold over which households are ineligible.

Below and around the threshold, the income tests are essentially an income tax. However, because the income tests are frequently applied to time intervals that are less than a calendar year, most unmarried households' only potential access to the program occurs during periods of time that they are out of work.[13] In this sense, and putting aside work requirements, antipoverty programs' income tests have a lot in common with employment taxes.

Take the SNAP program, which pays a benefit that is phased out at the rate of about 30 cents on the dollar with the recipient's income. The phaseout rate has hardly changed in recent history, giving the impression that the program's work disincentives haven't changed either. However, the vast majority of workers do not receive any SNAP benefits while they are working because their income from working is too high. For them, SNAP's disincentive to work is measured by the amount of the benefit, if any, available during times that they are out of work. The 30 percent phaseout is hardly relevant for that incentive. The SNAP program changes in and around the recession that expanded eligibility and benefits created opportunities for support when they were out of work, without adding to the support that they get while working. The same considerations apply to other antipoverty programs, the largest of which is Medicaid.

Measuring Combined Work Disincentives for Middle-Class Workers

As noted above, the new taxes are not uniform across people. Figure 2 shows an index of marginal tax rates for nonelderly household heads and spouses whose earnings capabilities—that is, the amount that they earn when they are working full-time—are in the middle of the distribution. The index is a population-weighted average over various ages, occupations, family situations, types of work decisions, and propensities to participate in subsidy programs. It includes both the employment taxes discussed above as well as income taxes (implicit and explicit). The index is expressed as a percentage of total compensation, including fringe benefits. The index also includes taxes on employers, such as the employer payroll tax, to the degree

Figure 2. Statutory Marginal Labor Income Tax Rates over Time

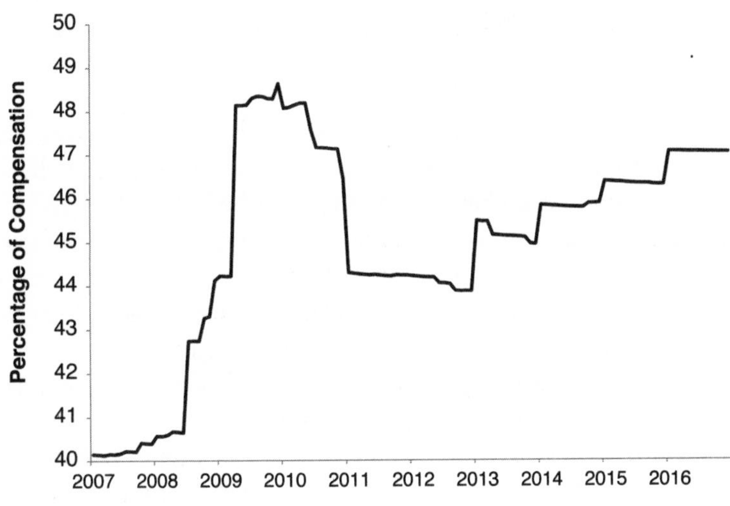

Source: Casey B. Mulligan, "The New Employment and Income Taxes," *Journal of Policy Analysis and Management* 34, no. 2 (2015): 466–73. It has been updated to reflect the end of most states' waivers of SNAP work requirements and to reflect the partial implementation of the ACA's employer penalty during 2015.

that the tax contributes to the overall wedge between the supply and demand prices of labor.

The 2009–10 peak for marginal tax rates comes from various provisions of the "stimulus" law and the 99-week duration of unemployment benefits in several states. At the end of 2012, and the last days of the payroll tax holiday, the marginal tax rate index reached its lowest value since 2008: less than 44 percent. One year later (January 2014), the index is almost 46 percent because multiple provisions of the Affordable Care Act are more than enough to offset the new incentives associated with the expiration of federal long-term unemployment assistance. The ACA employer penalty adds more than a percentage point in 2015 and 2016, while other ACA provisions strengthen their disincentives.

Because the Affordable Care Act is intended to be permanent, there are no plans laid in the federal statutes to significantly reduce the marginal rate after 2016. Typical marginal labor tax rates are therefore indefinitely scheduled to be about 7 percentage points greater than they were before the 2008–09 recession began.

As a result of implicit and explicit taxes, a worker costs his employer more than the worker receives; the federal and state treasuries get the difference as additional revenues or less program spending. Understanding the labor market thereby requires both of these wage measures: employer costs and employee rewards. Figure 3 displays them each as a quarterly inflation-adjusted index, normalized to 100 in the last quarter before the recession.[14]

The solid series in Figure 3 is the index of employees' financial reward to work after taxes and subsidies. It falls sharply and remains depressed. In contrast, the dashed employer cost series rises somewhat during the first two years. It is stable for the next two years, and falls slightly during 2011. By 2013, the employer cost index is roughly the same as it was before the recession began.[15] Thus, on the scale of changes in the reward to work, employer costs hardly fell, if at all.

Behavioral Consequences of Employment Taxes

The new national average employment taxes reduce employment and incomes below what they would be if the old lower rates of employment tax had continued.[16] Based on their size, the taxes should not be expected to reduce everyone's employment, or even most people's employment. The employment responses will be primarily among people at the margin between working and not working, and do so in multiple ways. They will cause middle-class people to spend more time in between jobs, for example, because now they can get taxpayer assistance with their health insurance during such times. There will be early retirements for similar reasons. Because many of the social programs make layoffs less painful, they will also make layoffs more common (that's the law of demand!).

Figure 3. Employer Costs and Employee Rewards

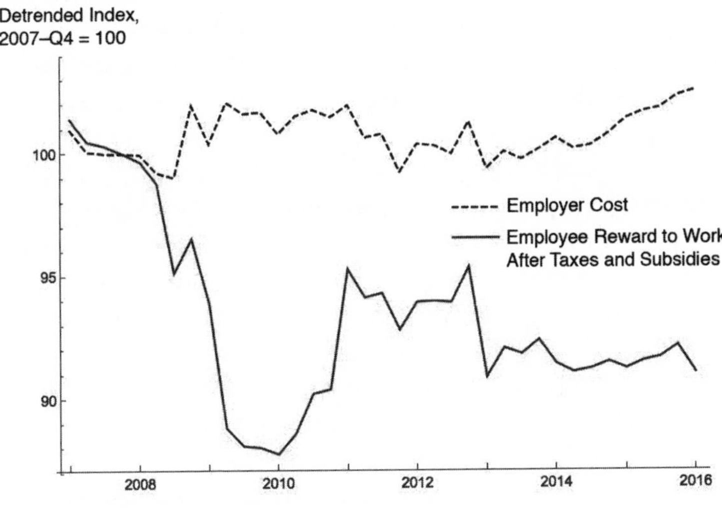

Source: Casey B. Mulligan, *Side Effects and Complications: The Economic Consequences of Health-Care Reform* (Chicago: University of Chicago Press, 2015).

The employment taxes in the health law apply specifically to full-time employment. The conventional wisdom says that the result will be shorter weekly work schedules, with employment rates *increasing* to "compensate" for work hours lost from taxes on full-time schedules. Under this view, more people working 29 hours rather than, say, 35, would mean that employers simply have to hire more or keep workers on the payroll longer in order to accomplish the tasks necessary to conduct their business. The conventional wisdom fails in two ways. First, the vast majority of workers will continue working full-time schedules despite the new taxes, and for them the tax is best avoided by working fewer weeks and working somewhat more hours during the weeks that they are at work. For example, having 100 employees working 42 hours per week creates less employer penalty than having 105 employees working 40 hours, even though both scenarios give the employer 4,200 total hours of work per week.

Second, even if full-time employment taxes were avoided by reducing weekly work hours, there would not be a commensurate increase in the employment rate because weekly hours would not be reduced for normal business or personal reasons, but rather to avoid penalties and implicit taxes. The penalties and implicit taxes make the business of an employer more expensive, or being an employee less rewarding, even in those cases when people avoid the new tax by adjusting their employment conditions rather than writing a check to the federal treasury. Some employers may go out of business, or never start their businesses in the first place, because of the extra cost of the tax (or the costs of adjustments needed to avoid the tax) or because of the additional costs (e.g., higher wages) needed to attract workers to positions that render them ineligible for exchange subsidies. The net result is that the labor market will involve fewer total hours, and that higher employment rates, if any, will not be enough to compensate for the reduced hours per week. This economic reasoning has been confirmed by empirical studies of previous public policies that raised the relative employer cost of weekly work hours and failed to create a commensurate increase in employment because the average hour worked by employees had been made more expensive or less productive.[17]

The new taxes are not uniform across groups, which means that the law's effects on employment and incomes will not be uniform. Several papers could be written about the dimensions of heterogeneity, but a fairly typical pattern is that the new social programs have much less effect on the work incentives of the most-skilled workers in the economy. By itself, this suggests that the programs will do more to reduce employment than to reduce national income.

However, the new programs, especially the ACA, reduce total factor productivity precisely because their taxes are not uniform across types of workers, sectors, employers, and regions. The heterogeneous tax rates encourage the private sector to sacrifice productivity in order to reduce their taxes and to enhance their subsidies. The "29er" phenomenon is a good example: employers and employees adopt 29-hour work schedules to avoid the ACA's employer penalty and to obtain premium assistance, even though 29-hour schedules are not the most productive way to arrange the workplace. With fewer and less-productive workers in the economy, we can also expect less capital to be accumulated (compared with what the capital stock would have been without the new programs).

A presumably unintended consequence of the recent safety net expansions has been to reduce the reward for working and thereby keep employment rates low, keep poverty rates high, and keep national spending low, longer than they would have been if safety net program rules had remained unchanged. None of this is to say that new social programs are undesirable. One can legitimately value the programs' insurance and redistributive aspects. But these benefits are far from free: they make a nation that works less, and works less productively.

Notes

1. As documented by, among others: Congressional Budget Office, *Effective Marginal Tax Rates for Low- and Moderate-Income Workers,* 2012; Jennifer L. Romich, Jennifer Simmelink, and Stephen Holt, "When Working Harder Does Not Pay: Low-Income Working Families, Tax Liabilities, and Benefit Reductions," *Families in Society: The Journal of Contemporary Social Services* 88, no. 3 (2007): 418–26; Stephen D. Holt and Jennifer L. Romich, "Marginal Tax Rates Facing Low- and Moderate-Income Workers Who Participate in Means-Tested Transfer Programs," *National Tax Journal* 60, no. 2 (June 2007): 253–77; and Robert A. Moffitt, "Multiple Program Participation and the SNAP Program," University of Kentucky Center for Poverty Research *Discussion Paper Series*, DP2014-04, February 2014, http://uknowledge.uky.edu/ukcpr_papers/10. It is common for low- and middle-income families to keep only a minority of what they earn at the margin. In some cases, families earning more actually have less to spend: their marginal tax rate exceeds 100 percent.

2. The first 30 full-time employees are to be ignored for the purposes of determining an employer's penalty. By "equivalent," I mean that, due to the differential business tax treatment of wages and penalties and the "premium adjustment percentage" as determined by the secretary of Health and Human Services, the 2017 employer penalty is the same as taking $3,449

out of wages and delivering that to the Treasury. See *Federal Register*, 12297; and Casey B. Mulligan, *Side Effects and Complications: The Economic Consequences of Health-Care Reform* (Chicago: University of Chicago Press, 2015).

3. The enhancements were not limited to the maximum duration for which benefits could be collected, which increased from 26 weeks to (in some states) 99 weeks in 2008 and 2009 and by the end of 2013 had returned to 26 weeks. The American Recovery and Reinvestment Act temporarily changed the tax treatment of unemployment benefits and added a weekly cash bonus. The act also paid states to (perhaps permanently) relax the eligibility criteria for collecting unemployment benefits. Unlike the basic state unemployment benefits, none of these enhancements were charged back to employers according to their former employees' participation in the programs.

4. See Casey B. Mulligan, *The Redistribution Recession* (Oxford University Press, 2012); and Mulligan, *Side Effects and Complications*.

5. Beginning calendar year 2016, only nine states remained eligible. For additional details, see Casey B. Mulligan, "The New Employment and Income Taxes," *Journal of Policy Analysis and Management* 34, no. 2 (2015): 466–73.

6. David H. Autor and Mark G. Duggan, "The Rise in Disability Rolls and the Decline in Unemployment," *Quarterly Journal of Economics* 118, no. 1 (February 2003): 157–206.

7. It is difficult to quantify subjective judgments, and my work is limited to statutory measures of program rules. But it is interesting that the ratio of DI application acceptances to denials increased with the unemployment rate in 1988 and 1992. See Congressional Budget Office, *Social Security Disability Insurance: Participation Trends and Their Fiscal Implications*, July 22, 2010.

8. The only exceptions are the increasingly rare cases where part-time positions are eligible for employer health coverage.

9. The incentives can be more complicated for dual-earner couples; see the ACA's "family glitch" in Mulligan, *Side Effects and Complications*.

10. N. Gregory Mankiw, "Supply-Side Ideas, Turned Upside Down," *New York Times*, November 1, 2009, BU14.

11. Casey B. Mulligan, "The New Full-Time Employment Taxes," *Tax Policy and the Economy* 29 (2015): 89–132.

12. The histograms differ according to the method used to calculate the value created per hour of employee work.

13. As noted above, the household income test makes unmarried households the primary program participants.

14. Both are also measured relative to a 0.5 percent per year trend to adjust for the fact that productivity and wages normally grow over time.

15. The employer cost index is compensation of employees from the national accounts deflated by the deflator for personal consumption expenditures. (St. Louis Federal Reserve database series COE and PCETCPI, respectively) and by aggregate work hours as measured for the public and private sectors by Mulligan, *Side Effects and Complications*.

16. As appropriate for employment taxes that generate revenue for transfers or for government purchases that are good substitutes for private purchases, my conclusion does not include any fully offsetting aggregate income effect.

17. Some studies even find that raising the employer cost of weekly work hours reduces employment. See the literature surveyed by Daniel S. Hamermesh, *Labor Demand* (Princeton, NJ: Princeton University Press, 1996), chap. 3; and Daniel S. Hamermesh, *Workdays, Workhours and Work Schedules: Evidence for the United States and Germany* (Kalamazoo, MI: Upjohn Institute for Employment Research, 1996), 106–07. For how employment taxes increase hours per employee, see Luis Garicano, Claire LeLarge, and John Van Reenan, "Firm Size Distortions and the Productivity Distribution: Evidence from France" (working paper, National Bureau of Economic Research, 2013).

VI

What Are the Economic Effects of Lesser-Skilled Immigration on Lesser-Skilled Native Workers?

Low-Skill Immigration

GEORGE J. BORJAS
Harvard University

Do low-skill immigrants harm the employment opportunities of low-skill native workers? And do low-skill immigrants "pay their way" in the welfare state, or are they a fiscal burden to native taxpayers? These questions regarding the consequences of low-skill immigration lie at the core of the contentious immigration debate in the United States today.

Although most receiving countries seem to encourage and welcome the entry of high-skill immigrants, most of these countries restrict the entry of low-skill immigrants. These restrictions are often imposed through "point systems," as in Australia or Canada, that effectively "grade" visa applicants on the basis of their observable skills, including education and occupation, and only grant an entry visa to those who get a passing grade. These restrictions are typically justified by arguing that they improve the economic well-being of native workers, as well as protect native taxpayers from the presumably sizable costs of providing assistance to perhaps millions of low-skill immigrants.

The major impetus for the resurgence of large-scale immigration to the United States came from the 1965 amendments to the Immigration and Nationality Act. Before 1965, immigration to the United States was guided by the national-origins quota system. This scheme limited the size of the immigrant flow and established quotas that allocated visas across countries, where the number of visas given to each country was based on the ethnic composition of the US population in 1920. As a result, 75 percent of all available visas were awarded to applicants from three countries: Germany, Great Britain, and Ireland. In addition, during the 1950s, preference was given to visa applicants whose skills were "urgently needed," and half of all visas were granted to such persons.

The 1965 amendments repealed the national-origins quota system. Along with subsequent minor legislation, the amendments set a higher worldwide numerical limit for immigration and enshrined a new objective for allocating entry visas among the many applicants: the reunification of families. Between 2000 and 2010, two-thirds of legal immigrants entered the country through the family preference system, and fewer than 15 percent entered through employment-based visas. The 1965 policy shift also had an historic impact on the number of immigrants admitted. Even though only 250,000 legal immigrants entered the country annually during the 1950s, almost 1 million were entering by the 1990s.

There has also been a substantial increase in illegal immigration. The large-scale entry of undocumented immigrants began in the late 1960s after the end of the *bracero* program, an agricultural guest worker program for Mexicans that was discontinued because of its perceived harm to the economic opportunities of competing native workers. As of January 2012, the Department of Homeland Security estimated that 11.4 million undocumented persons resided in the United States. It is worth emphasizing that there is no skill filtering of the undocumented population.

The lack of effective skill filters for both legal and undocumented immigrants has led to dramatic changes in the skill composition of the foreign-born population in the United States. Figure 1 illustrates the sharp decline in the educational attainment of newly arrived immigrants relative to that of natives. In 1960, the two groups had essentially the same education. By 1990, the recent immigrants had almost two fewer years of education. Not surprisingly, the lower relative skills of new immigrants led to a corresponding decline in their economic performance. In 1960, for example, the average newly arrived immigrant earned 11 percent less than natives. By 1970, immigrants earned 21 percent less, and by 2010, the wage disadvantage had grown to 28 percent.

Figure 1. Years of Educational Attainment of Immigrants at the Time of Entry, 1960–2010

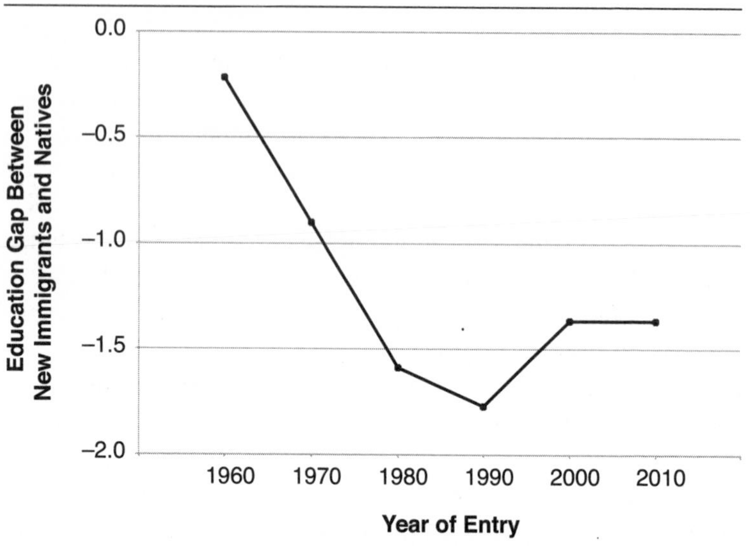

Source: George J. Borjas, *We Wanted Workers: Unraveling the Immigration Narrative* (New York: Norton, 2016).

The decline in the skills of immigrants, their worsening economic performance, and the implied growth in low-skill immigration raise many contentious questions in the current immigration debate. This essay summarizes what we have learned about the consequences of low-skill immigrants on native employment opportunities and on the welfare state.

The Impact on Native Wages

A central aspect of the immigration debate concerns the possibility that low-skill immigrants have a particularly harmful effect on the economic well-being of low-skill natives. The notion that low-skill immigrants can have adverse effects on low-skill natives follows trivially from the laws of supply and demand. After all, low-skill immigrants and natives tend to have similar skills and can perform the same types of jobs. An influx of low-skill immigrants gives employers a greater opportunity to "pick and choose" among the many workers who are looking for such jobs, inevitably reducing the wages of all low-skill workers.

Of course, not everyone loses out from low-skill immigration. The employers who hire low-skill immigrants will obviously benefit. They can now hire low-skill workers at lower prices. Moreover, high-skill native workers will probably also benefit. The low-skill immigrants fill jobs that free up the time of high-skill natives to concentrate on the types of activities that high-skill natives excel at. For example, instead of mowing the lawn or fixing the roof, high-skill natives can now devote more time to improving their coding skills. This complementarity makes high-skill natives more productive, increasing their wages.

The evidence indicates that these sensible implications of the laws of supply and demand are indeed confirmed by wage trends in real-world labor markets. For example, we can observe wages for specific skill groups defined by education and age (e.g., high school dropouts in their early 20s or college graduates in their late 40s) across many decades. We can then determine if the wage trends are correlated with the entry of immigrants into those skill groups. Presumably, those skill groups that experienced the largest "supply shocks" would be the ones for which wages either fell the most or grew the least.

Figure 2 demonstrates the strong link that exists between trends in the wages of native-born workers and immigration between 1960 and 2010. The data clearly shows a negative relation between the growth in weekly earnings and the number of immigrants entering a specific skill group. Put simply, weekly earnings in any particular decade grew most for workers in the skill groups least affected by immigration in that decade. In fact, the trendline suggests that, if immigrants increase the number of workers in a skill group by 10 percent, the average earnings of workers in that group falls by 3 to 4 percent. Because immigration during this period particularly increased the number of low-skill workers, it follows that low-skill wages were the ones most adversely affected by recent immigration.

Figure 2. The Impact of Immigration on the Earnings of Native Workers

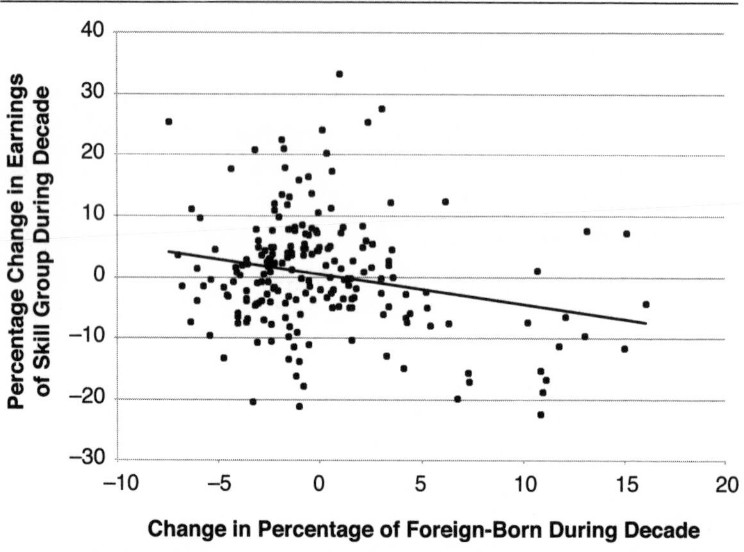

Source: George J. Borjas, *We Wanted Workers: Unraveling the Immigration Narrative* (New York: Norton, 2016).

An equally convincing link between low-skill wages and immigration is obtained by reexamining what happened to the low-skill labor market in Miami in the 1980s. On April 20, 1980, Fidel Castro declared that Cubans wishing to move to the United States could leave from the port of Mariel. The first Marielitos arrived on April 23. By June 3, over 100,000 Cubans had migrated, and Miami's workforce had grown by around 8 percent.

David Card's pioneering study, published in 1990, examined the *average* wages in Miami before and after the entry of the Marielitos, and compared this trend to how wages evolved in a set of comparison cities.[1] Surprisingly, there was little difference in wage growth between Miami and other cities, leading to the conclusion: "The distribution of non-Cubans' wages in the Miami labor market was remarkably stable between 1979 and 1985. . . . These data provide

Figure 3. Mariel and the Earnings of High School Dropouts

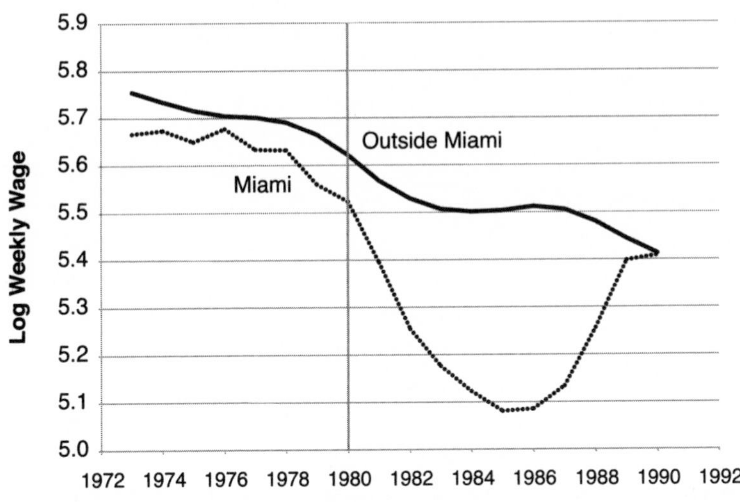

Source: George J. Borjas, "The Wage Impact of the Marielitos: A Reappraisal" (working paper, National Bureau of Economic Research, September 2015).

little evidence of a negative effect of the Mariel influx on the earnings of natives."

In retrospect, this conclusion was wrong. By looking at the trend in *average* wages, Card's analysis missed what was really going on. Immigration will tend to have laser-focused effects on *comparable* native workers. Almost two-thirds of the Marielitos were high school dropouts, so that the Mariel supply shock increased the number of high school dropouts in Miami by an astounding 20 percent in a matter of weeks. This obviously suggests that a good place to start would be to look at what happened to the wage of high school dropouts. As Figure 3 shows, the earnings of the workers most likely to be affected by the Mariel immigrants indeed took a dramatic nosedive after 1980, and it took a decade for that wage to fully recover.

In short, both the Mariel data and an examination of how wages have grown for different skill groups over the past few decades confirm that the laws of supply and demand hold—even when it comes to immigration. Moreover, the effect is numerically important, with a 10 percent increase in supply lowering wages by 3 to 4 percent in the national labor market, and by at least 10 percent in the exceptional context of the Mariel supply shock.

Although the evidence summarized in Figures 2 and 3 provides an easy-to-understand approach for measuring the labor market impact of immigration, it does not fully capture how immigration changes the wage structure. After all, the entry of immigrants into one skill group affects not only the wage of that skill group, but the wage of every other group as well. For example, the entry of young high school dropouts could influence the wages of young high school dropouts *and* the wages of young and old college graduates. The correct measurement of the wage impact of immigration should incorporate all of these potential complementarities.

The problem with measuring the magnitude of the cross-effects is that the empirical exercise quickly becomes intractable. Even if we only looked at, say, 10 skill groups, composed of 5 education groups and 2 age groups, we would need to worry about 100 potential wage effects if immigration into one group affected the wage of every other group. To measure the cross-effects, therefore, we need to reduce the dimensionality of the problem. The standard approach used by economists is to specify the production technology in the labor market by writing down specific formulas that describe how the various groups interact and produce output.

Table 1 summarizes the implications from this theory-based approach by showing how wages responded to the immigration that occurred between 1990 and 2010. These immigrants increased the supply of high school dropouts by 26 percent, and those of workers with more than a college degree by 15.0 percent.

Even after accounting for all interactions across skill groups, the large supply shock experienced by high school dropouts reduced the wage of that group by 6 percent in the short run and 3 percent in the long run. Similarly, the wage declines for the most highly skilled workers (those with more than a college degree) were 4 percent in the short run and 1 percent in the long run.

Table 1. Predicted Wage Impact of the 1990–2010 Immigrants, Accounting for Cross-Effects

	Percent Increase in Supply	Percent Wage Effect in Short Run	Percent Wage Effect in Long Run
Group:			
High School Dropouts	25.9	–6.3	–3.1
High School Graduates	8.4	–2.8	0.4
Some College	6.1	–2.3	0.9
College Graduates	10.9	–3.3	–0.1
Post-College	15.0	–4.1	–0.9
All Workers	10.6	–3.2	0.0

Source: George J. Borjas, *Immigration Economics* (Cambridge: Harvard University Press, 2014), 114.

The wage effects are attenuated in the long term because firms will expand to take advantage of the lower wages. This expansion raises the demand for labor, and the wage of the average native workers will remain unchanged in the long run (as long as technical assumptions about the production technology hold).[2] Nevertheless, it is still the case that even in the long run, low-skill natives suffer a 3 percent wage drop.

A 3 to 6 percent wage drop implies that the earnings of native high school dropouts, a group that makes up about 10 percent of the workforce, will fall by $900 to $1,700 annually. These workers are among the poorest Americans and include many minorities. Put bluntly, low-skill immigration can be quite detrimental for the most vulnerable among us.

Low-Skill Immigration and Welfare

The other controversial issue raised by low-skill immigration concerns the link between these immigrants and the welfare state. Milton Friedman made a famous quip that captures the concern: "It's just obvious you can't have free immigration and a welfare state." The underlying reason for the concern is obvious. The welfare state in the United States, although not as generous as that in many Western European countries, still provides a standard of living that far exceeds what would be available to many persons in poor countries. The welfare state, therefore, may play a magnetic role that particularly attracts low-skill immigrants.

Because of this potential attraction, the United States has long enacted statutes that limited immigrant access to welfare programs. Those statutes (which date back more than a century) prohibit the admission of "any persons unable to take care of himself or herself without becoming a public charge," and allow for the deportation of immigrants who become public charges within five years of entry.

More recently, the welfare reform legislation enacted in 1996 contained several provisions aimed specifically at the foreign-born population, including one that prohibits almost all newly arrived immigrants from receiving most types of federal assistance. This ban is lifted when the immigrant becomes an American citizen. In a sense, the legislation established a five-year "waiting period" before immigrants qualify. After five years, a legal immigrant can typically apply for naturalization. If the application is approved, the immigrant becomes an American citizen and is entitled to all federal benefits.

It turns out that despite these restrictions, the "wall" built around the welfare state does not seem to prevent many immigrants from qualifying for and receiving public assistance. The fundamental reason for the participation by many immigrant families in welfare programs is trivial. *By design*, welfare programs subsidize workers who have below-average incomes, and those subsides are paid for by workers who have above-average incomes. If the typical immigrant were a high-skill worker, that immigrant would help defray the costs of social assistance programs. But if the typical immigrant were a low-skill worker, that immigrant—assuming he or she qualifies for the benefits—would likely receive a net subsidy. Put bluntly, low-skill immigration is likely to be a drain on native taxpayers, while high-skill immigration is likely to be a boon to those taxpayers.

It is easy to document the evidence showing that immigrants, and particularly low-skill immigrants, have very high rates of participation in welfare programs. The Current Population Survey (CPS) is the premier monthly survey of the American population and is conducted by the Bureau of Labor Statistics. The March survey solicits information on a person's income in the previous calendar year, and on whether the person received particular types of public assistance. Since 1994, the CPS reports whether a particular person is foreign-born.

To simplify the exposition, being "on welfare" will mean receiving benefits from any one of three programs: Medicaid, food stamps, or cash benefits (which include Temporary Assistance for Needy Families, Supplementary Security Income, and "general" assistance given by cities and counties to persons in short-term dire need). There are obviously many other programs that could be thought of as being some type of welfare, but it is easy to illustrate the main point by concentrating on the three main programs that make up the safety net.

Figure 4 shows the trends in welfare use, reporting the fraction of households that receive some type of assistance. An immigrant household is one where the head of the household is foreign-born, and a native household is one where the head is native-born. Evidently, households headed by an immigrant have particularly high rates of welfare use, and the gap between immigrant and native households increased over time. By 2015, 37 percent of immigrant households were on welfare compared with only 24 percent of native households.

Figure 5 shows the very large difference in welfare use between low-skill and high-skill households, where the "skill" of the household is determined by the educational attainment of the household head. The head in a low-skill household lacks a high school diploma, while the head in a high-skill household has at least a high school diploma. It is evident that both low-skill immigrant households and low-skill native households have extremely high rates of welfare participation. In 2015, about half of low-skill households received some type of assistance, a far higher rate than the 20 to 30 percent among households where the head has at least a high school diploma.

Figure 4. Trends in Welfare Use Among Immigrant and Native Households, 1994–2015

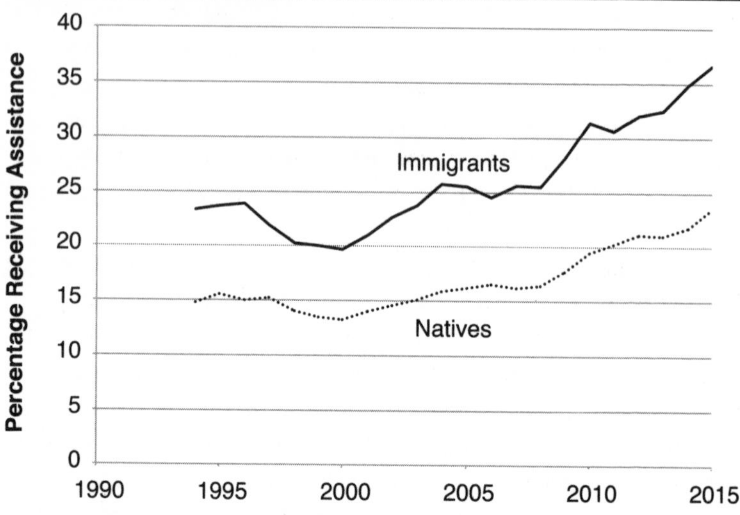

George J. Borjas, *We Wanted Workers: Unraveling the Immigration Narrative* (New York: Norton, 2016).

The fact that immigrants, on average, use welfare more often than natives is not that surprising. Welfare programs are designed to redistribute wealth from those who do well economically to those who do poorly. Because immigrants are disproportionally low-skill, a disproportionately high number of welfare recipients will be foreign-born. Some studies use the data on welfare programs and on the costs of other government programs to determine whether immigrants "pay their way" in the welfare state—that is, whether the taxes that immigrants pay cover the expenditures they trigger. Although this type of numerical exercise often leads to news headlines, either claiming that immigrants pay far more in taxes than they cost or that some types of immigrants, such as undocumented immigrants, are a drain on fiscal resources, it is wise to be skeptical of many of these claims.

The bottom line of the exercise often depends on assumptions. As an example, how exactly should one allocate expenditures in public goods, such as police and fire protection or national defense,

Figure 5. Welfare Use by Educational Attainment of Household Head, 1994–2015

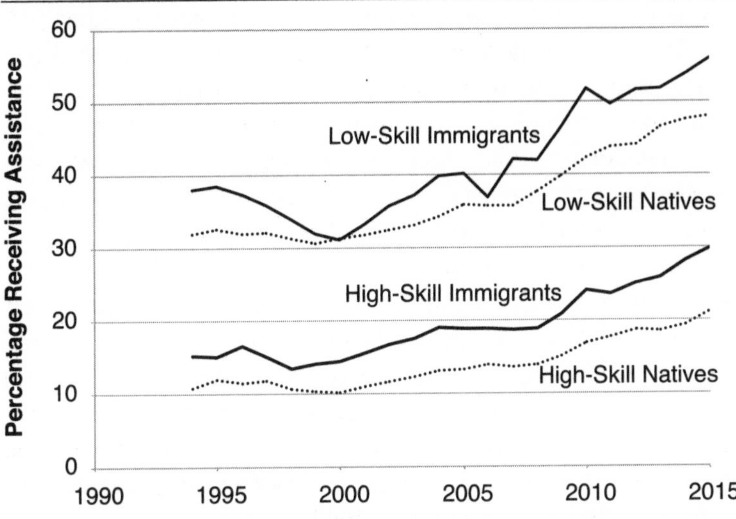

Source: Author's calculations from the 1994–2015 March Current Population Surveys. Low-Skill Immigrants are households where the foreign-born head lacks a high school diploma. High-Skill Immigrants are households where the household head has at least a high school diploma.

between immigrants and natives? The admission of *one* additional immigrant would probably not change the cost of these programs. That additional person can be covered by the current infrastructure. But it is far less likely that the admission of over 40 million immigrants would leave expenditures on public goods unchanged. The typical "do-immigrants-pay-their-way" exercise must make an assumption about how expenses on public goods are allocated, and that assumption will affect the bottom line substantially.

There is little doubt that low-skill immigration *must be* a fiscal burden for the native population. Low-skill immigrants have lower-than-average earnings and pay lower-than-average taxes. At the same time, low-skill immigrants will make relatively high use of the programs that are specifically designed to help disadvantaged persons through difficult times.

Implications

Low-skill immigration creates important challenges for public policy. Unfortunately, the solution to these challenges is far from clear.

The notion that the economic insights and empirical findings summarized in this essay can somehow lead to a purely technocratic determination of public policy ignores a simple fact of life. Many of us have particular policy preferences because we believe that what those policies are trying to accomplish is the right thing to do.

We all have different values and perceptions about what is right. Some of us believe that it is immoral to deny anyone the right to enter the United States in search of a better life. Some value the cultural diversity that immigrants introduce into our culture. Others contend that *this* particular type of immigrant is better than *that* other type. And still others want to substantially cut immigration, arguing that the continued entry of large numbers of immigrants will alter the country in fundamental and undesirable ways.

When thinking specifically about low-skill immigration, many participants in the public debate believe that immigration policy should protect the economic well-being of low-skill native workers and taxpayers. If we view the available data on the consequences of low-skill immigration from that perspective, it is obvious that public policy should be changed to greatly limit (or altogether restrict) low-skill immigration, as done by the point system that some other countries adopt.

Other participants in the debate, however, believe that immigration policy should give poor people abroad the opportunity to move to this country and partake in the American dream. That perspective might recognize that low-skill immigration imposes costs on low-skill native workers and taxpayers. But proponents of low-skill immigration would argue that, as a nation, we should be willing to bear those costs in return for the intangible benefit derived from giving many poor people the chance at a better life.

It is not possible to reconcile those two extreme views of what immigration policy *should* accomplish. They represent different values about who we are and who we care about. But, regardless of what we believe the world should look like, it is a *fact* that low-skill immigration creates winners and losers.

The existence of winners and losers suggests a new avenue for thinking about low-skill immigration and public policy. Perhaps it is time to conceive of immigration policy from a much broader viewpoint, a viewpoint that delineates more than just how many immigrants to admit and which types of immigrants to admit. If we are going to open the doors and admit many low-skill immigrants that specifically harm disadvantaged Americans, immigration policy should also describe how we will compensate those low-skill Americans for their economic suffering. In short, future discussions of immigration reform should begin to incorporate detailed proposals that would ensure the costs and benefits from low-skill immigration are more equitably shared by the American people.

Notes

1. David Card, "The Impact of the Mariel Boatlift on the Miami Labor Market," *Industrial and Labor Relations Review* 43, no. 2 (January 1990), 245–57.

2. The key assumption is that the production technology has "constant returns to scale": if we could double the number of workers and double the capital stock, output would also double.

Less-Skilled Immigration: Economic Effects and Policy Responses*

PIA M. ORRENIUS
Federal Reserve Bank of Dallas and American Enterprise Institute

MADELINE ZAVODNY
Agnes Scott College and American Enterprise Institute

Immigrants play an important role in the US labor market. Almost 26 million—one in six—workers are foreign born, and immigrants account for about one-half of labor force growth in recent years. They fill jobs ranging from CEOs, doctors, and computer programmers to fast-food workers, housekeepers, and farm laborers. They have spread out across the country, moving from traditional destinations into communities that had long been isolated from immigration.

Immigration creates both benefits and costs for the US economy and the communities where immigrants settle. Immigration increases the number of workers and hence total economic output, making the country as a whole richer. However, not everyone benefits equally. Immigrants themselves are the largest beneficiaries. Business owners, consumers, and complementary workers gain as well, but competing workers can experience losses, particularly in the short run. From a fiscal perspective, immigrants broaden the tax base, but they also consume government-provided services. Immigrants can bring vitality to waning areas, alleviate labor shortages, increase diversity,

*The views expressed here are those of the authors and do not reflect those of the Federal Reserve Bank of Dallas or the Federal Reserve System.

and slow the aging of the workforce. However, some Americans feel their jobs and way of life are threatened by the arrival of people who readily find work yet speak different languages, eat different foods, and practice different religions.

The economic benefits of immigration are more obvious for highly skilled immigrants than for less-skilled immigrants. Highly skilled immigrants typically earn high incomes and pay more in taxes than they receive in government-provided services. Many of them work in technology-intensive, knowledge-producing sectors that boost innovation and productivity growth. Meanwhile, less-skilled immigrants tend to earn less, pay less in taxes than they receive in government services, be less likely to speak English fluently, and be more likely to be unauthorized than highly skilled immigrants. However, less-skilled immigrants make a vital economic contribution in that they have very high employment rates and fill jobs that few Americans want while providing services that many Americans demand.

The most recent surge in immigration, sometimes called the Second Great Migration to distinguish it from the historic highs at the turn of the last century, has come during the last four decades, which have also been difficult times for many less-skilled American workers. The median inflation-adjusted income of US natives who are high school dropouts fell by almost one-half from 1970 to 2014.[1] Globalization and technological change have eroded labor market opportunities for less-skilled workers at the same time as immigration to the United States has surged. Despite the coincident timing, as this essay discusses, immigration has had little to do with the difficulties many less-skilled American workers face. Moreover, immigration policy has the potential to boost the economy by creating an orderly legal flow of vetted workers who enter when labor demand is strong. A sensible immigration policy would prioritize employment-based immigration while increasing fees on employers and allowing worker mobility. It would couple a legalization program for current unauthorized workers with a requirement that employers use E-Verify. Together, these changes would increase economic growth and enhance labor market efficiency while improving incentives for employers to treat workers right.

Economic Effects

Immigration affects the economy first and foremost by increasing the number of workers. The canonical economic model posits that this increase in labor supply due to immigration pushes down wages and increases output. The economy as a whole benefits, but wages and employment fall for competing workers. The canonical model assumes that foreign- and native-born workers are perfectly substitutable for each other. Models that relax this assumption predict smaller adverse wage and employment effects on competing native-born workers. Meanwhile, the influx of workers pushes up the return to capital, stimulating investment. The increase in income that accrues to owners of capital as a result of labor inflows—called the immigration surplus—is between 0.2 and 0.4 percent of GDP (about $35 to $70 billion).

A voluminous literature on the labor market effects of immigration has reached disparate conclusions, even when limited to studies of less-skilled immigration. Findings vary primarily because of differences in the techniques used, which in turn depend on the underlying assumptions. George Borjas shows that the simulated long-run effect of the inflow of less-skilled immigrants during 1990–2010 on less-skilled natives can range from +1.1 percent to −1.7 percent, depending on assumptions about the substitutability of immigrants for natives and of non–high school graduates for high school graduates.[2] There is, however, a general consensus that inflows of less-skilled immigrants have a sizable negative effect on the wages of earlier less-skilled immigrants. This makes sense since immigrants are likely to be more substitutable for each other than for US natives.

There are several reasons to believe that less-skilled immigration has had at most a relatively small adverse effect on similar US-born workers. One is the declining share of less-skilled US-born workers. Figure 1 shows the share of US natives ages 16–64 who have not (yet in some cases) completed high school during 1950 to 2010. This is arguably the group that competes the most intensely with less-skilled immigrants in the labor market.

Figure 1. Immigrants Are a Growing Share of Less-Skilled Workers

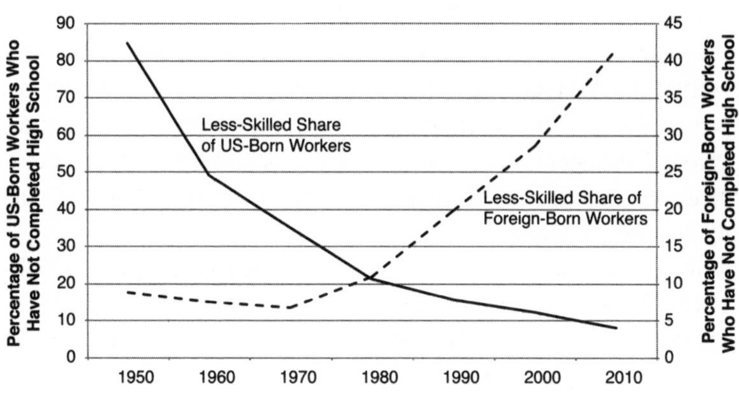

Source: Authors' calculations from 1950–2010 Census data on workers ages 16–64 from Integrated Public Use Microdata Series (IPUMS).

The share has fallen dramatically over time because of increased educational attainment across native-born cohorts—older generations that are much less likely to have completed high school are aging out of the workforce. Immigrants therefore account for a growing share of the least-educated workers.[3] In fact, immigrants now make up about one-half of the less-skilled adult workforce.[4]

Many low-skilled immigrants live in different areas and work in different occupations than low-skilled natives, softening competition between the two groups. Even among the least-skilled workers, immigrants and US natives tend to have different skill sets. In particular, US natives have comparative advantages in speaking English and being familiar with US customs. As a result, less-skilled US natives are much more likely than immigrants to work in jobs that involve customer contact, such as being a waiter or cashier. Less-skilled immigrants, meanwhile, tend to hold manual, labor-intensive jobs that involve little customer contact, such as being a cook, landscaper, or farmworker.

Further, less-skilled US natives have responded to immigrant inflows by upgrading their occupations. Giovanni Peri and Chad Sparber show that less-educated US natives have shifted toward occupations that emphasize communications skills and away from occupations that emphasize manual labor in response to immigrant inflows.[5] This shift mitigates the labor market competition between immigrants and natives, and it boosts US natives' wages since communications-intensive jobs tend to pay more than manual-labor–intensive jobs.

Businesses have responded to less-skilled immigrant inflows as well. Businesses change how they make products, what products they make, and where they make them in response to labor costs, among other factors. The influx of less-skilled immigrants has therefore likely slowed the substitution of capital for labor and the offshoring of labor-intensive jobs, preserving jobs for some less-skilled US natives. For example, Ethan Lewis shows that manufacturing plants have added technology more slowly in areas that have received larger numbers of less-skilled immigrants, helping explain why less-skilled immigration has had little effect on wages.[6]

Less-skilled immigration has positive effects on other aspects of the economy, such as consumers. Inflows of less-skilled immigrants have reduced the price of labor-intensive services such as child care, restaurant meals, housecleaning, and landscaping.[7] The decreased costs of such services has led to an increase in hours worked and fertility among high-earning or highly educated women.[8]

Meanwhile, a number of other major economic forces have contributed to worsening economic outcomes for less-skilled workers. Increased trade with labor-abundant countries, most notably China, has harmed the labor market prospects of US manufacturing workers.[9] Automation and technological change have hollowed out the middle of the labor market, with many rote tasks now done by machines instead of workers.[10] Changes in labor market institutions, namely declines in the unionization rate and in the inflation-adjusted federal minimum wage, have played a role in reduced wages for less-skilled workers as well.

Fiscal Effects

The fiscal impact of immigration is the difference between what immigrant families pay in taxes and consume in government-provided benefits. Tax contributions include sales, income, payroll, and property taxes, among others. Government services include public education, health care for the poor (Medicaid) and the elderly (Medicare), and programs such as cash welfare, food stamps, and housing assistance. As is true for US natives, less-educated immigrants have lower incomes and pay less in taxes than high-educated, high-income immigrants. Less-skilled immigrants also tend to have larger families and use more public services. As a result, they impose net fiscal costs over their lifetimes.[11]

It is important to note that, in the very long run, across generations, the negative fiscal impact of less-skilled immigration dissipates. The children and grandchildren of immigrants assimilate, reaching average education and income levels and "paying back" the costs imposed by earlier cohorts.[12] Rapid economic integration of the second and third generations of immigrants thus pays off not only in the labor market, but also in the public sector. Early-on costs can also be seen as human capital investments that boost education and health and earn returns in the long run, but this does not change the fact that taxpayers must still shoulder those additional expenses in the short run. Moreover, because educational and health care expenses are primarily the responsibility of state and local governments, the fiscal burden of immigration falls disproportionately on them, while the federal government gets more of the tax contributions in the form of payroll and income taxes.

Unauthorized immigrants, because they have relatively little education and low wages, tend to impose a net fiscal cost even though most unauthorized workers have taxes withheld from their paychecks.[13] They are also ineligible for most transfer programs and hence impose a lower fiscal burden than otherwise similar legal immigrants or US natives. In fact, the fiscal costs of unauthorized immigrants stem overwhelmingly from expenses related to their children, most of whom are US born and, hence, US citizens.

Policy Responses

Immigration policy needs to balance many interests, including national security, geopolitical relations, and humanitarian concerns. One of the overarching goals should be maximizing the economic benefits from immigration, which include—but are not limited to—minimizing harms to competing US-born workers.

Current US immigration policy is a mixed bag at best when it comes to maximizing the economic benefits from immigration. The United States allocates the great majority of permanent resident visas to family-based immigrants, who are less skilled than employment-based immigrants and less likely to be economically active. The United States prioritizes skilled immigrants in its allocation of employment-based visas, however. This is important since high-skilled immigrants make a larger economic and fiscal contribution than less-skilled immigrants do. From an economic perspective, admitting highly skilled immigrants, especially those who work in STEM fields, should be the top priority of immigration policy, and there is more the United States can and should do in that direction.

But prioritizing high-skilled immigration ignores a large segment of the nation's fastest-growing industries while making it very hard for less-skilled workers to legally migrate to the United States, especially if they are not an immediate relative of a US citizen (the only category of immigrants that is not numerically restricted). The result has been 11-plus million unauthorized immigrants. Addressing unauthorized immigration is an important component of immigration policy reform.

Unauthorized immigration, fiery rhetoric aside, actually has several economic advantages. Unauthorized immigrants arrive in the country in larger numbers when demand for their labor is booming, and they tend to rapidly move to areas where job growth is strong and, as a result, have very high employment rates.[14] If they cannot readily find work, they tend to leave the country since they are ineligible for virtually all government-funded transfer programs. From a fiscal perspective, they are less costly than similarly educated legal immigrants. In addition, legal immigration is typically much less responsive to market forces—immigrants are admitted with long bureaucratic delays and primarily on the basis of family ties, so their skills may not match employers' demands.

Despite some of the macroeconomic benefits of illegal immigration, unauthorized immigrants have limited upward mobility and may exert downward pressure on wages and working conditions. Their lack of legal status hampers their ability to bargain for higher wages or better working conditions and makes them vulnerable to abuse by employers. This harms competing US natives and legal immigrants as well as unauthorized immigrants and their families. It also creates an unfair playing field for employers who do not violate the law in sectors that have a large share of workers who are unauthorized, such as agriculture and construction.

Deporting all unauthorized immigrants or building a wall to keep them out is not the best answer. Doing so would be prohibitively expensive as well as extremely disruptive to the economy—many employers have come to depend on unauthorized workers, who make up 5 percent of the US labor force, and would have difficulty filling labor market gaps in the short-to-medium run.

Instead, the United States needs to create more and better legal channels for less-skilled workers to enter the country. This requires expanding existing temporary foreign worker programs or creating new ones. Those programs should admit more workers when demand for labor is strong and involve fewer bureaucratic hurdles and shorter lags than current programs do. They should include workers in year-round jobs, not just the temporary or seasonal jobs covered by the current H-2A and H-2B temporary foreign worker programs. They should allow workers to easily move across jobs, which gives workers more bargaining power and helps reduce labor market bottlenecks. Temporary foreign workers should not be precluded from using existing pathways to adjust to permanent resident status.

The United States should allow most unauthorized workers and their families who are already here to adjust to legal status. Deporting over 11 million immigrants is cost prohibitive and nonsensical, given most are long-term US residents and hold jobs, and many have pending applications for lawful permanent residence. It would also allow them to invest in job training or further their education, improve their bargaining position with employers, and enable them to move into better jobs, increasing their productivity and wages and easing downward pressure at the bottom of the income distribution.

It is important to also consider family-based immigration policy when thinking about less-skilled immigrants. About two-thirds of legal permanent residents are admitted based on family ties, and many of them are less skilled.[15] Family-based immigrants have the advantage of a ready network of family members to help them find a job, but they do not necessarily have the skills that employers want or go to areas where the economy is growing. From an economic perspective, it would be better to prioritize immigrants who come with a job in hand, either on a permanent or a temporary basis, over those admitted solely based on family ties.

Immigration programs should involve higher fees on employers. After all, employers and especially immigrants themselves reap benefits from immigration. Higher fees would incentivize employers to make more efforts to hire American workers before turning to foreign workers. If the goal is to maximize revenue, the federal government could auction off permits to hire temporary or permanent foreign workers or even the right to immigrate.[16] The revenues could be used for training programs for US-born workers who are adversely affected by immigration and to offset costs incurred by communities that attract large numbers of less-skilled immigrants.

Higher fees also increase employers' incentive to turn to unauthorized immigrant workers, so it is important to couple an increase in fees with an increase in enforcement, particularly worksite enforcement. The United States has opted to focus its enforcement efforts along its borders and has massively increased border enforcement in recent years. The US Border Patrol program budget rose to $3.8 billion in FY 2015 from $2.1 billion in FY 2006, while its agent staffing rose by 64 percent during that period.[17] Worksite enforcement has not increased commensurately and indeed became less of a priority under the Obama administration than under the Bush administration.

One key way to increase worksite enforcement would be requiring all employers to use E-Verify to check workers' employment eligibility and then penalize employers who hire workers who are not eligible to work in the United States. More generally, oversight of employers to ensure they do not violate labor laws—ranging from workplace safety laws to overtime regulations—is necessary, and employers who violate labor laws should not be allowed to participate in programs that allow businesses to bring in foreign workers on a temporary or permanent basis.

Immigrants are not the source of the many challenges faced by less-skilled American workers. "Closing the border" and reducing the number of low-skilled immigrant workers in the United States would do little to help blue-collar American workers who have faced stagnating wages and declining opportunities for decades. Research convincingly shows that technology and globalization have forever changed the labor market, leaving many US workers in the lurch. But cutting off immigration can do nothing to reverse the inflow of goods produced more cheaply overseas or the substitution of machines and computer programs for workers. If anything, immigration by less-skilled workers reduces offshoring, props up domestic production, and slows down automation. Better ways to help less-skilled American workers include more education funding, targeted training programs, grants to less-skilled workers who move from declining to booming regions, and an expansion of the earned income tax credit to make work more worthwhile and to help offset the substantial decline in income many less-skilled workers have witnessed during the last four decades.

Conclusion

The cornerstone of present-day US immigration policy—the 1965 Immigration and Nationality Act—turned 50 last year. It may be no surprise then that the nation's immigration framework is going through somewhat of a midlife crisis. Since the 1965 law was passed, the world economy has completely transformed. Technological change and globalization now rule the day, and the advanced industrial economies of North America, Western Europe, and Japan have lost power, productive capacity, and prominence to the rapid rise of emerging nations such as China, Mexico, and India. US workers, particularly those in manufacturing, have been adversely affected as factories have come to rely more on technology and offshoring.

It is largely futile to resist the forces of change that pervade today's labor markets. Policymakers must instead figure out how to make those forces work to the nation's advantage. This is also true for less-skilled immigration. Dwindling numbers of low-skilled US-born workers and proximity to the pent-up supply of underutilized workers in Mexico and Central America call for sensibly tapping that resource rather than building more barriers to keep out such workers, a strategy that has led to illegal immigration and a booming smuggling industry.

There are many economic benefits to less-skilled immigration, and incorporating it into comprehensive immigration reform is the best way to address the sources of illegal immigration once and for all. A well-designed temporary foreign worker program can incorporate all the advantages of a market-driven labor flow—expanding in booms, contracting in busts—while mitigating the fiscal costs and backlash against illegal inflows. This requires legalizing much of the existing unauthorized immigrant population and raising fees as well as using broad interior enforcement mechanism, such as E-Verify, to ensure workers are funneled through legal channels and employers are complying with the rules.

Policymakers should prioritize market forces when it comes to responses to immigration, preserving flexible wages and prices and limiting labor market regulations that prevent the efficient reallocation of resources over time. Sensible policies might include funneling employer fees to retrain domestic workers or help them relocate to growing areas and implementing policies that encourage entrepreneurship and business investment by US natives and immigrants alike.

The United States is a nation of immigrants—high- and low-skilled, family- and employment-based, legal and illegal—all of whom have played a role in the country's growth and prosperity. Much of the

United States' success in attracting and integrating immigrants is due to allowing foreign workers access to the labor market. The importance of foreign workers will only grow as Americans age and the forces of technological change and globalization march on. Now is the time to devise policies to ensure that the United States will have the less- and more-skilled immigrants it will increasingly need in the years and decades to come.

Notes

1. Authors' calculation of total personal income among US-born non–high school graduates ages 20–64 using Integrated Public Use Microdata Series (IPUMS) data from the 1970 Census and the 2014 American Community Survey, deflated using the CPI-W.

2. George J. Borjas, *Immigration Economics* (Cambridge, MA: Harvard University Press, 2014).

3. If less skilled is defined to include high school graduates, then immigrants account for a much smaller share of the less skilled—8.7 percent in 1950 and 23.2 percent in 2010. Expanding the definition to include high school graduates weakens negative estimates of the effect of immigration on similarly educated US natives. See David Card, "Immigration and Inequality," *American Economic Review: Papers & Proceedings* 99, no. 2 (2009): 1–21.

4. Pia M. Orrenius and Madeline Zavodny, *From Brawn to Brains: How Immigration Works for America: Federal Reserve Bank of Dallas 2010 Annual Report*, Federal Reserve Bank of Dallas, 2011.

5. Giovanni Peri and Chad Sparber, "Task Specialization, Immigration, and Wages," *American Economic Journal: Applied Economics* 1, no. 3 (2009): 135–69.

6. Ethan Lewis, "Immigration, Skill Mix, and Capital Skill Complementarity," *Quarterly Journal of Economics* 126, no. 2 (2011): 1029–69.

7. Patricia Cortés, "The Effect of Low-Skilled Immigration on US Prices: Evidence from CPI Data," *Journal of Political Economy* 116, no. 3 (2008): 381–422.

8. Patricia Cortés and José Tessada, "Low-Skilled Immigration and the Labor Supply of Highly Skilled Women," *American Economic Journal: Applied Economics* 3, no. 3 (2011): 88–123; and Delia Furtado, "Fertility Responses

of High-Skilled Native Women to Immigrant Inflows," *Demography* 53, no. 1 (2016): 27–53.

9. See, for example, David H. Autor et al., "Trade Adjustment: Worker-Level Evidence," *Quarterly Journal of Economics* 129, no. 4 (2014): 1799–860.

10. See, for example, David H. Autor, "Why Are There Still So Many Jobs? The History and Future of Workplace Automation," *Journal of Economic Perspectives* 29, no. 3 (2015): 3–30.

11. James P. Smith and Barry Edmonston, eds., *The New Americans: Economic, Demographic and Fiscal Effects of Immigration* (Washington, DC: National Academies Press, 1997).

12. Mary C. Waters and Marisa G. Pineau, eds., *The Integration of Immigrants into American Society* (Washington, DC: National Academies Press, 2015).

13. Congressional Budget Office, *The Impact of Unauthorized Immigrants on the Budgets of State and Local Governments*, 2007.

14. Gordon H. Hanson, *The Economic Logic of Illegal Immigration*, Council on Foreign Relations, April 2007.

15. Our calculations using data from the 2008 Survey of Income and Program Participation suggest that about two in five less-skilled immigrants are unauthorized. The rest are legally present in the United States, most of them permanent residents or naturalized US citizens. Those data also suggest that over one-fourth of immigrants who are a permanent resident or a naturalized US citizen have not completed high school, and another one-fifth have a high school diploma or equivalent but have not attended college.

16. Pia M. Orrenius and Madeline Zavodny, *Beside the Golden Door: US Immigration Reform in a New Era of Globalization* (Washington, DC: American Enterprise Institute Press, 2010).

17. See US Border Patrol, "Enacted Border Patrol Program Budget by Fiscal Year," https://www.cbp.gov/sites/default/files/documents/BP%20Budget%20History%201990-2015.pdf; and US Border Patrol, "Border Patrol Agent Staffing by Fiscal Year," September 9, 2015, https://www.cbp.gov/sites/default/files/documents/BP%20Staffing%20FY1992-FY2015.pdf. Budget figures are in nominal dollars.

VII

Would Cutting the Corporate Tax Rate Significantly Increase Jobs in the US?

Would Reducing the US Corporate Tax Rate Increase Employment in the United States?

MARTIN FELDSTEIN
Harvard University

Reducing the corporate tax rate and changing the rules for taxing the foreign earnings of US corporations would have many favorable effects, including an increase of employment in the United States.

First, a brief description of the current corporate tax arrangements. The federal government now imposes a statutory tax rate on corporate profits of 35 percent, the highest tax rate among all the industrial countries of the world. In addition, the individual states levy corporate tax rates that average 9 percent. Since that state tax is a deductible expense in calculating income subject to the federal corporate tax, the combined tax rate is approximately 40 percent.

Profits that are paid out to shareholders as dividends are subject to an additional personal income tax at both the federal and state levels. The federal tax on dividends is now 20 percent, and the state taxes average about 5 percent. Profits that are not paid out increase the value of the corporation and are subject to capital gains tax when shareholders sell their shares.

Countercyclical Increases in Employment

The labor market in the United States works well at matching individuals and jobs, unencumbered by monopoly labor unions, large state-owned enterprises, and the kinds of labor rules that impede employment in other industrial countries. The result is that high rates of unemployment in the United States are a temporary condition of business-cycle downturns. There has been no trend in the rate of unemployment during the 50 years that I have been studying the American economy. In contrast, the unemployment rate in Western Europe has increased from less than 5 percent in the early 1970s to more than 10 percent now.

Reductions in the corporate tax rate can stimulate demand and reduce unemployment during periods of cyclically high unemployment. The lower tax rate increases available net profits that firms can use to finance investment in structures and equipment, leading to increases in employment in those industries. When Congress wants to use reductions of the effective rate of corporate tax to stimulate employment demand, it has traditionally done so by changing depreciation rules and by introducing investment tax credits rather than by reducing the statutory corporate rate.

Such changes in the tax treatment of corporate investment provide a direct incentive for corporations to increase the rate of investment in new plant and equipment. Over the years, Congress has enacted accelerated depreciation rules, allowing companies to reduce taxable income by investing in new equipment. For some smaller firms, the accelerated depreciation has allowed an immediate expensing of their outlays for new investment. Accelerated depreciation has been supplemented by investment tax credits, an explicit tax reduction as a fraction of the amount that the firm spends on new equipment.

A substantial body of empirical research has shown the effectiveness of such reductions in the effective corporate tax rate achieved through changes in depreciation rules and investment tax credits. Those policies lead to increased spending on investment and therefore an increased demand for labor at times of high unemployment.

Inducing Increased Labor Supply and Employment

But lowering the statutory corporate tax rate can increase employment over and above the countercyclical effect that I have just been discussing. A lower corporate tax rate increases the after-tax profitability of corporate investment, encouraging more investment in the corporate sector. Some of that additional investment in the corporate sector is financed with funds that would otherwise have gone to financing investment in owner-occupied real estate. Some of the additional investment is done with funds that would otherwise be invested outside the United States. And some of the additional investment is done with increased saving that is induced by the higher rate of return.

The increased investment in the corporate sector raises the marginal product of labor in the corporate sector and therefore the real wages that firms will pay to attract employees. As a result, there is an increase in the labor force participation rate and in the ratio of employment to population.

The effect of increased investment on the marginal product of labor is more complex than generally assumed. The traditional textbook view of the role of capital formation is that increased capital per worker means more and better industrial equipment, leading to higher productivity and therefore higher real wages. That continues to be true, but it is only a small part of the story about the potential role of increased investment in businesses today.

The data teach us that investment in industrial equipment is just a small part of the investment that firms do today. Last year, total business investment, other than inventory investment, totaled $2.3 trillion. Only 10 percent of this investment was spent on industrial equipment ($234 billion). Firms spent nearly 50 percent more on information processing equipment ($323 billion) and more than three times as much on software and other intellectual property products ($729 billion).

The accelerated depreciation and investment tax credits encourage spending on information processing equipment in the same way that they encourage investment on industrial equipment. Reductions in the corporate tax rate provide the cash flow to invest in software and other intellectual property products and also make such investments more profitable. These newer forms of investment contribute directly to higher productivity and therefore to higher real wages, thus inducing an increase in the labor force participation rate and in the employment-population ratio.

All forms of investment require additional financing. As I have already noted, some of the additional funds can come from transferring capital that would otherwise be invested outside the United States, and some of it can come from investments in housing, a form of investment that does little to raise the marginal product of labor. Both of those sources of funds for investing in the corporate sector will be increased by the higher net-of-tax rate of return that would result from a reduction of the corporate tax rate.

The major source of funds for corporate investment is saving by households. There is a lot of talk in some quarters about the existence of a savings glut—i.e., about how high the rate of saving is. I do not see the evidence for such a high rate of national saving. It's clearly not high in the household sector. Indeed, it is much lower now than it was in the past. In the quarter century from 1960 to 1985, households saved an average of 9 percent of their after-tax incomes. The annual saving rate in those 25 years ranged from a low of 7 percent to a high of 11 percent. Now the official saving rate is just about 5 percent. But even that number is misleadingly high because the government statisticians changed the way we now measure the saving rate in the national income accounts. By the old definition, today's saving rate would be only about 3 percent or one-third of the average of the earlier quarter century. So there is no evidence of any excess amount of household saving.

A lower corporate tax rate would induce more household saving by increasing the return on additional saving. Some of the extra saving would be the result of households deciding to reduce current consumption because of the higher return on saving. But some of it would be a more mechanical effect by which a higher return on saving would cause saving balances to grow more rapidly.

Changing the Taxation of Corporations' Foreign Earnings

Corporate investment in the United States is depressed not only by the high rate of tax on corporate profits but also by the unusual way in which US firms are taxed on overseas incomes. Firms in every country pay taxes on the profits they earn in the country where those profits are earned. But if that is not the home country of that firm, the firm must also pay some tax on the profits that they chose to bring back to their home country.

Generally, however, foreign firms pay only a small token tax if they bring their after-tax profits back to their home country. But that's not how it works for American firms. Our companies must pay the difference between the US tax rate and the tax that they have already paid.

For example, French and American firms that invest in Ireland pay a corporate tax of only 12.5 percent to the Irish government. The French firm can then bring its after-tax profit back to France by paying less than 5 percent on those repatriated profits while an American firm would have to pay 22.5 percent, the difference between our 35 percent corporate tax and the 12.5 percent Irish tax.

The extra tax that American firms must pay when they repatriate foreign profits encourages those firms to leave profits abroad, investing those funds to expand foreign operations instead of bringing that money back to invest in new plants and equipment at home. That increases the demand for employees by US firms in those foreign countries at the expense of employment in the United States. The result is that real wages are lower in the United States, and therefore fewer potential employees seek work in the United States.

The extra tax paid by US firms when repatriating profits also raises the effective cost of capital to American firms operating in other countries, making them less able to compete in those markets. That shrinks the scale of their global production, reducing the cost savings that would result from spreading domestic R&D and other fixed costs over a larger volume of sales. That also reduces the demand for employees in the United States, lowering real wages in the US and therefore employment.

American firms are also at a disadvantage in obtaining new technology by acquiring high-tech firms abroad. Because of the high cost of capital of US firms, foreign firms can often afford to pay more in bidding to acquire those firms and their technology.

Fortunately, shifting the US method of taxing foreign profits to the "territorial" method used by all other industrial countries would have little adverse effect on corporate tax revenue. According to the 2010 Report on Tax Reform Options of the President's Economic Recovery Advisory Board, the Treasury estimates that a territorial system might cost only $130 billion over 10 years but could be structured in a way that actually raises revenue. Even the $130 billion estimate ignores the favorable revenue effect of the resulting increase in profitable corporate investment in the US.

Shifting to the territorial method of taxation would increase investment in the United States, thereby increasing the real wages of American workers and inducing an increased supply of those workers. The increased flow of capital to the US and the increased productivity of American firms would generate new tax revenue that would offset some of the direct revenue loss caused by a lower corporate tax rate. And since the increased stock of capital in the US would raise productivity and wages, personal income tax revenue would also rise.

Several US firms have responded to the existing rules for taxing foreign profits by engaging in what is known as corporate "inversions." The basic idea of an inversion is to merge with a foreign firm so that the profits earned abroad are technically earned by a foreign firm. That firm can then pay dividends to shareholders in the United States without first distributing them to a US parent company and incurring the incremental US corporate tax. The Treasury Department has recently cracked down on this type of behavior, making it more difficult to make such inversions.

The Organisation for Economic Co-operation and Development (OECD) has recently developed a plan designed to avoid what they label as "Base Erosion and Profit Shifting" in Europe and the United States. The basic idea of the OECD plan is focused on what they see as mobile capital, such as patents and software, where the income earning potential is easily shifted among countries. The OECD has proposed to limit this shifting of profits to low-tax countries by requiring that a company have substantial economic activity in a country to claim that its profits should be taxed there. The US

Treasury Department originally supported the OECD strategy but has more recently come to oppose it when it became clear that it would have the effect of inducing US firms to shift management and production from the United States to low-tax jurisdictions in order to qualify for paying tax in that jurisdiction.

If the OECD plan were enacted by the member countries, there would be a strong incentive for US firms to shift investment and substantial employment to the low-tax jurisdictions. That OECD plan may not happen, but if it were to prevail, the best way to maintain demand for labor in the United States would be to reduce the US corporate tax rate and adopt a territorial system of taxation.

Business Tax Reform and the Labor Market

JASON FURMAN
President's Council of Economic Advisers

BETSEY STEVENSON
University of Michigan

There is widespread agreement that the US system of business taxation needs reform. The current system has one of the highest statutory rates in the developed world, and this has coincided with loophholes and structural features of the US system that substantially lower effective tax rates—in fact, the US average effective tax rate is below the average among the other G-7 countries. A high statutory rate with the ability to achieve a low effective rate through loopholes creates distortions that hurt economic growth and workers, as too many business decisions are shaped by tax incentives, rather than where the economic returns are highest.

Business tax reform has the potential to improve the labor market by reducing these distortions and improving the allocation of resources, including the allocation of labor. When capital and labor are better allocated, productivity is higher, and productivity is an important driver of higher wages for workers. Business tax reform could also reduce the severity of recessions, which themselves can be highly damaging to workers' future earnings and employment. While none of these effects are very large, reform that addresses them merits a place as one among many policies to boost productivity, output, and wages.

The challenge is that the primary goal of business taxes—to raise revenue—cannot be sacrificed. Both businesses and workers rely on government investment and spending to help spur growth and ensure shared prosperity. And higher deficits could come at the expense of capital formation and foreign borrowing, either of which would lower national income in the future. The same incentives that have created the current inefficient set of loopholes and tax preferences are in play in any discussion of business tax reform. Business tax reform could easily go wrong, creating exploding deficits, forcing the elimination of essential government services, or simply creating new distortions in response to the pressure from industries seeking special treatment. Eliminating some distortions in the current system would not bring enough benefits to the US economy and American workers to make up for the costs of a significant reduction in revenue. So while revenue-neutral business tax reform has the potential to improve the US economy and increase opportunities for workers, it must be done correctly to reap these gains.

Reducing Distortions

The economy functions efficiently when capital and labor are allocated to the industries and firms where they are most productive. In a stylized model of perfectly competitive markets with no externalities, owners seeking the highest profits and workers seeking the highest wages would bring about this allocation. In reality, distortionary tax systems are unavoidable, and market imperfections are common. The goal of taxation is therefore to minimize the distortions that create a wedge between optimal private choices and optimal social choices. In particular, the business tax system can be designed to help ensure that business decisions are made on the basis of the highest social returns, not the greatest tax advantages.

While many calls for business tax reform center on our high statutory rate, the primary challenge with the current system is a highly distortionary system that results in much lower effective marginal tax rates for some businesses. The United States has an average 39.0 percent statutory tax rate on corporations including state-level taxes, the highest of any advanced economy and well above the 29.6 percent average for the other G-7 economies, as shown in Table 1.

Table 1. G-7 Statutory Corporate Tax Rates (Percentage)

	Statutory Corporate Tax Rate	Effective Marginal Tax Rate[a]	Effective Actual Tax Rate
	(Including Subnational Taxes)		
	2015	**2015**	**2006–09**
Canada	26.3	12.5	21.6
France	34.4	24.0	23.1
Germany	30.2	21.2	27.9
Italy[b]	31.3	5.2	29.1
Japan	32.1	24.5	38.8
United Kingdom	20.0	19.0	23.6
United States	39.0	18.1	27.7
G-7 Average Excluding the US[c]	**29.6**	**19.4**	**29.2**

Notes: (a) EMTRs reported in this table include temporary incentives for investment, including 50 percent bonus depreciation in the United States. (b) The statutory rate for Italy includes the 3.9 percent IRAP regional production tax not in the reported OECD rate. (c) The G-7 averages for 2015 tax rates are calculated using 2014 gross domestic product (in current US dollars) as weights.

Sources: Organisation for Economic Co-operation and Development; US Department of the Treasury, Office of Tax Analysis; and Barack Obama, "Economic Report of the President," White House, February 2015.

But our effective marginal tax rate is 18.1 percent, just below the 19.4 percent average effective marginal tax rate for the other G-7 economies. The US effective average actual tax rate was 27.7 percent from 2006 to 2009, also somewhat lower than the 29.2 percent average for other G-7 economies.

The difference between the relative statutory rate and the relative effective marginal rate indicates the pervasive ways in which the US tax base is narrowed by loopholes and other tax preferences, some benefiting narrowly targeted industries (e.g., preferential treatment for oil and gas extraction), some benefiting broader sets of industries (e.g., more accelerated depreciation schedules than most other advanced economies), and some rewarding effective tax planning (e.g., a very negative effective tax rate on debt-financed investment and an ability to shift profits overseas in order to avoid taxation).

As a result, effective tax rates vary across a range of economic activities. Examining average effective tax rates between 2007 and 2010, as shown in Table 2, shows that the effective actual federal corporate tax rates range from 14 percent on utilities to 30 percent on construction. Effective marginal tax rates also vary by asset type, with the effective marginal tax rate ranging from 22 percent for intangibles to 29 percent for structures to 39 percent for inventories. Parallel calculations by the Congressional Budget Office (CBO) further illustrate the impact that targeted tax preferences can have on investments in more narrowly defined asset classes. CBO estimates that the effective marginal corporate tax rate on mining structures owned is only 1 percent, while the effective marginal corporate tax rate on prepackaged software is 30 percent. Taken together, some businesses clearly manage to avoid the high US statutory rates quite effectively, while others are less able to do so.

Different tax rates may indeed be warranted based on differences in market imperfections such as externalities. However, the differences in our current system are mostly driven by haphazard decisions and complex interactions in the tax system, or created and maintained at the behest of beneficiaries of the preferences—such as the tax preference for fossil fuels.

As a result of these disparities, for any given level of the capital stock, firms will pursue low-return projects in tax-preferred sectors rather than higher-return projects in tax-disadvantaged sectors. Shifting to a corporate tax system with a broader base and lower rates would reduce these distortions, allowing the economy to shift production and employment toward higher productivity and thus higher wage areas even with no change in the level of investment and savings. One recent study of 11 advanced economies including the United States concluded that 4 percent of the aggregate capital stock appears to be misallocated as a result of corporate tax distortions.[1]

Table 2. Effective Actual Federal Corporate Tax Rates by Industry, 2007–10

Industry	Effective Actual Corporate Tax Rate
Utilities	14.5
Leasing	17.7
Transport and Warehouse	18.6
Mining	21.6
Agriculture, Forestry, Fishing	22.0
Real Estate	22.4
Manufacturing	22.4
Insurance	23.1
Finance	23.1
Information	24.2
Wholesale-Retail	27.9
All Services	29.4
Construction	30.3
Average Effective Actual Tax Rate	**23.3**

Source: US Department of the Treasury, Office of Tax Analysis.

Encouraging Businesses to Efficiently Take into Account Any Broader Costs They Impose

Market imperfections such as externalities provide an opportunity to raise revenue while improving economic efficiency. A well-designed tax system should take every opportunity to use the tax system to improve efficiency by ensuring that private decision makers take into account the full costs of their actions for society. One example is environmental externalities, most notably carbon pollution and particulate matter, which cause both harmful global warming and localized health problems and other harms. While broader policies that put a price on carbon are the optimal way to deal with this externality, in the absence of such policies, steps that subsidize renewable energy such as the Production Tax Credit and the Investment Tax Credit are justified.

The financial sector can also impose negative externalities.[2] Large and risky bank portfolios can increase economy-wide risk, as seen most recently in the 2007–09 financial crisis. While Wall Street reform has greatly reduced these risks, a financial fee on liabilities or the riskiness of liabilities could help create further incentives to internalize these externalities. Moreover, eliminating tax preferences for certain financial activities has the potential to improve allocative efficiency within the sector. For instance, the tax preference for carried interest effectively subsidizes hedge fund management compared with other jobs within the financial sector. Closing the carried-interest loophole, like other loopholes, would thus potentially increase allocative efficiency.

Encouraging Research and Development to Increase Labor Productivity Growth

Business taxes also have a role to play in addressing positive spillovers. A notable example is the broader benefits to society of spending on research and development, as innovations by one company have substantial spillovers for other companies. Thus social benefits can substantially exceed the returns to the company that undertook the research, resulting in underinvestment in research and development relative to the socially optimal levels. Public policy provides a number of tools to address this issue including public funding of research and intellectual property rights to create temporary monopoly power for innovators, but the tax system also has a potentially important role to play.

Through encouraging research and development, tax reform has the potential to impact not only productivity at a point in time, but its growth rate as well. Policies that have the potential to raise labor productivity growth are potentially even more important than policies that raise the level of output in creating the necessary conditions for sustained increases in real wages. Historically the large swings in productivity growth over sustained periods have come from different rates of total factor productivity (TFP) growth, the amount of output for a given amount of inputs, not from variations in the growth rate of capital services or labor quality. One way to increase TFP growth is through more research and development.

The United States does this through the Research and Experimentation (R&E) tax credit, which provides a subsidy for the input costs of research and allows expensing of research expenditures. This approach is supported by a wide range of research conducted in several countries over many years. Research has found that tax credits for research are highly effective in increasing research spending—each dollar of forgone tax revenue due to the credit generally leads firms to invest at least one dollar in research and development, with some studies finding much larger effects.[3] Studies find elasticities of research in response to tax changes of roughly one and often as high as two. This all suggests further benefit from expanding the R&E tax credit.

An alternative approach is an innovation box or a patent box, which has been adopted by the United Kingdom, France, and the Netherlands and proposed in the United States. Instead of subsidizing inputs, this approach would subsidize outputs by applying a separate, lower tax rate to income attributed to patents and other types of intangible business property, such as copyrights, trademarks, trade secrets, and other forms of intellectual property. This approach is relatively new and does not have the same body of supporting research as do approaches that subsidize research inputs. In fact, there are a number of reasons to believe that an innovation box would increase cost and complexity without a commensurate boost to innovation.[4] This is because an innovation box rewards factors such as luck and market power along with higher and more effective research expenditures. It also provides a windfall for past investments and a larger subsidy for activities with a higher private return, often the activities that actually have smaller externalities. An innovation box also has an uncertain and potentially high cost that is not necessarily a function of the amount of additional research it encourages, but instead depends on the degree of tax planning it encourages and the effectiveness of the complex new compliance rules that would be needed to prevent even larger revenue loss.

Reducing the Severity of Business Cycles by Reducing Incentives for Leverage and Improving Countercylical Policy

In addition to increasing the level of output and raising its growth rate, business tax reform can play a role in reducing the severity of economic fluctuations. These fluctuations can be very damaging for workers, including leading to long-lasting reductions in wages and lack of participation in the labor market.[5]

Specifically, the current US system of business taxation imposes a significantly higher tax burden on equity-financed investment than debt-financed investment. Tax reform that reduces this disparity can reduce overleveraging, which increases financial fragility since firms have less of a cushion in downturns, and it can prevent fire sales, contagion, and larger and less efficient macroeconomic fluctuations.[6] Firms' decisions about financing their investments also affect bankruptcy risk, the extent to which investment risk is distributed in the population, and potentially also the management quality of the firm itself.[7] The tax advantage for interest arises because firms can deduct interest payments but not dividend payments from taxable income while individuals must pay tax on both interest and dividend income, although they pay tax on dividends at a reduced rate.

The Treasury Department estimates that the marginal corporate tax rate on equity-financed investment is 27.3 percent, while the marginal corporate tax rate on debt-financed investment is –38.9 percent, as shown in Figure 1. This tax rate on debt-financed investment in machinery is among the lowest in the OECD. Counting individual-level taxes, the disparity is still large, with a 35.5 percent tax rate on equity-financed investment and a –0.2 percent tax rate on debt-financed investment.

By reducing the statutory rate, business tax reform would moderate the debt-equity disparity. Since the statutory rate determines the value of an additional deduction and interest payments are deductible, a reduction in the statutory rate reduces the value of the deduction for interest payments. Additional reforms to the treatment of interest expense could further moderate the disparity, for example,

Figure 1. Effective Marginal Tax Rates by Source of Financing, 2015

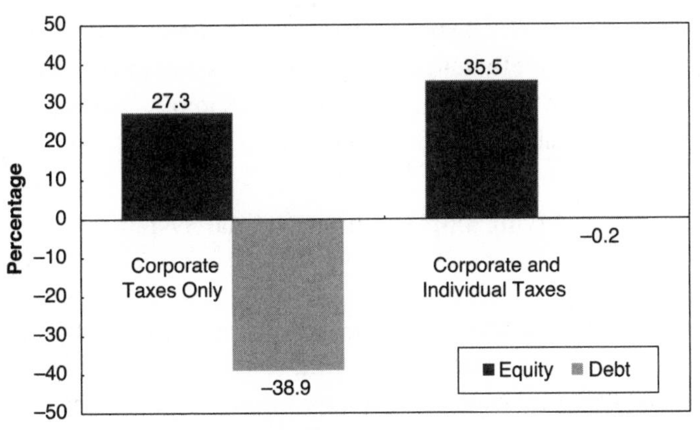

Source: US Department of the Treasury, Office of Tax Analysis.

by reducing the deductibility of interest expenditures as has been done in Germany.

In addition, business taxes can play a role in countercyclical policy, either on a discretionary basis or potentially even through automatic triggers. Specifically, policies that temporarily reduce effective marginal tax rates on business investment, such as bonus depreciation or expensing for small businesses, can play an important role in increasing the quantity of investment and output in the short run, when the economy is operating below its potential. These policies can work both by reducing the cost of capital and also by improving the cash flow for firms that have difficulty accessing capital in financial markets, something that may be particularly important in a financial crisis. Research by Eric Zwick and James Mahon found that bonus depreciation increased investment by 17 percent between 2008 and 2010, with the largest effects among small and financially constrained firms.[8] Moreover, the cost to the federal government was very low—effectively the lost time value of money because of the faster depreciation allowances. As a result, such policies can provide an important additional fiscal tool for responding to recessions. However, such policies are likely more feasible if they are built into business tax reform with explicit triggers based on the performance of the economy. When such policies are left to pass on an as-needed basis, it is difficult to both get the policy passed in time and to undo the policy as the economy recovers. (For example, bonus depreciation will not fully phase out under current law until 2020.)

Fixing a Broken International System

Perhaps nothing exemplifies the broken US tax system more than the taxation of income that is labeled as coming from overseas. In theory the United States has a worldwide international tax system that taxes US multinationals on their income regardless of where in the world it is earned. In practice, however, the US system is more akin to a "stupid territorial" system in which we collect relatively little taxes on income that is labeled as coming from overseas, one of the reasons that the overall US corporate tax rate is relatively low. At the same time, however, our system imposes distortions on US companies that go through accounting and other efforts, including changing their capital structures, to avoid paying these taxes. In theory, it should be possible to push out the revenue-efficiency frontier.

There is an economic argument for shifting to a pure worldwide tax system that eliminates the deferral of taxation on foreign income that exists in the current system, resulting in economic activities being taxed in the same manner in the United States, a low-tax country, or a high-tax country, and thus satisfying the condition of "capital export neutrality" by ensuring that production is located wherever it is most efficient. There is also an economic argument for shifting to a pure territorial system that eliminates taxation on foreign income altogether, which in theory would not lose much revenue compared with the current system, would eliminate the distortions in capital structures, and would satisfy the condition of "capital ownership neutrality" by ensuring that a foreign subsidiary of a US company would not be disadvantaged relative to the foreign subsidiaries of other companies.[9]

It is impossible to satisfy both of these reasonable neutrality principles simultaneously. A lower statutory tax rate would help relieve the pressure on both of them, one reason why comprehensive business tax reform is preferable to international-only reform. But there will always be other countries with lower statutory rates, especially in a world where some small island nations have effective zero rates. As a result, the right response to the contradictory pressures from maximizing on two different margins is to adopt a hybrid system that is some convex combination of a pure worldwide and pure territorial system. This could be done with a rate intermediate between the full US rate and the zero territorial rate, for example a minimum tax along the lines proposed by President Barack Obama, former House Ways and Means Chairman Dave Camp, and Senator Rob Portman.

The theoretical ideal territorial system where domestic US income is taxed at US rates and foreign income is taxed at foreign rates is impossible to implement in the real world. In practice, companies can use a variety of techniques to lower the taxes they pay on foreign income, well below the tax rates in those countries, for example through aggressive transfer pricing, earnings stripping, intellectual property location, and other techniques. But it is not only about the income earned abroad, a subject of legitimate debate; these same techniques are also used extensively to shift income that is genuinely earned in the United States to foreign jurisdictions in order to avoid paying taxes on it here or perhaps even anywhere as in the case of "stateless income."[10]

Harry Grubert and Rosanne Altshuler analyzed a reformed system in which the United States lowered its statutory tax rate to 30 percent and then considered investments in a low-tax country (with a 5 percent rate) and a high-tax country (with a 25 percent rate).[11] The case for a territorial system rests on foreign income actually being taxed at those respective rates in those countries, but they found that adding the essential elements of a territorial system to the current US system would open up such opportunities for tax reduction that the actual rate on typical activities in the low-tax country would be –30 percent and the actual tax on typical activities in the high-tax country would be 11 percent as shown in Figure 2. While various

Figure 2. Effective Marginal Tax Rates in Several Tax Systems

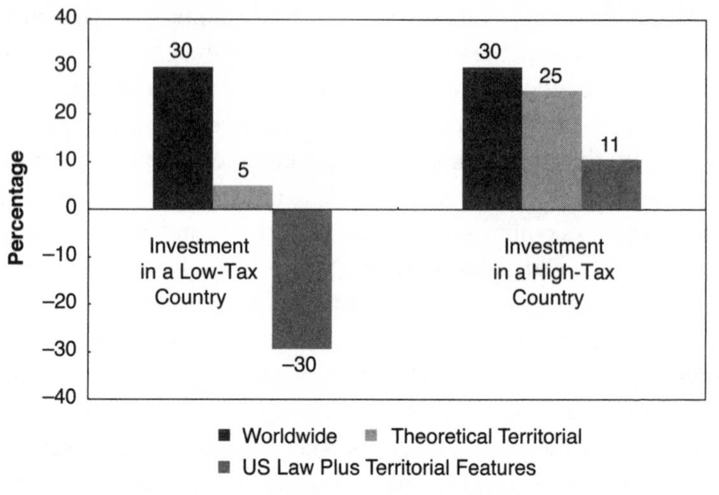

Note: US Law Plus Territorial Features is Grubert and Altsuler's dividend exemption scenario.

Source: Harry Grubert and Rosanne Altshuler, "Fixing the System: An Analysis of Alternative Proposals for the Reform of International Tax," *National Tax Journal* 66, no. 3 (2013): 671–712.

anti-abuse rules could potentially curb some of the resulting revenue loss, such rules would be complicated and inevitably incomplete given the incentives businesses face to avoid taxes. Not only would such a rate structure lead to highly inefficient allocations of capital and wasted effort on avoidance, it would also require substantially higher domestic rates to make up for the revenue loss—compounding the problem with today's tax system rather than ameliorating it.

Business Tax Reform Done Wrong: Revenue Losses and Lower Individual Rates

All of these potential benefits of business tax reform are worthwhile, but they can be realized only by getting tax reform right. Business taxes raise important revenue, and reform that significantly reduces revenue will result in large costs that more than offset potential gains.

Tax reform can improve the *quality* of capital, shifting it toward its most efficient uses and toward a greater investment in innovation. Innovation has historically been much more important in driving improvements in labor productivity and living standards than changes in the *quantity* of capital. Tax reform that results in substantial revenue loss can increase deficits, reduce national savings, and crowd out investment or increase foreign borrowing—costs that would outweigh any direct benefits from tax reform. In fact, business tax reform should replace the revenue that was recently lost by making tax extenders permanent without paying for them or, alternatively, should offset some of the losses already built into the baseline, which assumes increased tax planning activities.

Some reforms risk revenue losses through gimmicks, such as plans that appear to be paid for in the traditional 10-year budget window but that actually raise the deficit on a present-value basis by shifting costs outside the window, for example by lengthening depreciation schedules.

The other significant issue in business tax reform is the treatment of the top individual tax rate. Some have called for reducing this rate in tandem with the corporate rate, arguing that pass-throughs, a category that includes many small businesses, pay taxes at the individual rate, not the corporate rate. However, cutting the top individual rate suffers from three large drawbacks. First, pass-throughs currently face a lower average effective tax rate, 25 percent, as compared with the 30 percent average effective tax rate for C corporations that face taxation at both the business level and at the individual level when dividends and capital gains are paid. Cutting the individual rate would widen this disparity, undermining neutrality and thus introducing greater inefficiency into the tax system. Second, most of the income earned at the individual rate is genuinely earned by individuals—including, in some cases, income that appears to be business income such as the salaries of partners in accounting or law firms. Cutting taxes for high-income individuals is unrelated to business tax reform and also unlikely to be economically beneficial, and attempts to limit these cuts to genuine small businesses are doomed to some combination of failure and significant complexity. Finally, cutting the individual rate is extremely expensive, substantially reducing the amount that the statutory rate could be reduced or increasing the likelihood of reform that is not revenue neutral.

It is certainly possible to design reforms that simplify and cut taxes for small businesses and small pass-throughs if desired, but doing so does not require cutting the top individual rate and instead can be done by, for example, expanding Section 179 expensing for small businesses.

Conclusion

A sensibly designed business tax reform that focuses on the genuine economic problems of a system that is highly distortionary, does not properly address externalities, does not sufficiently encourage research, and leads to over-indebtedness and financial fragility has benefits that make it an important part of a broader strategy to create more high-paying jobs and improve the functioning of the labor market and the economy more broadly. But to the degree that business tax reform actually leads to significant revenue losses or is a pretext for the unrelated enterprise of cutting the top individual tax rate, it would be counterproductive.

Notes

1. Serena Fatica, *Do Corporate Taxes Distort Capital Allocation? Cross-Country Evidence from Industry-Level Data*, European Commission Economic Papers, September 2013.

2. For example, see Luigi Zingales, "Does Finance Benefit Society," *Journal of Finance* 70, no. 4 (2015): 1327–63.

3. Nick Bloom, Rachel Griffith, and John Van Reenen, "Do R&D Tax Credits Work? Evidence from a Panel of Countries 1979–1997," *Journal of Public Economics* 85, no. 1 (2002): 1–31; Bronwyn Hall, "R&D Tax Policy During the Eighties: Success or Failure?" in *Tax Policy and the Economy*, vol. 7, ed. James Poterba (Cambridge: MIT Press, May 1993), 1–35; and James R. Hines Jr., "On the Sensitivity of R&D to Delicate Tax Changes: The

Behavior of US Multinationals in the 1980s," in *Studies in International Taxation*, ed. Alberto Giovannini, R. Glenn Hubbard, and Joel Slemrod (Chicago: University of Chicago Press, 1993), 149–94.

4. International Monetary Fund, *Fiscal Monitor: Acting Now, Acting Together*, April 2016.

5. Steven J. Davis and Till von Wachter, *Recessions and the Cost of Job Loss*, Brookings Papers on Economic Activity, Fall 2011, 1–72.

6. Ruud A. de Mooij, *Tax Biases to Debt Finance: Assessing the Problem, Finding Solutions*, International Monetary Fund, May 3, 2011; and Joel Slemrod, "Lessons for Tax Policy in the Great Recession," *National Tax Journal* 62, no. 3 (2009): 387–97.

7. Alfons Weichenrieder and Tina Klautke, "Taxes and the Efficiency Costs of Capital Distortions" (working paper, CESifo, October 2008).

8. Eric Zwick and James Mahon, "Tax Policy and Heterogeneous Investment Behavior" (working paper, National Bureau of Economic Research, January 2016).

9. Mihir A. Desai and James R. Hines Jr., "Evaluating International Tax Reform," *National Tax Journal* 56, no. 3 (2003): 487–502.

10. Edward Kleinbard, "Stateless Income's Challenge to Tax Policy," *Tax Notes* 132, no. 1021 (2011): 1021–42.

11. Harry Grubert and Rosanne Altshuler, "Fixing the System: An Analysis of Alternative Proposals for the Reform of International Tax," *National Tax Journal* 66, no. 3 (2013): 671–712.

VIII

What Should We Do About Those Americans Who Are Especially Difficult to Employ?

Making Work a Priority for Working-Age People with Disabilities*

RICHARD V. BURKHAUSER
Cornell University and University of Texas

MARY C. DALY
Federal Reserve Bank of San Francisco

Political discourse regarding people with disabilities has shifted considerably over the last three decades. The need to protect the less-abled has been replaced with a recognition that with appropriate support, most everyone, regardless of their differences, can participate in the economy and society. This change in mindset is reflected in the 1989 Americans with Disabilities Act and supported by medical and technological innovations that have made work more available and possible for those with disabilities. Against this positive backdrop stand two troubling trends regarding the economic integration of people with disabilities. Since 1989, the employment rate of working-age (ages 18–64) people with disabilities has fallen almost continuously, hitting a low of 22 percent in 2012. Adults with disabilities now work less than many other vulnerable groups targeted by public policy, such as poor single mothers and African American youth and young adults. As their employment rates have fallen, the share of adults with disabilities relying on federally

*The contents of this paper do not necessarily represent the policies of the Federal Reserve Bank of San Francisco or the Federal Reserve Board of Governors, and readers should not assume their endorsement.

provided disability benefits has increased, reaching nearly 50 percent in 2012.

We argue that the growing divergence between the change in political discourse and the economic integration of adults with disabilities into the workforce is a shortcoming of US policy related to the failure to reform the two main public programs for adults with disabilities: Social Security Disability Insurance (SSDI) and Supplemental Security Income (SSI).[1] Established in 1956 and 1972, respectively, these programs continue to require their applicants to prove they cannot work before granting access to benefits including rehabilitative services and work incentive programs. For the average applicant this means a long period out of the labor force while their case is decided. Not surprisingly, this long work absence has a significant negative effect on the subsequent employment odds of both accepted and rejected applicants.[2] As such, the design of these programs effectively forces adults with disabilities to choose early on between work and public support (cash assistance plus health insurance).

Unfortunately, the data reveal that an increasing fraction of working-age adults with disabilities are choosing the latter option and applying for permanent disability benefits.[3] This has significant consequences for both the disability system, which is being tasked with supporting an increasing number of beneficiaries, and for the economy, which is losing significant numbers of potentially work-capable adults from the labor force.

Here we review trends in employment, benefit receipt, and the household income for adult Americans with disabilities. We show that while their income has been growing, the share of it they earn from market sources has declined relative to adult Americans without disabilities. We then argue that this outcome relates more to policy design than to changes in health or population composition, suggesting there is room for change. We conclude by comparing US outcomes with those of other countries. While the share of adults receiving disability-based social insurance has increased substantially in many industrialized nations, several have been proactive in reversing these trends. The reform experiences in these countries provide useful lessons for US policymakers focused on matching policy language with policy action.

Employment, Benefits, and Economic Well-Being

We begin by reviewing trends in employment, benefit receipt, and household size-adjusted income for adults with and without disabilities. Our discussion is based largely on analysis done by Burkhauser, Larrimore, and Lyons[4] and Lyons, Burkhauser, and Larrimore,[5] using data from the Current Population Survey.[6] Figure 1 plots the employment rates of adults with and without disabilities from 1980 through 2012. NBER-based recession years are shaded. As the figure shows, during the 1980s, employment rates for adults with and without disabilities moved with the business cycle, declining when the economy contracted and increasing when the economy expanded. Employment rates for both populations fell again in the early 1990s, but in contrast to adults without disabilities, the employment rates of adults with disabilities never recovered and, in fact, continued to decline. In 2012, just 22 percent of working-age adults with disabilities were employed, compared to 40 percent in 1989.

This decline in employment has been accompanied by a steady rise in the fraction of adults with disabilities receiving federal disability benefits and publicly provided health insurance (Figure 2). In 1982, the first year in the sample, about 27 percent reported having income from SSDI or SSI. By 2012, the last year in the sample, this number had risen to 49 percent. The same pattern can be seen for their public (Medicare or Medicaid) versus private health insurance coverage. Adults with disabilities have consistently moved from private health insurance coverage to public programs associated with federal disability benefits.

Figure 3 shows how these trends in employment and benefit receipt have affected the relative household size-adjusted income of adults with and without disabilities. The figure plots two lines. The first line shows the median household size-adjusted market (e.g. wages, rents, interest, dividends, etc.) income of adults with disabilities relative to the median household size-adjusted market income

Figure 1. Trends in the Employment Rate of Working-Age Adults (Ages 18–64) with and Without Disabilities

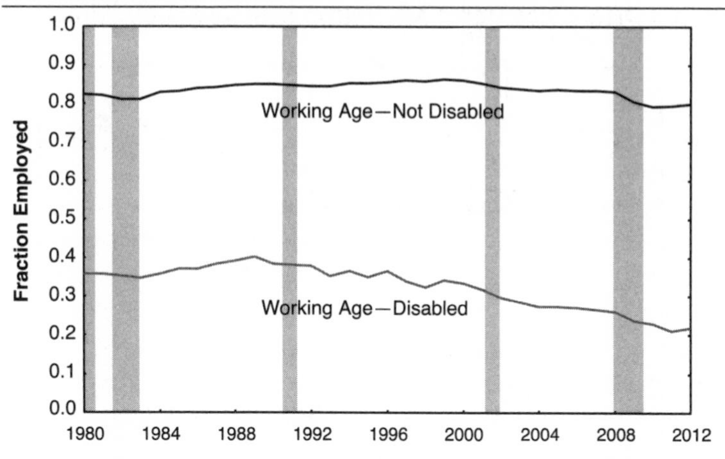

Note: Employment includes full- and part-time.
Source: Sean Lyons, Richard V. Burkhauser, and Jeff Larrimore, "Accounting for the Growing Importance of Access to Health Insurance in the Household Income of Working-Age People with and Without Disabilities" (working paper, Cornell University, 2016).

Figure 2. Trends in the Take-Up Rate of SSDI/SSI and Private and Public Health Insurance for Working-Age Adults (Ages 18–64) with Disabilities

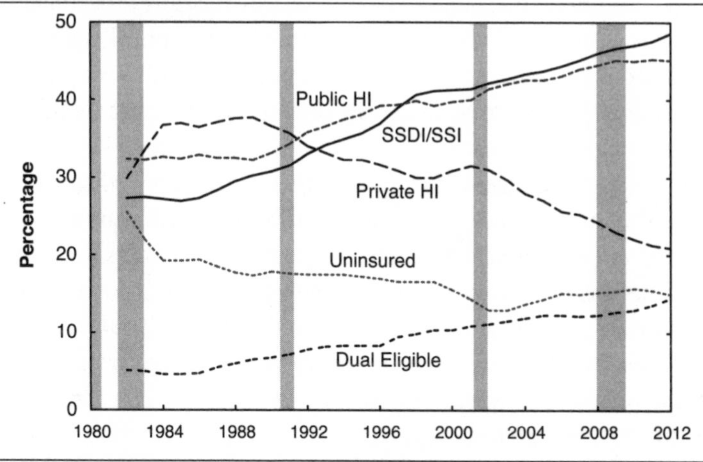

Source: Richard V. Burkhauser, Jeff Larrimore, and Sean Lyons, "Measuring Health Insurance Benefits: The Case of People with Disabilities" (working paper, National Bureau of Economic Research, October 2015).

Figure 3. Trends in the Ratio of Median Household Size-Adjusted Income of Working-Age Adults (Ages 18–64) with and Without Disabilities Using Alternative Measures of Income

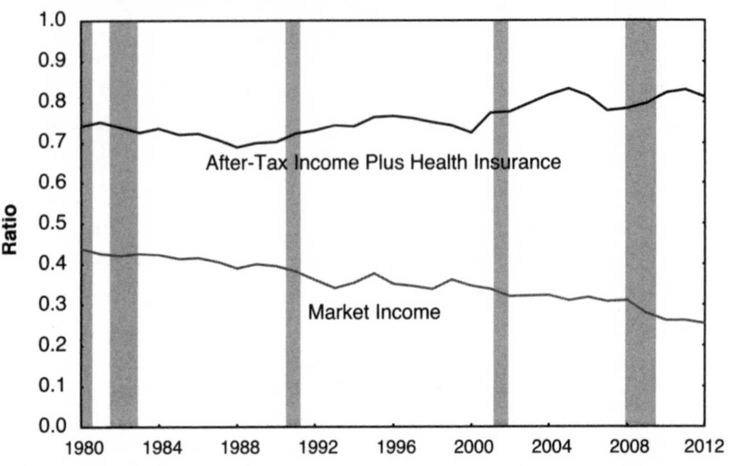

Source: Sean Lyons, Richard V. Burkhauser, and Jeff Larrimore, "Accounting for the Growing Importance of Access to Health Insurance in the Household Income of Working-Age People with and Without Disabilities" (working paper, Cornell University, 2016).

of adults without disabilities. Based on this measure, the relative income of adults with disabilities fell almost continuously over the period, from 44 percent in 1980 to 25 percent in 2012. This pattern is consistent with the relative decline in employment rates for adults with disabilities.

The picture changes when government taxes and transfers as well as the market value of public and private health insurance are included in household size-adjusted income.[7] In all years the addition of government taxes and transfers improves the income of the median adult with disabilities relative to the median adult without disabilities. But the size of this improvement has varied considerably over the period. During the 1980s, the increase in government taxes and transfers was not enough to offset the decline in relative market income, and hence relative disposable income (i.e., market plus government transfers net of taxes) fell. However, since 1988, with few exceptions the increase in government transfers net of taxes has more than offset the decline in relative market income. As a result, relative disposable income of adults with disabilities has risen from 74 percent in 1980 to 81 percent in 2012. Burkhauser, Larrimore, and Lyons show that the vast majority of this offset comes from the value of employer- and government-provided health insurance for those with disabilities.[8]

These results provide both good and bad news. The good news is that once fully counted, the declines in relative median market income of working-age people with disabilities have been largely offset by the combined benefits of SSDI, SSI-disabled benefits, Medicare, and Medicaid. The bad news is that access to these programs requires recipients to demonstrate they can't work before being granted benefits and provides them with systematic disincentives to reengage in employment. This effectively means that most adults who start to receive disability benefits permanently leave the US labor force and forgo their opportunity to fully engage in the economy. This and other flaws in US disability policy stand in the way of a fuller integration of adults with disabilities into the American workplace.

The Role of Health and Aging on Disability Benefit Growth

To the extent that the shift from employment to the disability rolls reflects a rise in disability prevalence or deterioration in health among adults with disabilities, these outcomes are less worrisome. However, little evidence suggests that this is the case. Figure 4 shows the fraction of adults reporting a work limitation between 1980 and 2012. Although there are fluctuations in the prevalence from year to year and a modest drift upward, it is not consistent with the patterns observed for disability benefit receipt. Additionally, data from the National Health Interview Survey show either no change or substantial improvement in health among adult Americans.[9]

The most obvious potential driver of SSDI growth is the aging of the adult population. Since SSDI benefits are conditioned on having a disability, and disability generally rises with age, the aging of the baby-boom generation will, on net, push up the SSDI

Figure 4. Trends in the Share of Working-Age Adults (Ages 18–64) Reporting a Work Activity Limitation

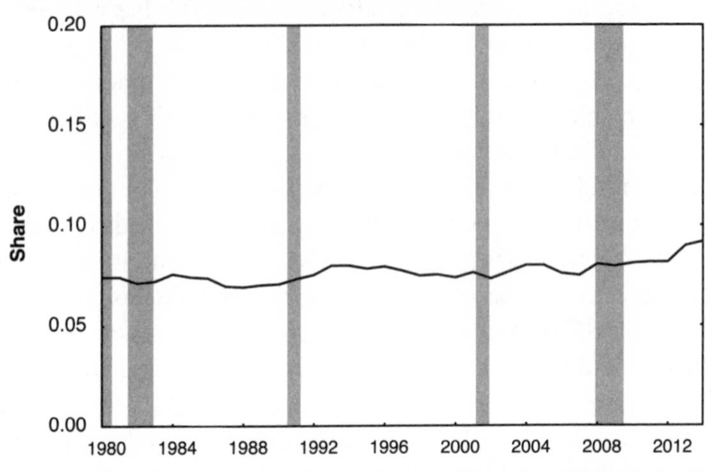

Source: Authors' calculations using March data from the Current Population Survey.

rolls. Calculations by Duggan and Imberman show that, holding age-specific rates of disability benefits at their 1984 levels, the aging of the population explains about 6 percent of the growth in disability receipt between 1984 and 2004.[10] Daly, Lucking, and Schwabish update these calculations to take into account the growing importance of aging and find that, holding disability recipiency rates at their 1980 base, the aging of the population accounted for about 18 percent of SSDI recipiency growth between 1980 and 2012. In their fuller model they also control for the increasing SSDI coverage of women and changes in Old-Age and Survivors Insurance (OASI) normal retirement age and still find nearly one-half of the increase may be explained by policy changes.[11]

The Role of Policy

In the late 1970s and early 1980s SSDI caseloads per adult population fell, first because program gatekeepers were urged to more strictly interpret existing rules and then because Congress, in 1980, required the Social Security Administration (SSA) to reevaluate all current recipients to see if they still met the medical standards. This rule change, which was rigorously enforced by SSA at the start of the new Reagan administration, resulted in a drop in the SSDI rolls per adult population despite a major recession. By 1983 the widespread reevaluation of those already on SSDI was halted as the courts and then Congress restricted the SSA's power to reevaluate beneficiaries. Furthermore, in 1984, responding to a backlash against restrictive cuts imposed in the Social Security Disability Amendments of 1980, policymakers expanded the ways in which a person could medically qualify for the SSDI program. The 1984 legislation moved away from a strict medical listing determination of eligibility to one that also considered an applicant's overall medical condition and ability to work. These changes meant that applicants could qualify for SSDI based on having multiple conditions, even when no single condition would meet the SSDI eligibility threshold. In addition, the legislation allowed for symptoms of mental illness and pain to be counted when assessing SSDI eligibility, regardless of whether the person had a verifiable medical diagnosis.

The expansion of eligibility to more-difficult-to-measure impairments that do not precisely meet the medical listings means that SSA has increasingly been tasked with making more subjective decisions about the impact that presenting impairments might have on an applicant's work ability. For applicants who do not meet or exceed the medical listings, program administrators consider a set of vocational criteria. While these criteria have not changed over the history of the SSDI program, their use by program gatekeepers to determine benefit eligibility has risen dramatically since 1991. Currently, they are used to justify the majority of new awards, especially among those with the more-difficult-to-determine conditions of mental illness and musculoskeletal conditions—the primary condition of more than 50 percent of all newly enrolled beneficiaries.[12]

The effect of this growing share of marginal applicants is a substantial variation in the flow of applicants onto the rolls. This variation comes both from fluctuations in applicant inflow and variations in decision making among SSDI gatekeepers. For example, Maestas,

Mullen, and Strand using SSA administrative records find that at the initial Disability Determination Stage (DDS) of decision making, 23 percent of new applicants in 2005 were marginal cases whose admittance into the program was determined by the luck of drawing an easier rather than a stricter DDS gatekeeper. Importantly, when they compare the subsequent work histories of those who entered the program in this way with a matched set of applicants who drew a stricter DDS gatekeeper, they find the latter group's employment was on average 20 percentage points higher. This difference is even greater for those with less severe medical conditions.[13] This research suggests that, increasingly, applicants admitted to the SSDI rolls on these looser criteria have greater work capacity than assumed for those receiving SSDI benefits.

The differences in allowances are important, especially when one considers how application rates fluctuate with economic conditions. Plots of the SSDI application rate and the national unemployment rate show that, with the exception of the double-dip recession in the 1980s, application rates are highly correlated with the business cycle. They rise during recessions and fall during periods of economic growth. Disability application rates hit record highs during the Great Recession and have only modestly declined since then. Most research on the consequence of business cycles on application rates finds that economic conditions play a substantial role in SSDI application and award patterns over time.[14]

In sum, a significant fraction of disability benefit growth has been driven by factors other than an aging workforce, declines in population health, the increasing SSDI coverage of women, and changes in the OASI normal retirement age. Loosening of program rules in the 1980s has made it more difficult for gatekeepers to judge eligibility and increased the likelihood that applicants facing rising replacement rates or declining economic opportunities will apply for SSDI benefits. A growing number of individuals allowed onto the rolls could work in some capacity and would do so if they were not judged eligible for benefits.

Figure 5. Growth in Disability Recipiency Across Countries

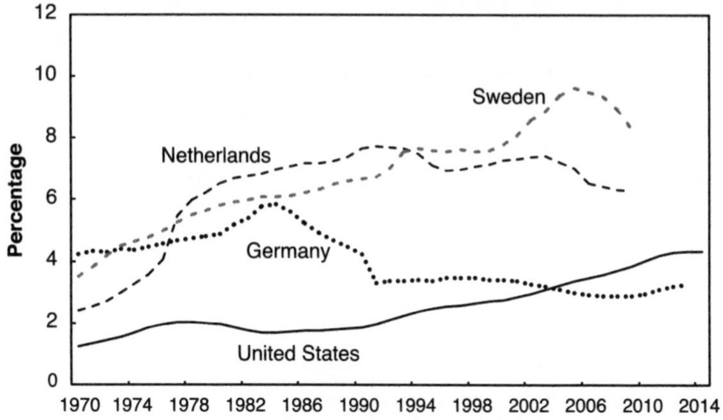

Source: Richard V. Burkhauser, Mary C. Daly, and Nicholas Ziebarth, "Protecting Working-Age People with Disabilities: Experience from Four Industrialized Nations" (working paper, Federal Reserve Bank of San Francisco, June 2015), http://www.frbsf.org/economic-research/publications/working-papers/wp2015-08.pdf.

Integrating Americans with Disabilities into the Work Force: Lessons from Other Countries

As in the United States, the number of workers receiving disability-based social insurance has increased substantially in many other industrialized nations over the past 40 years. Population growth accounts for part of this increase, but disability caseloads as a share of the working-age adult population—the disability recipiency rate—also have risen substantially. This can be seen in Figure 5, which shows disability recipiency rates in four countries—Germany, the Netherlands, Sweden, and the United States—beginning in 1970 through the last year of public data in each country.[15]

In 1970, disability recipiency rates in our three EU nations (4.2 percent in Germany, 2.4 percent in the Netherlands, and 3.5 percent in Sweden) were considerably higher than they were in the US (1.2 percent). Since then disability recipiency rates have risen substantially in each country with the exception of Germany. However,

Table 1. Average Annual Growth in Disability Recipiency by Decade and Country

	Germany	Netherlands	Sweden	United States
1970–79	1.69	11.45	5.49	5.65
1980–89	–1.79	1.79	1.59	–0.91
1990–99	–2.30	–0.34	1.44	4.10
2000–Final	–1.61	–1.25	1.00	3.17
1970–Final	**–0.93**	**2.69**	**2.30**	**2.96**

Source: Richard V. Burkhauser, Mary C. Daly, and Nicholas Ziebarth, "Protecting Working-Age People with Disabilities: Experience from Four Industrialized Nations" (working paper, Federal Reserve Bank of San Francisco, June 2015), http://www.frbsf.org/economic-research/publications/working-papers/wp2015-08.pdf.

as Figure 5 highlights, they have done so along significantly different trajectories. To see these dynamics more clearly, Table 1 provides average annual growth rates in disability recipiency by decade and over the entire sample. As the table shows, disability recipiency rates rose in all countries during the 1970s, with especially rapid growth in the Netherlands and more modest growth in Germany. In contrast, in the 1980s, recipiency rates grew more modestly and even fell in the US and Germany. By the 1990s, growth in the Netherlands and Germany ended and disability recipiency rates, on balance, fell over the decade. During the 2000s, disability recipiency rates continued to fall in the Netherlands and Germany and grew less quickly in Sweden. Growth in the US slowed slightly but remained quite high relative to the EU countries in our sample.

The final average (1970–final) shows that smoothing through the fluctuations in growth that have occurred over the decades, the US experienced the highest average annual growth rate over the sample period. The rapid growth in our three EU countries brought on program reforms and a tempering or reversal of the path of disability recipiency. In contrast, with the exception of the 1980s, growth in US disability recipiency has been nearly continuous over the sample period.

Accounting for These Trends. Burkhauser, Daly, and Ziebarth argue that neither changes in underlying health nor changes in population characteristics can account for all of the cross-country differences in disability recipiency rates, either levels or trends.[16] They then show how changes in disability policy and its implementation in each country are correlated with the dynamics of disability recipiency rates in Figure 5. While their comparative descriptive analysis falls short of establishing a causal effect of policy on the disability rolls, it is suggestive of the potential impact of policy design on the trends in disability benefit receipt across and within these countries. A systematic look at the policies in place during the disability recipiency growth years in Germany, the Netherlands, and Sweden reveals disability programs focused on providing cash assistance in lieu of full-time work without a careful consideration of the unintended consequences of such a policy. This design was based on several assumptions: (1) People with disabilities are incapable of work; (2) it is easy to determine who is and is not disabled; and (3) the behavior of individuals, program managers, and employers is not affected by program rules and incentives.

For instance, in both Germany and the Netherlands those with only partial disabilities who were unemployed but could have worked were admitted onto the disability rolls with full benefits. This mission creep increasingly made their disability programs "unemployability" programs and resulted in very rapid increases in recipiency rates.

The single most important factor in reducing recipiency rates in all three countries was a shift to work-first policies that slowed the movement of disabled workers onto the rolls by ensuring that accommodation and rehabilitation were explored before workers were even considered for long-term disability transfer benefits. This was done in Germany by substantially increasing the bar for entry onto the public disability program and reducing benefits—but also by requiring employers to implement a workplace reintegration program. Changes in the eligibility criteria for government-provided disability benefits resulted in major growth in the private disability market. In 2012, 61 percent of employed men and 42 percent of employed women were covered by private disability insurance.[17] Because private disability is experience rated, it encourages workers and employers to look to rehabilitation and accommodation first since they now more directly bear the costs of a movement onto the disability rolls.

In the Netherlands disability eligibility standards were also raised and benefits reduced, but an even larger shift to work-first policies took place. Employers are now mandated to provide the first two years of disability benefits to their disabled workers. In addition, employers must demonstrate an effort to provide accommodation and rehabilitation to their workers, and their workers must show a willingness to use them. Only when such efforts are shown not to be effective are workers allowed to apply for government disability benefits and their employers allowed to stop directly paying their private disability benefits. This change in policy has also resulted in major growth in the private disability market, and these experience-rated payments further ensure that accommodation and rehabilitation are tried before a worker moves onto the disability rolls. Furthermore, even the government-run disability program is now financed by experience-rated payments by firms.

In Sweden, despite considerable opposition from various advocacy groups, significant reforms were put into place whose driving principle was that work support, rather than cash assistance in lieu of work, was the primary goal of disability policy. To achieve this, the government merged the sickness benefits and disability systems and began a series of changes to standardize and enforce the administration of these now joint systems. Most notable among them was the centralization of screening processes. This allows policymakers to better regulate the gatekeepers and enforce the strategy of promoting participation in work before offering cash benefits. Employers are also required to work with disability administrators to create a rehabilitation plan. And gatekeepers now have the power to demand that employers prove they provided worker accommodations. Most recently Sweden has established a timeline for the provision of rehabilitation services under the sickness absence program with checkpoints at 3-, 6-, and 12-month increments to align assessment of work capacity and a reduction of the cash value of sickness benefits for those who did not return to work.[18]

Lessons for the US. An important issue for policymakers in all countries facing the challenges of providing protection for workers with disabilities is that disability programs, even if not generous, are essential income for many individuals. In the US, where other components of the social safety net are weaker or less generous, disability benefit programs are even more difficult to challenge.

However, the policy outcomes of Germany, the Netherlands, and Sweden show this is a very static view that assumes in the absence of benefits individuals with disabilities would remain out of the labor market, dependent on other forms of public or private assistance for support. While more research is needed to assess the full impact of disability reforms in these countries, their reform experience shows that a significant number of people with disabilities, who would otherwise have moved on to long-term cash benefits, were able, with reasonable levels of support, to return to work. While it is always the case that tightening the criteria for disability benefits runs the risk of denying disability benefits to those who will not be able to find work, on balance the EU experience suggests that reasonable pro-work policies will both substantially reduce disability recipiency rates and increase the employment of those who would otherwise have been on the long-term disability rolls.

Another concern is that programs like disability insurance are especially important in economic downturns where individuals with limited work capacity are not only more likely to be laid off but less likely to find a new job. Past experience of EU countries, especially Germany and the Netherlands, which intentionally or unintentionally used this logic to turn their long-term disability programs into more general unemployment programs, suggests that it can be a very expensive and ultimately ineffective policy decision. Indeed, many EU nations continue to struggle to regain control over their disability systems, which for many decades have been used as long-term unemployment insurance programs. A key message from the EU experience is that explicitly divorcing long-term "unemployability" insurance from disability insurance is critical to effectively targeting resources toward both populations.

Together the experiences of other nations suggest that it is possible to balance the competing goals of providing social insurance against adverse health shocks during working age and maximizing the work effort of all working-age adults with and without disabilities. Past disability policies in both the United States and EU countries have focused more on the former than the latter, resulting in rapid growth in disability transfer populations that outpaced growth in the economy. Efforts to shift to more pro-work policies over the last decade in Europe suggest that fundamental disability reforms, if done well, can lower projected long-term costs for taxpayers, make the job of disability administrators less difficult, and, importantly, improve the short- and long-run opportunities of Americans with disabilities to work.

Acknowledgments

We thank Sean Lyons and Andrew Houtenville for providing data for this paper and Catherine van der List for excellent research assistance.

Notes

1. For a more detailed discussion of the SSDI and SSI programs, see Richard V. Burkhauser and Mary C. Daly, *The Declining Work and Welfare of People with Disabilities: What Went Wrong and a Strategy for Change* (Washington, DC: American Enterprise Institute, 2011).

2. David H. Autor et al., "Does Delay Cause Decay? The Effect of Administrative Decision Time on the Labor Force Participation and Earnings of Disability Applicants" (working paper, January 2015).

3. Application rates rise and fall with economic conditions but have been trending up since the late 1990s. Data on applications can be found at https://www.socialsecurity.gov/policy/docs/statcomps/supplement/2015/ (SSDI, Table 6.C7) and http://www.socialsecurity.gov/policy/docs/statcomps/ssi_asr/2014/ (SSI, Table 57).

4. Richard V. Burkhauser, Jeff Larrimore, and Sean Lyons, "Measuring Health Insurance Benefits: The Case of People with Disabilities" (working paper, National Bureau of Economic Research, October 2015).

5. Sean Lyons, Richard V. Burkhauser, and Jeff Larrimore, "Accounting for the Growing Importance of Access to Health Insurance in the Household Income of Working-Age People with and Without Disabilities" (working paper, Cornell University, 2016).

6. US Department of Commerce, Current Population Survey, various years.

7. Since 2012 the Congressional Budget Office (CBO) has included an estimate of the market value of government-provided health insurance coverage (Medicare and Medicaid) in its measure of household income to more fully identify how government taxes and expenditures (transfers) are distributed across the income distribution. These estimates reflect the additional market price individuals would pay for this health insurance in the private market. A small academic literature shows that the inclusion of the market value of health insurance will primarily affect US income levels but have a smaller effect on their trends except at the bottom tail of the distribution. For a fuller discussion, see Burkhauser et al., "Measuring Health Insurance Benefits."

8. Ibid.

9. Burkhauser and Daly, *The Declining Work and Welfare of People with Disabilities*; and Mark Duggan and Scott A. Imberman, "Why Are the Disability Rolls Skyrocketing? The Contribution of Population Characteristics, Economic Conditions, and Program Generosity," in *Health at Older Ages: The Causes and Consequences of Declining Disability Among the Elderly*, ed. David M. Cutler and David A. Wise (Chicago: University of Chicago Press, 2008), 337–79.

10. Duggan and Imberman, "Why Are the Disability Rolls Skyrocketing?"

11. See Mary C. Daly, Brian Lucking, and Jonathan A. Schwabish, "The Future of Social Security Disability Insurance," Federal Reserve Board of San Francisco Economic Letter, June 24, 2013, http://www.frbsf.org/economic-research/publications/economic-letter/2013/june/future-social-security-disability-insurance-ssdi/. Liebman finds a greater role for aging and other factors unrelated to policy, but those findings are sensitive to the particular years selected for the analysis. See Jeffrey B. Liebman,

"Understanding the Increase in Disability Insurance Benefit Receipt in the United States," *Journal of Economic Perspectives* 29, no. 2 (Spring 2015): 123–50.

12. For fuller discussion see Burkhauser and Daly, *The Declining Work and Welfare of People with Disabilities.*

13. Nicole Maestas, Kathleen J. Mullen, and Alexander Strand, "Does Disability Insurance Receipt Discourage Work? Using Examiner Assignment to Estimate Causal Effects of SSDI Receipt," *American Economic Review* 103, no. 5 (August 2013): 1797–29.

14. Richard.V. Burkhauser and Mary C. Daly, "Social Security Disability Insurance: Time for Fundamental Change," *Journal of Policy Analysis and Management* 31, no. 2 (Spring 2012): 454–61.

15. The US disability recipiency rate only includes beneficiaries receiving SSDI. When SSI-disabled adults and SSDI program beneficiaries are combined, the level of the US disability recipiency rate is higher, but the patterns over time are roughly the same.

16. Richard V. Burkhauser, Mary C. Daly, and Nicholas Ziebarth, "Protecting Working-Age People with Disabilities: Experience from Four Industrialized Nations" (working paper, Federal Reserve Bank of San Francisco, June 2015), http://www.frbsf.org/economic-research/publications/working-papers/wp2015-08.pdf.

17. Beneficiaries of private disability insurance may also receive government-provided disability benefits if eligible. In contrast, in the US private insurers may reduce payments dollar for dollar for recipients of public SSDI. This means that private insurers in Germany have more of an incentive to return beneficiaries to work than do those in the US.

18. Boeheim and Leoni review all EU countries disability policies. They include Germany, the Netherlands, and Sweden among the subset of these countries characterized by their combination of strong employment-oriented policies and comparatively high protection levels. See Rene Boeheim and Thomas Leoni, "Disability Policies: Reform Strategies in a Comparative Perspective" (working paper, National Bureau of Economic Research, April 2016).

How to Help the Hard-to-Employ: A Focus on Young Men, Especially the Ex-Incarcerated

TIMOTHY M. SMEEDING
University of Wisonsin–Madison

The overall US economy is in fairly good shape. But large pockets of the country, as well as the young and least skilled, are still in need of jobs. Many who need help in the labor market are single parents caring for young children. For these parents, "the deserving poor," work is often part-time and involves responsibilities for child raising, and the rewards to market work have grown because of refundable tax credits and other income and work support.[1] The longer-term solution here is some additional but modest amount of income support leading to decreased income volatility, quite possibly in the form of a universal child allowance.[2]

Many of these children have an absent parent, usually a father under the age of 30, who has poor job skills and poor job prospects, and who lacks the economic wherewithal to help support his children.[3] These include the ex-incarcerated and young men of color, ages 18–34, who have a high school degree or less and many who are currently not in employment, education, or training (NEET). Many face immediate penalties from legal work due to garnishment of earnings for child support or prison-related penalties and costs.[4] Indeed they are the forgotten poor and the invisible men who are a serious drag on the economy, with huge social and economic costs.[5] Arguably these are the hardest to employ in our nation, and they are the focus of this essay.

Our work is much in the spirit of the recent AEI-Brookings report, *Opportunity, Responsibility and Security*, which summarized the problems we address here as follows: "Some groups of Americans (like less-educated men generally and black men specifically) are working considerably less than they once did. Stagnant wages and low work participation among some groups of workers are blocking progress. Both must be addressed."[6] The report goes on to say that we need to expand opportunities for the disadvantaged by making more jobs available, at wages that pay better than they did in 2015, in large part by making work requirements and opportunities for the hard-to-employ that combine both carrots and sticks to promote opportunities to work and the independence and responsibility that hopefully follows. The report also recognizes as do we that markets alone won't generate the desired level of work-based learning that is in both the private and public interest.[7] Hence, governments will need to offer some assistance in the form of tax credits and technical assistance to promote work programs and to make work pay.

The major thrust of this paper is aimed at the young and hard-to-employ and what we should do to help them become stably and gainfully employed. We begin with the state of the current labor market and identifying those men who are the hard-to-employ. These include young men ages 18–34, those who have only a basic education at best, those who are in locations where few jobs are available, and especially the ex-incarcerated. Some call them the "lost generation."[8] Many of these fall into the NEET category, also known as the "disconnected," and are notable only in the fact that they are not participants in today's legal economy.

Next, we review the characteristics of successful jobs programs and consider three programs that might help increase employment: a jobs-of-last-resort guarantee for those able to work but with quid pro quos on both the employment side (e.g., employer involvement and child care provision) and the client side (e.g., child support and some legal payments); a major infrastructure project with federal-state job assistance to place workers in such projects; and finally relocation assistance to where jobs are available—a new Homestead Act.[9] One key to all of these enterprises is better involvement of employers in both training and hiring workers. We conclude on what to do next to build on bipartisan support for greater government and non-profit involvement in worker training, placement, and support for the hard-to-employ.

While this essay is about how to get under-skilled youth into jobs and keep them in jobs that pay a sufficient wage to escape poverty and reliance on income support systems, we must realize that unless and until we can build human capital for the low skilled and under-educated, we will still need income support to help make ends meet.

The Labor Market and the Difficulties of Younger Less-Skilled Men

The staggering problem of chronic joblessness among young and especially minority men is visible all over the United States and especially in large central cities. In places like Los Angeles and New York City about 30 percent of 20- to 24-year-old black men were out of work and out of school in 2014.[10] According to a number of employment measures, teens and young adults are still struggling to gain traction in the labor market after the Great Recession. Labor force participation and employment rates continue to trend downward, as do median annual earnings for less-skilled younger men. This decline in labor force participation and employment rates is particularly pronounced among teens and young adults, where those without postsecondary credentials fare the worst. Employment rates for teens fell by 17 percentage points between 2000 and 2014, compared to a drop of 5 percentage points among 20- to 24-year-olds and 3 percentage points among those age 25 and older.[11] After three decades of high and generally rising returns to college education, the employment and earnings opportunities of the other two-thirds of our workforce (i.e., the non-college workers), particularly the younger cohort disadvantaged by the Great Recession, is our main concern at present.

The continuing recovery is generating more high-wage jobs—but it is not creating new opportunities for those whose jobs disappeared or never appeared. The growth in low-wage jobs far outpaces high-skill ones. Young unskilled and under-skilled workers are at the greatest disadvantage. Autor shows how, in the period between 1999 and 2007, the share of low-wage occupations increased greatly while middle- and high-wage occupations were basically flat.[12] Since the recovery from the Great Recession, there has been an even larger growth in especially low-wage occupations, while middle-wage occupations have continued to lose ground. Overall between 2007 and 2015, low-wage occupations grew as a share of the labor market by 0.6 percent, middle-wage occupations shrank by 4 percent, and high-wage occupations grew by 0.3 percent. Further, the least-well-paid workers are making less money than they were before the recession: median wages for low- and middle-earning occupations sank 1.5 and 1.8 percent, respectively, from 2007 to 2015.[13]

Finding basic, steady work for the NEET population will increase self-sufficiency but by itself is not liable to be enough to escape poverty or pay bills. Hence, income support, including the proposed higher EITC for single people now being tested in New York City, will still be needed.[14]

The recovery has also been geographically uneven. Many regions of the country are struggling to adjust in the wake of the recession. Migration is one channel by which labor markets adjust, but even factoring in out-migration, employment remains depressed in many severely affected metro areas more than five years after a major employment dislocation shock or plant closing. In fact, adjustment is occurring so slowly that at the current pace of normalization, flat employment rates amount to more than a relative "lost decade" of depressed employment for large segments of the country, especially the youngest and hardest to employ.[15]

Finally, there is growing evidence that poor education, limited transportation, and criminal backgrounds combine to create significant barriers to employment for the hard-to-employ. For instance, a recent Federal Reserve Bank of Chicago Community Development forum reviewed six employment and training programs in Milwaukee designed to move low-income workers into jobs.[16] Criminal backgrounds were the most important issue for a majority of men

Figure 1. Share of Young Men Who Were Jobless and Share Who Were Incarcerated

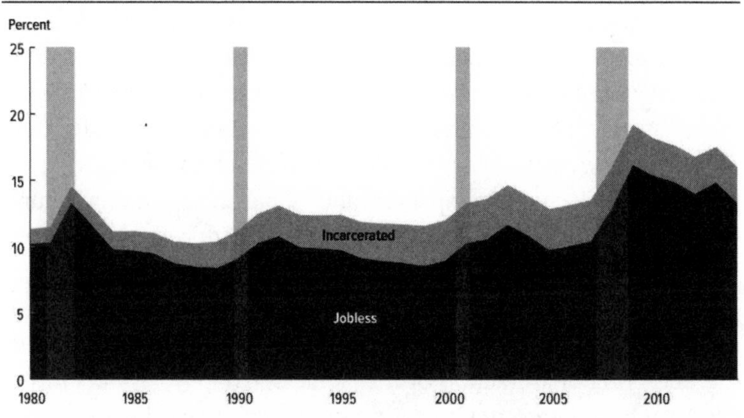

Note: Young men are those ages 18–34. People are counted as jobless if they are neither in school nor working, whether or not they are looking for work. Shaded vertical bars indicate periods of recession, which extend from the peak of a business cycle to its trough.
Source: Congressional Budget Office, "Trends in the Joblessness and Incarceration of Young Men," May 2016, 2, https://www.cbo.gov/publication/51495.

(60 percent) who participated in these workforce programs, with lack of a high school diploma or GED an issue for far fewer people (23 percent). Ex-offenders were also more likely to have multiple barriers, including lack of transportation or failure to hold a valid driver's license.

The Ex-Inmate Underclass

Among the most difficult to employ and to monitor are the ex-incarcerated. A recent Congressional Budget Office report shows that in 2014, there were 38 million men in the United States between the ages of 18 and 34; about 5 million of those young men were jobless, and 1 million were incarcerated (Figure 1).[17] The share of young men who are jobless *or* incarcerated has been rising for more than three decades. In 1980, 11 percent of young men were jobless or incarcerated; in 2014, 16 percent were, and the fraction of all such men who were incarcerated rose from 1 to 3 percent, suggesting that among lowly educated young men the long-run increases in joblessness are to some extent because so many are currently incarcerated.

What is unknown is how these two factors are related to each other, because people with criminal records often have a hard time finding employment. That is, some large fraction of the increase in labor force nonparticipation and joblessness among young men with an inadequate education has been due to the increase in post-incarceration joblessness among these same young men. Whether people who leave prison avoid recidivism depends most of all on whether they get jobs quickly and work steadily.[18] This begs the question, what fraction of the "jobless" 18–34-year-olds in the CBO study who are not currently incarcerated (see Figure 1) has been incarcerated or penalized by the criminal justice system in the recent past?

But first we should establish the important constraint that a criminal record puts on obtaining a job. Prison and jail inmates have very low levels of formal educational attainment, with 66 percent of state prisoners, 56 percent of federal prisoners, and 55 percent of local jail inmates having less than a high school degree.[19] African Americans are heavily overrepresented among the incarcerated, accounting for 43 percent of state prisoners, 46 percent of federal prisoners, and approximately 50 percent of jail inmates, compared with 13 percent of the US population as a whole. Finally, most of the incarcerated are in prime-working-age ranges for men, ranging from their late 20s to their early 40s.[20]

Recent surveys find that over 70 percent of employers and almost 9 in 10 large companies conduct criminal background checks, roughly double the rate during the 1990s.[21] While felony convictions were most "influential" in determining the hiring decision of the employers surveyed, misdemeanors also play a key role in the hiring process.[22] Serving time in prison reduces wages for men by approximately 11 percent, annual employment by nine weeks, and annual earnings by 40 percent compared with similar workers without a history of incarceration.[23]

Job application experiments find that those with criminal records were 50 percent less likely to receive an interview request or job offer, relative to identical applicants with no criminal record, and these disparities were larger for black applicants. Collateral consequence studies have addressed the effects of criminal justice involvement on employment prospects.[24] While private employers are often reluctant to hire ex-offenders, it is a violation of federal Equal Employment Opportunity law for any employer to have a blanket policy of not hiring ex-offenders without regard to the requirements of the job or the nature of the felony. "Ban the box" ordinances, which forbid employers from asking about criminal records in written applications, are growing, but while they show some promise, they are likely not enough to help most ex-offenders to find jobs and may make the situation worse.[25] Employers can still use the Internet to identify criminal history in any case, and where jobs are scarce, the low-skill ex-incarcerated are at a significant disadvantage. Individuals with criminal records are frequently barred from obtaining occupational licenses; according to the American Bar Association, there are over 1,000 mandatory license exclusions for individuals with records of misdemeanors and nearly 3,000 exclusions for felony records.[26]

In a recent comprehensive study of labor markets and the ex-incarcerated, Mueller-Smith finds that among a sample of over 1.0 million Texas men there is clear evidence of lasting negative effects on economic self-sufficiency.[27] Incarceration generates net increases in the frequency and severity of recidivism, worsens labor market outcomes, and strengthens dependence on public assistance. Negative effects on post-release employment and earnings indicate that inmates face significant barriers to job re-entry. Each additional year behind bars reduces post-release employment by 3.6 percentage points. Among felony defendants with stable pre-charge earnings incarcerated for one or more years, post-release employment drops by at least 24 percentage points. These results are paralleled by an increased take-up of SNAP and other welfare. In other words, the ex-incarcerated have many unique employment barriers that need to be addressed.

Nearly one in three adults in 2010 had a serious misdemeanor or felony arrest that can show up on a routine background check for employment, and a substantial share of discouraged workers report a felony conviction.[28] Most offenders emerging from prisons at the end of their sentences or on parole are in the disadvantaged group of younger low-skilled men, many of whom are first-time offenders. The prison outflow now exceeds 650,000 a year.[29]

Shannon et al. extend national estimates of former prison or felony probation populations and compile the first-ever state-level estimates of these populations from 1980 to 2010.[30] These ex-felon estimates complement prior estimates of ex-prisoners but also include the large number of people in the United States who have not served time but experience many of the same consequences of a felony conviction as ex-prisoners.[31] Ex-prisoners and ex-felons, including those under correctional supervision, numbered over 7.0 million in 2010 and have increased since the recent decarceration movement has begun to shrink the prison population. Based on life table estimates, over 5.1 million former prisoners and 15 million former felons, a total of 20 million such individuals, were found in the US population in 2010.[32] As with prisoners, a dramatically higher percentage of African American adults in most states were under correctional supervision for felonies in 2010, at which time the rate exceeded 5 percent of African American adults in 24 states, and no state had less than 2.5 percent of its adult African American population under supervision for felony convictions. States such as Oregon, Rhode Island, and Wisconsin had especially high rates of African American correctional supervision (more than 8 percent of adults). In Florida about 10 percent of the total adult population had spent time under felony-level correctional supervision by 2010.[33]

Importantly, while imprisonment is a serious consequence of a felony conviction, most people with felony convictions never enter prison but instead serve their sentences in jail or on probation in the community.[34] Nationwide, about 8 percent of all adults have had a felony conviction, but 33 percent of African American adult males have a felony conviction history (as compared with 13 percent of all men). Depending on the state, between 1 in 10 and 1 in 3 African American adults are confronting the daily reality of limited citizenship rights, diminished job prospects, and stigmatization.[35]

These men are overrepresented in the younger male population in Figure 1, especially among men of color. Community policing and similar practices have led to high rates of initial contact with the criminal justice system in poor minority neighborhoods. Recently some have estimated the likelihood of experiencing arrest, noting that almost half of all black men will be arrested prior to the age of 23.[36] For example, one study estimated that in 2009, of black men 30 to 34 years old who had less than a high school education, 68 percent had spent at least some time incarcerated.[37] Low-income boys who grow up in high-poverty, high-minority areas work significantly less than girls in these same places. These areas also have higher rates of crime, suggesting that boys growing up in concentrated poverty substitute from formal employment to crime.

While these statistics and data are hampered by inconsistencies in age, race, time period, and education, a safe and conservative estimate is that *up to half of the 5 million 18–34 year old jobless men in Figure 1* who were not in jail or prison in 2014 had some type of previous criminal justice system involvement. As prisoners continue to be recycled into the community by the decarceration movement, these numbers will continue to grow. The policy lesson is clear: if we want to cure the joblessness of young men, we must confront the labor market issues of ex-felons and the ex-incarcerated.

Mass incarceration harms not only the offenders, but also the families and communities they leave behind.[38] There is good reason to believe that the aggregate presence and relative size of former felon populations have spillover effects on social institutions and processes, especially in communities of color.[39] A population of this size—16 million nationwide as of 2004 and 20 million in 2010—can be expected to substantially affect not only labor markets, but also politics, health care, education, and institutional functioning more generally.[40]

The increase in the joblessness and incarceration of young men between 1980 and 2014 has immediate implications for federal and state budgets. Jobless young men have no earnings on which to pay taxes or child support as arrears grow due to incarceration or continued joblessness. About 65 percent of all men under age

30 with no more than a high school education are fathers, and less than half of them live with all of their children.[41] Also, the jobless and ex-incarcerated and their families receive more federal benefits—such as benefits from Medicaid, unemployment insurance, and SNAP—than employed young men and their families receive. Young men who are jobless or incarcerated today are less likely to marry, less likely to stay married, and less likely to have children who live in two-parent households than their counterparts who are employed or in school. Because the earnings of the next generation are likely to be affected by the families in which they grow up, adverse consequences for today's families have long-run economic impacts as well.[42]

Effective Employment Policies for the Hard-to-Employ

Finding jobs for young undereducated and NEET men, especially the ex-incarcerated, is not an easy task. In particular, there is very little systematic research on training and placing the ex-incarcerated. But there have been some limited successes more generally in placing the hard-to-employ upon which we can build. Young people with stronger skills, which may include some work experience and a secondary school credential, can experience periods of engagement and then disengagement. They may work in a series of low-wage jobs with gaps in between spells, start classes at a community college but then drop out, or a combination of the two. Growing evidence suggests that programs that take career pathways approaches and connect training to identifiable opportunities in the local labor market are more likely to achieve strong employment outcomes for the young and disconnected population.[43]

Three such programs have shown some success, though mainly for those without criminal records at this time.

Career Academies has successfully worked to take non-four-year-college-bound individuals and connect them with training and employment, producing higher marriage rates for young men as well.[44]

The Massachusetts Career and Technical Employment programs have also had successes by identifying areas of employer need (computing, health care, and advanced manufacturing) and connecting young people to the training needed for these occupations.[45] Both of these programs provide career pathways with strong links among partners in education, training, hiring, and the job market. It is not difficult to imagine how such a program might work in a jail or prison, making many of the same connections.

Year Up, a nonprofit organization dedicated to improving the lives of young people, provides participants ages 18 to 24 with six months of training in information technology and finance, followed by a six-month internship.[46] Participants need to have some type of secondary credentials (high school diploma or GED) to qualify for the program. Each participant receives a stipend tied to a performance contract during both the training and internship phases. Staff advisers help young people with both personal and professional issues, and each participant is also paired with a mentor. Evaluations of the program by Abt Associates suggest significant positive effects of the initial program.[47] Efforts are now underway at Year Up to move to a larger nationwide scale.

While these three programs have impacts that may be modest or short-lived, all three successful programs share some common features. These include connecting with local employers to understand their job-skill needs to obtain meaningful internships and employment opportunities for paid work and using financial incentives to increase work effort and financial employment support as part of the program or after the training programs end.[48]

Dutta-Gupta et al. have completed an extensive review of subsidized-employment programs and suggest that a national subsidized-employment policy could target low-income, disadvantaged workers experiencing long-term unemployment by offering subsidies to third-party employers—private, public, or nonprofit—who in turn provide jobs to eligible workers at reasonable cost.[49] The goal of this type of project would be to increase the number of quality job opportunities available to individuals with serious or multiple barriers to employment, including ex-offenders and the undereducated.

Programs that combine the on-the-job training of apprenticeships with the attainment of a credential, such as a certificate in a high-demand field, would also improve the attractiveness of the training to students and the portability of the skills acquired across employers and economic sectors. But if employers are not involved, training certificates for areas where there are no jobs stifle the will to succeed.[50] The lack of employer involvement in hiring less-qualified men is also typified by the very poor take-up of paid internships for less-skilled youth in the United States.[51]

While targeted education and jobs programs can be effective tools to prevent crime, they rarely deal with the ex-offender population.[52] Summer youth employment can help prevent the start-up of criminal behavior of disadvantaged youth.[53] While multiple evaluations have found that in-school behavioral therapy can help reduce criminal activity, evaluations of programs specifically targeted at ex-offenders are rare.[54]

In order to better prepare young workers for the jobs that need to be filled, we need an increase in incentives for high schools, community colleges, and even prison learning programs to partner with employers so we can better match worker skills with employment needs. These might well include more targeted investment for technical education in K–12 to incorporate courses such as computer programming and data analytics to better prepare graduates for the changing workforce, and technical training in chronic health care to meet the needs of the growing elder population.[55]

Three Programs That Might Work

With these caveats in mind, we turn to a combination of programs and policies that might help make headway in creating, finding, and maintaining jobs for the hard-to-employ, especially young ex-incarcerated men.

A jobs-of-last-resort guarantee for those able to work could match public benefit receipt with quid pro quos on both the employment side (employer involvement and job guarantees) and the client side (beginning child support payments). Many able-bodied young persons living without dependents (so-called ABAWDS) are being ordered to work to keep their SNAP benefits. But many are under-skilled and live in places without jobs or, especially for the ex-incarcerated, without job offers. If we require more work as a condition of receiving public benefits, we should support policies expanding work availability to those who need it, especially in depressed regions of the country. These jobs should not be "workfare" but subsidies for employment over a definite period (up to a year) with a private or nonprofit organization that promises employment in return for good behavior by the employee.

They may also involve national service. Stein and Sagawa suggest an interesting public-sector twist on the job-guarantee strategy for the young in the form of government service.[56] National statewide service programs could pay participants a modest living allowance to address a variety of national needs in fields such as education, conservation, and affordable housing. They argue that there is evidence that such programs can also successfully engage young people with criminal records, who have some of the highest barriers to employment.[57]

In the words of the AEI-Brookings report, these programs combine "help and hassle," in the tradition envisioned by Mead, but with job guarantees.[58] Young men who are promised work need to show up and work. Young fathers should begin to pay past-due child support. A good additional step is to allow fathers who owe past-due support to have their debt forgiven or reduced if they work steadily and consistently pay their current child support from the earnings on the new job.[59] Many of the ex-incarcerated also need a plan for repaying their nontrivial incarceration-related costs or having them forgiven in return for continued work and meeting post-incarceration supervision requirements.[60]

A major infrastructure project linked with federal job assistance to place workers in such projects appears to have broad bipartisan support, but there are no active plans to actually carry it out. One reason is that such investment projects require careful planning and long-term commitments to continue the operation. Alpert effectively argues that there is a prevailing oversupply of labor in today's economy and that the solution on the demand side is an intensive revitalization of our public infrastructure.[61] Stiglitz also argues that underinvestment by the US government in infrastructure and technology is a major issue, even as it would be highly complementary to private capital.[62]

To achieve such an end, the US government would use its credit to borrow the capital necessary to make such an investment and then deploy it wisely across states and localities to promote jobs and growth. Both Alpert and Stiglitz argue that such an investment could be financed through an infrastructure bank such as the European Investment Bank, which has proven to be an effective way of financing cost-effective infrastructure on a large scale across that continent.

Kane and Towner argue that not every infrastructure occupation requires above-average knowledge.[63] In total, nearly 5.8 million workers across 19 infrastructure occupations require less specialized knowledge and have lower infrastructure knowledge scores as a result. With a greater focus on administration and customer service, couriers, ticket agents, transportation attendants, and packers and packagers are among the larger infrastructure occupations that rely on alternate types of skills and face fewer detailed knowledge requirements overall. While workers in infrastructure occupations require knowledge across a variety of areas and use many different tools and technologies, 93 percent of these jobs do not require a bachelor's degree. The educational barriers to entry in these occupations are therefore relatively low because most infrastructure workers develop skills through on-the-job training and gain expertise through related work experience, while still earning competitive wages along the way. The key ingredient is to make sure that the ex-incarcerated and other longer-term jobless young people get some of the new job slots that will be opened up by the infrastructure inititative

Relocation assistance to where jobs are available with some assistance to becoming settled would be the third piece of the puzzle—in effect a new Homestead Act.[64] This is spurred in part by falling levels of geographic mobility in the United States, and the unlikely result that Hurricane Katrina, like Moving to Opportunity, led to worker relocation and better economic lives for displaced low-skill populations.[65] But moving across state lines is increasingly rare. Cadena and Kovak find that that native-born Americans with only a high school degree or less do not move for jobs, as large-scale declines in local employment produced very little if any measurable supply response among less-skilled workers.[66] More likely it ended in withdrawal from the labor force.[67]

This new Homestead Act would need some form of compensation and temporary income support, along with at least a temporary job guarantee to achieve worker mobility. The federal tax code could also be reformed to encourage less-affluent people to move. A refundable credit for moving expenses could be offered to those who took up work elsewhere. For those who have become dependent on food stamps, Medicaid, and other targeted programs, people for whom moving would provide the greatest opportunity are precisely those for whom the prospective loss of benefits or the difficulty in continuing them provides the greatest barrier to their deciding to risk moving.

Olsen's Homestead Act would start to solve this problem by systematically reforming our safety net to make the benefits fully transportable across state lines so that the fear of temporarily losing their benefits is no longer a reason to be immobile. State and local governments could experiment with trade-school vouchers or offer tax credits to businesses that support apprenticeships. However, factoring in the ex-incarcerated would be difficult as those who require supervision are not easily relocated without some type of innovative policy that allowed ex-inmates to move more easily across state or county lines. Experimental programs in Delaware and Maryland have shown some promise in terms of within-state relocation with community support services.[68] But relocation across state lines is difficult if not impossible for the ex-incarcerated.

Complementarities

There are several ways that these three policies could work together to reinforce one another. A more active role in infrastructure building complements active labor market policies by ensuring that jobs are created for the workers involved in training and in jobs-of-last-resort programs. These investments would create long-term employment opportunities available to prospective workers and create clearer career pathways for training and recruitment that would not only benefit infrastructure assets in need of maintenance or replacement, but also open up more enduring economic opportunities specifically for the 18–34-year-old hard-to-employ who were guaranteed jobs.

While the federal government and a number of other national actors represent crucial partners, states and metropolitan areas are well-positioned to take the lead with specific programs and tasks. Having already launched a variety of customized training initiatives, coordinated development strategies, and innovative partnerships, these regions should look to further experiment with and accelerate such efforts, with some federal support.

Given the wide-ranging variation in economic recovery with employable Americans staying in low-growth or declining areas, a national relocation experiment, involving the states as hubs and focusing on youth in need of jobs, might be one strategy to mix training and employment, as well as give them a fresh start.[69] For instance, Florida has lost 10 percent of its total employment and has a huge share of the nation's ex-convict population. In Florida about 10 percent of the total adult population had spent time under felony-level correctional supervision by 2010.[70] A national service or infrastructure grant to Florida, with buy-in from employers and sub-state regional authorities, might offer young ex-offenders a chance to find employment within that state.

What to Do Next

We need a national subsidized-employment policy effort that will work with states and localities to target low-income, disadvantaged workers, especially young men, experiencing long-term unemployment by offering subsidies to third-party employers—who in turn provide jobs to eligible workers. These policies could be part of a guaranteed jobs program, linked to relocation of workers (if necessary) and to large-scale infrastructure projects.

There are calls for a permanent employment fund that would enable states to both build their own subsidized jobs programs and take advantage of fully funded national service or infrastructure jobs that the federal government would directly create, targeting populations like the jobless young, the long-term unemployed, or people with criminal records, who are struggling in today's labor market and who will struggle even more in the next recession.[71]

There is wide agreement across the political spectrum that job creation is important and that job creation ought to be targeted at workers with less than a college education.[72]

We desperately need to experiment with jobs for the ex-incarcerated and jobless under-skilled youth, which would deter them from recidivism, close huge racial gaps in employment and parenting, and build stronger families, as prison, idleness, disconnected parents, and reliance on public-income supports would all be positively impacted by such programs. These should be at the very top of the jobs agenda. We have laid out at least three complementary paths that could be followed to reach these ends. They would all take a substantial and long-term public investment agenda in human capital, labor mobility, and infrastructure. In fact we know most of what we have to do. But as with so many similar issues in America, we need the political leadership and will to carry out the task.

Acknowledgments

The author thanks Molly Dahl, Mike Massoglia, Steve Raphael, Devah Pager, John Laub, and Chris Uggen for helpful discussions about the size and composition of the ex-incarcerated. He also thanks AEI for their support of this work. The author assumes responsibility for all errors of omission and commission.

Notes

1. Robert A. Moffitt, "The Deserving Poor, the Family, and the US Welfare System," *Demography* 52, no. 3 (2015): 729–49, http://link.springer.com/article/10.1007%2Fs13524-015-0395-0.

2. Irwin Garfinkel et al., *Doing More for Our Children: Modeling a Universal Child Allowance or More Generous Child Tax Credit*, Century Foundation, March 16, 2016, https://tcf.org/content/report/doing-more-for-our-children/.

3. Timothy M. Smeeding, Irwin Garfinkel, and Ronald E. Mincy, eds.,

"Young Disadvantaged Men: Fathers, Families, Poverty, and Policy," *Annals of the American Academy of Political and Social Science* 635 (May 2011): http://www.irp.wisc.edu/newsevents/conferences/fathers2009.htm.

4. Maria Cancian, Carolyn J. Heinrich, and Yiyoon Chung, "Discouraging Disadvantaged Fathers' Employment: An Unintended Consequence of Policies Designed to Support Families," *Journal of Policy Analysis and Management* 32, no. 4 (2013): 758–84, http://lbj.utexas.edu/sites/default/files/file/JPAM%202013%20Discouraging%20Disadvantaged%20Fathers%20Employment%5b2%5d.pdf; Alexes Harris, Heather Evans, and Katherine Beckett, "Drawing Blood from Stones: Legal Debt and Social Inequality in the Contemporary United States," *American Journal of Sociology* 115, no. 6 (2010): 1753–99, http://www.journals.uchicago.edu/doi/10.1086/651940; and Alexes Harris, *A Pound of Flesh: Monetary Sanctions as a Permanent Punishment for Poor People* (New York: Russell Sage, 2016).

5. Congressional Budget Office, *Trends in the Joblessness and Incarceration of Young Men*, May 2016, https://www.cbo.gov/sites/default/files/114th-congress-2015-2016/reports/51495-YoungMenReport.pdf; and Becky Pettit, *Invisible Men: Mass Incarceration and the Myth of Black Progress* (New York: Russel Sage Foundation Press, June 2012); and Council of Economic Advisers, "The Long-Term Decline in Prime-Age Male Labor Force Participation," June 2016, https://www.whitehouse.gov/sites/default/files/page/files/20160620_cea_primeage_male_lfp.pdf.

6. Lawrence Aber et al., *Opportunity, Responsibility, and Security: A Consensus Plan for Reducing Poverty and Restoring the American Dream*, AEI/Brookings Working Group on Poverty and Opportunity, December 2015, 42, https://www.aei.org/wp-content/uploads/2015/12/opportunity_responsibility_security_doar_strain_120315_FINAL.pdf.

7. Eduardo Porter, "Government Must Play a Role Again in Job Creation," *New York Times*, May 10, 2016, http://www.nytimes.com/2016/05/11/business/economy/as-jobs-vanish-forgetting-what-government-is-for.html; and Council of Economic Advisers, "The Long-Term Decline in Prime-Age Male Labor Force Participation."

8. Adam Clark Estes, "More Signs That American Youth Are a Lost Generation," *Atlantic*, September 22, 2011, http://www.thewire.com/national/2011/09/american-youth-lost-generation/42814/.

9. Henry Olsen, "A New Homestead Act—To Jump Start the US

Economy," *National Interest*, January–February 2016, http://nationalinterest.org/feature/new-homestead-act%E2%80%94-jumpstart-the-us-economy-14618.

10. Teresa L. Córdova, Matthew D. Wilson, and Jackson C. Morsey, *Lost: The Crisis of Jobless and Out of School Teens and Young Adults in Chicago, Illinois and the US*, University of Illinois at Chicago Great Cities Institute, 2016, https://greatcities.uic.edu/wp-content/uploads/2016/02/ASN-Report-v4.pdf.

11. Martha Ross and Nicole Prchal Svajlenka, "Employment and Disconnection Among Teens and Young Adults: The Role of Place, Race, and Education," Brookings Institution, May 24, 2016, http://www.brookings.edu/research/reports2/2016/05/24-teen-young-adult-employment-recession-ross-svajlenka.

12. David Autor, "Polanyi's Paradox and the Shape of Employment Growth" (working paper, National Bureau of Economic Research, September 2014), http://papers.ssrn.com/sol3/papers.cfm?abstract_id=2496241.

13. Lydia DePillis, "The Recovery Is Generating More High-Wage Jobs—But Does That Matter?" *Washington Post*, February 24, 2016, https://www.washingtonpost.com/news/wonk/wp/2016/02/24/the-recovery-is-generating-more-high-wage-jobs-but-does-that-matter/.

14. Rachel Pardoe and Dan Bloom, *Paycheck Plus: A New Antipoverty Strategy for Single Adults*, MDRC, May 2014, http://www.mdrc.org/sites/default/files/PaycheckPlus.pdf.

15. Danny Yagan, "The Enduring Employment Impact of Your Great Recession Location," University of California, Berkeley, and National Bureau of Economic Research, May 2016, http://eml.berkeley.edu/~yagan/EnduringImpact.pdf.

16. Public Policy Forum, *Barriers to Employment: Who Are Milwaukee's Unemployed Jobseekers?* May 12, 2016, https://custom.cvent.com/FAEFFF2A52AD4604952FF81E1F7992AE/files/Event/2a120f6949974e40a42fb1d3f55efc35/98e7c28db18c4e1e83d02f12f1378a05.pdf.

17. Congressional Budget Office, *Trends in the Joblessness and Incarceration of Young Men*.

18. Council of Economic Advisers, *Economic Perspectives on Incarceration and the Criminal Justice System*, April 2016, https://www.whitehouse.gov/sites/default/files/page/files/20160423_cea_incarceration_criminal_justice.pdf.

19. Ibid.; and Elizabeth Jacobs, "The Declining Labor Force Participation Rate: Causes, Consequences, and the Path Forward," testimony before the Joint Economic Committee, US Congress, July 15, 2015, http://www.jec.senate.gov/public/_cache/files/3d9668e5-804e-40da-bc6c-0f954b34f80e/jacobs-lfpr-testimony-for-jec-hearing-final.pdf.

20. Magnus Loftstrom and Steven Raphael, "Crime, the Criminal Justice System, and Socioeconomic Inequality," *Journal of Economic Perspectives* 30, no. 2 (Spring 2016): 103–26, http://pubs.aeaweb.org/doi/pdfplus/10.1257/jep.30.2.103; Congressional Budget Office, *Trends in the Joblessness and Incarceration of Young Men*; Pettit, *Invisible Men*; and Cherrie Bucknor and Alan Barber, "The Price We Pay: Economic Costs of Barriers to Employment for Former Prisoners and People Convicted of Felonies," June 2016, http://cepr.net/images/stories/reports/employment-prisoners-felonies-2016-06.pdf?v=5.

21. Harry J. Holzer, Steven Raphael, and Michael A. Stoll, "Perceived Criminality, Criminal Background Checks and the Racial Hiring Practices of Employers," *Journal of Law and Economics* 49 (2006): 451–80, https://gspp.berkeley.edu/assets/uploads/research/pdf/Holzer,_etal-PerceivedCriminality-oct2006.pdf; and Society for Human Resources Management, "Background Checking: The Use of Criminal Background Checks in Hiring Decisions," July 19, 2012, https://www.shrm.org/research/surveyfindings/articles/pages/criminalbackgroundcheck.aspx.

22. Society for Human Resources Management, "Background Checking."

23. Council of Economic Advisors, *Economic Perspectives on Incarceration and the Criminal Justice System*; John Schmitt and Kris Warner, "Ex-Offenders and the Labor Market," Center for Economic and Policy Research, November 2010, http://www.cepr.net/documents/publications/ex-offenders-2010-11.pdf.

24. Jeffrey Grogger, "The Effect of Arrests on the Employment and Earnings of Young Men," *Quarterly Journal of Economics* 110, no. 1 (1995): 51–71, http://qje.oxfordjournals.org/content/110/1/51.short; Holzer, Raphael, and Stoll, "Perceived Criminality, Criminal Background Checks, and the Racial Hiring Practices of Employers"; Devah Pager, "The Mark of a Criminal Record," *American Journal of Sociology* 108, no. 5 (2003): 937–75, http://scholar.harvard.edu/files/pager/files/pager_ajs.pdf; Michael Mueller-Smith, "The Criminal and Labor Market Impacts of Incarceration" (working paper,

University of Michigan, Department of Economics, August 2015), http://sites.lsa.umich.edu/mgms/wp-content/uploads/sites/283/2015/09/incar.pdf; and Bruce Western, *Punishment and Inequality in America* (New York: Russell Sage Foundation, 2007).

25. Jennifer L. Doleac and Benjamin Hansen, "Does 'Ban the Box' Help or Hurt Low-Skilled Workers? Statistical Discrimination and Employment Outcomes When Criminal Histories Are Hidden," July 1, 2016, http://ssrn.com/abstract=2812811.

26. Mark E. Wojcik, ed., *The State of Criminal Justice, 2016* (Washington, DC: American Bar Association, 2016).

27. Mueller-Smith, "The Criminal and Labor Market Impacts of Incarceration."

28. Maurice Emsellem and Jason Ziedenberg, "Strategies for Full Employment Through Reform of the Criminal Justice System," Center on Budget and Policy Priorities, March 2015, http://www.cbpp.org/research/full-employment/strategies-for-full-employment-through-reform-of-the-criminal-justice; and Jacobs, "The Declining Labor Force Participation Rate."

29. Peter Wagner and Leah Sakala, *Mass Incarceration: The Whole Pie*, Prison Policy Initiative, March 12, 2014, http://www.prisonpolicy.org/reports/pie.html.

30. Sarah Shannon et al., "The Growth, Scope and Spatial Distribution of America's Criminal Class, 1948–2010," *Demography* (forthcoming); and Christopher Muller and Christopher Wildeman, "Geographic Variation in the Cumulative Risk of Imprisonment and Parental Imprisonment in the United States," *Demography* (forthcoming).

31. Pettit, "Invisible Men."

32. Shannon et al., "The Growth, Scope, and Spatial Distribution of America's Criminal Class." See also Tables 1 and 2.

33. Ibid.

34. Christopher Uggen and Robert Stewart, "Piling On: Collateral Consequences and Community Supervision," *Minnesota Law Review* 99, no. 5 (2015): 1871–910, http://www.minnesotalawreview.org/wp-content/uploads/2015/09/Uggen_4fmt_PDF.pdf.

35. Shannon et al., "The Growth, Scope, and Spatial Distribution of America's Criminal Class"; and Loftstrom and Raphael, "Crime, the Criminal Justice System, and Socioeconomic Inequality."

36. Robert Brame et al., "Demographic Patterns of Cumulative Arrest Prevalence by Ages 18 and 23," *Crime & Delinquency* 60, no. 3 (2014): 471–86, http://cad.sagepub.com/content/60/3/471.

37. Bruce Western and Becky Pettit, "Incarceration and Social Inequality," *Dædalus* 139 (Summer 2010): 8–19, https://www.amacad.org/content/publications/pubContent.aspx?d=808.

38. Jeremy Travis, Bruce Western, and Steve Redburn, eds., *The Growth of Incarceration in the United States: Exploring Causes and Consequences* (Washington, DC: National Academies Press, 2014).

39. Jason Schnittkera, Michael Massogliaa, and Christopher Uggen, "Incarceration and the Health of the African American Community," *Du Bois Review* 8, no. 1 (April 2011): 133–41; Sara Wakefield and Christopher Uggen, "Incarceration and Stratification," *Annual Review of Sociology* 36 (August 2010): 387–406; and Claire Herbert et al., "Residential Instability Among the Formerly Incarcerated," University of Michigan, National Poverty Center, *Policy Brief* no. 42, April 2016, http://www.npc.umich.edu/publications/policy_briefs/brief42/policybrief42.pdf.

40. Christopher Uggen, Jeff Manza, and Melissa Thompson, "Citizenship and Reintegration: The Socioeconomic, Familial, and Civic Lives of Criminal Offenders," *Annals of the American Academy of Political and Social Science* 605 (May 2006): 281–310, http://users.soc.umn.edu/~uggen/Uggen_Manza_Thompson_ANNALS_06.pdf; and Shannon et al., "The Growth, Scope, and Spatial Distribution of America's Criminal Class."

41. Smeeding et al., "Young Disadvantaged Men."

42. Congressional Budget Office, "Trends in Joblessness and Incarceration of Young Men"; Bruce Western and Christopher Wildeman, "The Black Family and Mass Incarceration," *Annals of the American Academy of Political and Social Science* 621 (January 2009): 221–42, http://dx.doi.org/10.1177/0002716208324850; Sara McLanahan, Laura Tach, and Daniel Schneider, "The Causal Effects of Father Absence," *Annual Review of Sociology* 39 (July 2013): 399–427, http://www.annualreviews.org/doi/abs/10.1146/annurev-soc-071312-145704; Raj Chetty et al., "Childhood Environment and Gender Gaps in Adulthood" (working paper, National Bureau of Economic Research, January 2016), http://www.nber.org/papers/w21936; and Bucknor and Barber, "The Price We Pay."

43. Louisa Treskon, "What Works for Disconnected Young People: A Scan

of the Evidence" (working paper, MDRC, February 2016), http://www.mdrc.org/sites/default/files/What_works_for-disconnected_young_people_WP.pdf.

44. James J. Kemple and Cynthia J. Willner, *Career Academies: Long-Term Impacts on Labor Market Outcomes, Educational Attainment, and Transitions to Adulthood*, MDRC, June 2008, http://www.mdrc.org/sites/default/files/full_50.pdf.

45. Shaun Dougherty, "The Effect of Career and Technical Education on Human Capital Accumulation: Causal Evidence from Massachusetts" (working paper, Neag School of Education, University of Connecticut, 2016), http://chasp.lbj.utexas.edu/2015/04/24/the-effect-of-career-and-technical-education-on-human-capital-accumulation/files/2015/04/EffectofCareerandTechnicalEducation.pdf.

46. Gerald Chertavian, *Year Up* (New York: Viking, 2012).

47. Treskon, "What Works for Disconnected Young People."

48. Robert H. Haveman, Carolyn J. Heinrich, and Timothy M. Smeeding, *Jobs, Skills, and Policy for Lower-Wage Workers*, Fast Focus, Institute for Research on Poverty, University of Wisconsin–Madison, June 2011, http://www.irp.wisc.edu/publications/fastfocus/pdfs/FF10-2011.pdf.

49. Indivar Dutta-Gupta et al., *Lessons Learned from 40 Years of Subsidized Employment Programs*, Center on Poverty and Inequality, Georgetown Law, Spring 2016, https://www.law.georgetown.edu/academics/centers-institutes/poverty-inequality/current-projects/upload/GCPI-Subsidized-Employment-Paper-20160413.pdf.

50. Haveman et al., *Jobs, Skills, and Policy for Lower-Wage Workers*; and Kemple and Willner, *Career Academies*.

51. Harry J. Holzer and Robert I. Lerman, "Work-Based Learning to Expand Opportunities for Youth," *Challenge* 57, no. 4 (2014): 18–31, http://www.tandfonline.com/doi/abs/10.2753/0577-5132570402?journalCode=mcha20.

52. Council of Economic Advisors, *Economic Perspectives on Incarceration and the Criminal Justice System*.

53. Sara B. Heller, "Summer Jobs Reduce Violence Among Disadvantaged Youth," *Science* 346, no. 6214 (December 2014): 1219–23, http://science.sciencemag.org/content/346/6214/1219; and Alexander Gelber, Adam Isen, and Judd B. Kessler, "The Effects of Youth Employment: Evidence

from New York City Lotteries" (working paper, National Bureau of Economic Research, December 2014), http://www.nber.org/papers/w20810.

54. Sara B. Heller et al., "Thinking, Fast and Slow? Some Field Experiments to Reduce Crime and Dropout in Chicago" (working paper, National Bureau of Economic Research, May 2015), http://www.nber.org/papers/w21178; and YouthBuild USA, *Life After Lock-Up: A Special Report on Successful Recidivism Reduction*, January 2016, https://www.youthbuild.org/sites/default/files/Life%20After%20Lockup%20final%20report%201-16%20(1).pdf.

55. Ben Backes, Harry J. Holzer, and Erin Dunlop Velez, "Is It Worth It? Postsecondary Education and Labor Market Outcomes for the Disadvantaged" (working paper, National Center for Analysis of Longitudinal Data in Education Research, September 2014), http://www.caldercenter.org/sites/default/files/WP117.pdf; Ann Huff Stevens, Michal Kurlaender, and Michel Grosz, "Career Technical Education and Labor Market Outcomes: Evidence from California Community Colleges" (working paper, National Bureau of Economic Research, April 2015), http://www.nber.org/papers/w21137; and US Department of Health and Human Services, Administration for Children and Families, "Office of Family Assistance," http://www.acf.hhs.gov/office-of-family-assistance.

56. Harry Stein and Shirley Sagawa, *Expanding National Service to Address Long-Term Unemployment*, Center for American Progress, January 2016, https://www.americanprogress.org/issues/economy/report/2016/01/14/128837/expanding-national-service-to-address-long-term-unemployment/.

57. YouthBuild USA, *Life After Lock-Up*.

58. Aber et al., *Opportunity, Responsibility, and Security*; and Lawrence Mead, *Expanding Work Programs for Poor Men* (AEI Press, 2011).

59. Cancian et al., "Discouraging Disadvantaged Fathers' Employment."

60. Harris, *A Pound of Flesh*; and Travis et al., *The Growth of Incarceration in the US*.

61. Daniel Alpert, *GLUT: The US Economy and the American Worker in the Age of Oversupply*, Third Way, April 4, 2016, http://www.thirdway.org/report/glut-the-us-economy-and-the-american-worker-in-the-age-of-oversupply.

62. Joseph E. Stiglitz, "How to Restore Equitable and Sustainable Economic Growth in the United States," *American Economic Review* 106, no. 5 (2016): 43–47, http://econpapers.repec.org/article/aeaaecrev/v_3a106_3ay

_3a2016_3ai_3a5_3ap_3a43-47.htm.

63. Joseph Kane and Adie Towner, *Infrastructure Skills: Knowledge, Tools, and Training to Increase Opportunity*, Brookings Institution, May 13, 2016, http://www.brookings.edu/research/reports2/2016/05/13-infrastructure-skills-kane-tomer.

64. Olsen, "A New Homestead Act."

65. Malcom Gladwell, "Starting Over," *New Yorker*, August 24, 2015, http://www.newyorker.com/magazine/2015/08/24/starting-over-dept-of-social-studies-malcolm-gladwell/.

66. Brian C. Cadena and Brian K. Kovak, "Immigrants Equilibrate Local Labor Markets: Evidence from the Great Recession," *American Economic Journal: Applied Economics* 8, no. 1 (2016): 257–90, http://dx.doi.org/10.1257/app.20140095.

67. Andrew Foote, Michel Grosz, and Ann Huff Stevens, "Locate Your Nearest Exit: Mass Layoffs and Local Labor Market Response" (working paper, National Bureau of Economic Research, October 2015), http://www.nber.org/papers/w21618.

68. For example, see The Way Home, "About," https://thewayhomeprogram.wordpress.com/.

69. Yagan, "The Enduring Employment Impact of Your Great Recession Location."

70. Shannon et al., "The Growth, Scope, and Spatial Distribution of America's Criminal Class."

71. Ben Spielberg, "How to Prepare for the Next Recession," *New York Times*, April 29, 2016, http://www.nytimes.com/2016/04/29/opinion/how-to-prepare-for-the-next-recession.html.

72. Ibid.; Aber et al., *Opportunity, Responsibility, and Security*; Michael R. Strain, "A Jobs Agenda for the Right," *National Affairs* 18 (Winter 2014): http://www.nationalaffairs.com/publications/detail/a-jobs-agenda-for-the-right; Datta-Gupta et al., *Lessons Learned from 40 Years of Subsidized Employment Programs*; No Labels, *No Labels Policy Playbook for America's Next President*, 2015, https://2o16qp9prbv3jfk0qb3yon1a-wpengine.netdna-ssl.com/wp-content/uploads/2016/05/NoLabels_PolicyPlaybook_Pages-1.pdf; and Alpert, *GLUT*.

VIII

Should We Be Concerned About Income Inequality?

Is the Concept of Inequality the Best Way of Thinking About Our Economic Problems?

TYLER COWEN
George Mason University

Recent debates have made it clear that something has gone wrong with economic growth, but what is the best conceptual toolbox for understanding current problems?

I find it useful to compare the productivity slowdown and the increase in income inequality. It seems the productivity slowdown has been of much greater consequence for human welfare, including for lower-income groups. For instance, if American productivity growth had not slowed after 1973, today the median household would earn $30,000 more each year. Alternatively, if income inequality had not accelerated after 1973, today the median household would earn an extra $9,000 more. That is less than one-third of the loss from the productivity slowdown.[1]

To be sure, that is a rough and ready comparison. The notion of a world without a rise in income inequality, or a fall in productivity, and nothing else changed, is a pure abstraction which does not correspond to a possible scenario. Furthermore, the rise in income inequality and decline in productivity may in some way be related phenomena. Still, it is striking how much we hear about income inequality, and how little we hear about the productivity slowdown, most of all when lack of opportunity is the topic under consideration. Most likely, the productivity slowdown is a bigger problem.

I believe this discrepancy is for reasons that are political, cognitive, and possibly even biological. Many observers and commentators are programmed to respond to examples of inequality or unfairness,[2] and those tendencies may be present even when inequality is not the real problem at stake. Many political and economic problems thus end up framed as inequality problems in a misleading manner.

I wish to suggest a simple hypothesis: income inequality (or for that matter wealth inequality) is not the real problem. Rather, the problem is that many Americans are not seeing their lives improve as much as we would like. *This is a problem whether or not the top 1 percent is seeing big gains*. The problem has to do with the low *level* of earnings or health or well-being or opportunity for some individuals, not the disparity *per se*. That is a simple point, but it is difficult to communicate in today's discourse on these issues, and it turns out to have significant concrete implications for how we should seek remedies.

Princeton philosopher Harry Frankfurt put it fairly bluntly in his recent book on the idea of inequality, *On Inequality*. In a summary of that book, he wrote:

> The false belief that economic equality is morally important leads people to take too seriously a question that is inherently rather insignificant—namely, the question of how their economic status compares with the economic status of others. In this way the doctrine of equality contributes to the moral disorientation and shallowness of our time.[3]

He continued:

> Inequality is, ultimately, a purely formal characteristic; and from this formal characteristic of the relationship between two items, nothing whatever follows as to the desirability or value of either, or of the relationship between them. Surely what is of genuine moral concern is not *formal*, but *substantive*. It is whether people have good lives, and not how their lives compare with the lives of others.[4]

Inequality *would* be a primary problem if for instance lower earners were consumed with envy and displeasure at the earnings of Bill Gates and Warren Buffett. Then the problem would result from the disparity in well-being rather than from the low absolute level of earnings of the poorer person. There may be *some* of that envy, but that would be the main scope of the inequality problem, and it would not run much further. Instead many "absolute level problems" are reclassified as inequality problems, which again is a categorical mistake, and it leads us to think incorrectly about the relevant policy issues.

Practically speaking, that conceptual mistake misdirects the focus to making people or their outcomes more alike, rather than elevating opportunity for those at the bottom and also in the middle.

In fact, opening up enterprise and opportunity for large numbers of people often increases measured income inequality, even when it makes life better for most people, including those at the bottom. Let's say for instance that global markets were opened up to additional trade, or occupational licensure were relaxed and new commercial opportunities were created. Some people could use these new opportunities to earn much more than others, perhaps millions or even billions more. Probably most people would be better off, but since measured inequality might well rise, analysts who focus on inequality are likely to overlook or undervalue these potential remedies. Keep in mind that the larger a market economy, the larger a country, and the higher the level of aggregate wealth, the higher the level of inequality is likely to be for purely natural reasons; if everything and everyone is clustered at or near zero, inequality just can't get very high.

Just How Much Has Inequality Gone Up? And Inequality of What?

Inequality can be defined across many metrics, including inequality of income, inequality of wealth, inequality of consumption, and inequality of well-being, to name a few. There is also inequality of health, life span, and other social indicators.

It is odd that so much of the debate concerns *income* inequality. By most plausible standards, if one is to accept inequality as a relevant standard at all, the relevant inequality is one of inequality of well-being, or perhaps happiness, or some other direct measure of individual well-being.

When it comes to that metric, it is striking how little we know about whether the inequality of happiness is going up or down. For instance, one study found that inequality of happiness was largely unchanged in the United States, and that is in a period when measured income inequality was rising sharply. The United States also seems to have levels of happiness inequality roughly comparable with those of Sweden or Denmark.[5]

I am not suggesting these results are definitive, as, for one thing, they rely on measures that simply consist of asking people how happy they are. Those questionnaire methods might be flawed, or they might just be picking up framing effects about the questions themselves. Still, it is not the case that better studies have established a big uptick in the inequality of happiness—quite the contrary. We are thus left with a rather embarrassing truth: when it comes to "the inequality that matters," we don't even know if it is going up or down, or if it is especially pronounced in the United States.

It's also worth noting that, by common consensus among researchers and contrary to many common impressions, the rate of income mobility in the United States has been roughly unchanged for many decades.[6] We may well prefer rising mobility to that state of affairs, but again the actual state of opportunity is not as bad as many of the inequality critics make it out to be, and mobility is arguably a more relevant concept than inequality. People at the bottom of the income ladder usually care more about their chances of getting ahead and improving their lives than they care about the absolute gap between themselves and the very wealthy.

Economic income aside, numerous plausible metrics suggest life in the United States is getting better for a lot of people, not just the very wealthy, over say the last 30 years. Crime rates are way down, the divorce rate is down, unwanted pregnancies seem to be down, gender inequality seems to be down, there is near-universal access to the Internet at low cost, and there is much greater tolerance for many minorities than before, including LGBT individuals. To be sure, there is bad news as well, such as the trauma from the financial crisis, lower marriage rates for some groups, persistent segregation in poor neighborhoods, and a high ongoing rate of incarceration. Still, it is by no means crazy to think that the inequality of happiness might be going down at the same time while the inequality of income is going up. We just don't know, but again that implies current debates about inequality are missing the biggest and most important parts of the overall picture.

If we look at the inequality of consumption, rather than income, and count government benefits as a relevant part of income, it turns out actual inequality is considerably lower than many popular or even academic discussions might indicate.[7]

Furthermore, comparisons between inequality in the United States and other nations are typically misleading. Economically larger nations typically have higher income inequality, all other things equal, because their top producers are selling to a larger home market. Being the most successful producer in an American market is simply worth much more than holding the same status in Denmark. In addition, the United States is racially and ethnically more diverse than many parts of the world. An alternative comparison would be between the United States and the entirety of the European Union, which is an economic unit of roughly comparable size. In that instance the measured income inequality in the United States doesn't appear so outlandish at all.

Another striking and under-discussed feature of the inequality debates is that global income inequality has been going down for over 20 years.[8] The very poorest people in the world are now much wealthier than before, and significant portions of China, India, Africa, and other developing parts of the world now belong to a growing global middle class. Several billion people have been lifted out of extreme poverty into better circumstances, and over time we can expect the emerging economies to grow at faster rates than the wealthy ones, which will limit inequality all the more. At the same time, scourges such as malaria, polio, and other diseases have for the most part lost ground, most of all in poorer countries. *The last 20 to 30 years are probably the most egalitarian time, in terms of income, the world has ever seen*. So to the extent income equality is important, we should be celebrating like never before. More specifically, every discussion of income inequality, if it is to be accurate and scientific, should open by framing its worries in the context of a time that has made unparalleled strides toward limiting income inequality overall. Of course for political reasons that is not a popular presentation, but it is an accurate one.[9]

There may in fact be *some* reasons why we should worry about income inequality within individual nations. For instance, income inequality might make a successful politics difficult to run, as I'll discuss further below. But again, most of the news on the inequality front, all things considered, is positive, and that is the single most important piece of news for egalitarians, or at least it should be.

Also keep in mind that some of the increase in income inequality is from demographics alone. As people get older, their fates deviate relative to when they were younger. This is a natural principle of logic, and there doesn't have to be anything sinister about it. By one account,[10] these demographic effects account for about three-quarters of the observed rise in income inequality for men, and 69 to 95 percent of the observed rise in income inequality for women. Note that this estimate does not cover the last decade of our experience.

Finally, a lot of the inequality most relevant to people's actual lives, or happiness, is local inequality. Academics are resentful of colleagues who receive higher wages, husbands worry that their wives' friends or sisters' husbands may enjoy greater renown and success, and people think back on how well they did relative to their high school or college class. Arguably those phenomena are more important for well-being than the poor or middle class envying or resenting the rich. If that is the case, public policy cannot easily remedy those misery-inducing inequalities, and in fact some supposedly egalitarian policies may make them worse. The more equal we are supposed to be, and the closer we live together, perhaps the more we worry about the remaining differences because we absorb the message that we belong to all sorts of relevant peer groups. Note also that in this story, the relevant "inequality villain" is not capitalism or the market per se, but perhaps Facebook, social media, and even the telephone.

We do not in a rigorous way know how much envy and well-being comparison is local in this way. Still, the fact that this point hardly ever comes up in inequality debates again suggests those debates aren't about inequality at all. If they were, a lot of the usual political discussions, such as calls for more progressive taxation and redistribution, would be replaced by a study of how we might use social media to make ourselves happier rather than more obsessed with the doings of others in an alienating way. It's a kind of joke to suggest, "tax Facebook use, not Mark Zuckerberg," but maybe it's not so far from what a properly specified theory of inequality ought to imply. Again, we need to resist the temptation to apply standard rich versus poor tropes to these issues, as that is a politically popular lens but often a distorting one.

Why Has Income Inequality Gone Up?

Let's look at a few of the key drivers of the increase in inequality. We'll see that it makes sense to disaggregate "the inequality problem," as a lot of it isn't a problem at all, or again it is a problem of some kind other than an inequality problem. This will help us disaggregate inequality issues and turn them into more useful propositions and understandings. We'll see that some of the causes of inequality are positive or useful, while others are not and can be remedied, although not always by traditional egalitarian means. This disaggregation will then have policy implications, as I will consider further below.

Global Markets. The rise of global markets is a significant reason why some kinds of income inequality have gone up. It's pretty straightforward. The creators of the iPhone now are selling to the entire world, rather than just to North America, Western Europe, and Japan, as would have been the case a few decades ago. The larger the world market, the higher the returns to the most successful entrepreneurs, namely those who can build firms geared to export.

This cause of income inequality seems mostly positive, as it provides useful goods and services, most of all to relatively poor countries, and it motivates creators to innovate. Furthermore, these innovations arguably *lower* global inequality overall, by improving the variety of goods and services available around the world and lowering prices to most consumers.

Skills-Biased Technical Change. Another factor behind inequality, much discussed by economists, has to do with the shift away from manufacturing jobs toward information technology jobs in the developed economies, including the United States. In earlier decades it was relatively easy for males without a college degree, or without an advanced degree, to get a middle-class job in manufacturing. Today, information technology skills are more important, but those are less evenly distributed throughout the population. They may require not only a high amount of formal training, but also the ability to retrain oneself rapidly over time, since a lot of information technologies evolve quite rapidly, more rapidly than current systems of higher education can keep up. Yet not all individuals are so good at retraining themselves at such a rapid pace, and that skews the wage structure in an inegalitarian way.[11]

In sum, fewer individuals earn more, and that contributes to income inequality. At the same time, those new information technologies increase the reach of good managers (e.g., managing by teleconference and email), making it easier to export and manage foreign investment, and so they also contribute to the higher earnings of the top 1 percent.

Now let's break down where exactly the problem lies, to the extent there is a problem. First, it is good that information technology makes some workers much more productive, and it is good for consumers, too. Second, it is bad that some individuals do not work well with information technology, and that does harm their wages and future opportunities. But the problem part of that equation is not an inequality problem; it is an education problem and a retraining problem. It is a problem we should work harder to fix, but it is easy enough to pinpoint that what has gone awry is not the inequality per se. One also might say it is an "information technology should be easier to interact with" problem. That is true, too, and eventually ease of use may go up. That is also another problem we can and should work on.

Rent-Seeking. Another source of higher income inequality is public policy, the exercise of political privilege, and the use of government to transfer resources from one group of people to another. Over time the American government is spending more money on the elderly, who are relatively wealthy, and investing less in the young, who are relatively poor. On top of that is a long litany of topics, including overprotection of intellectual property rights, excessive occupational licensure, subpar public goods (such as lead in water supplies, as in Flint, Michigan, or bad inner-city schools), barriers to price transparency in health care, and many others. Not everyone agrees on all of these issues, but almost everyone grants that some of these policies are significant problems. They reduce efficiency and also contribute to income inequality.

Again, it is not so helpful to identify "income inequality" as the core problem here, even if that may be one of the negative consequences of these interventions. The core problem is instead that laws and policies are restricting economic opportunity for many people and destroying efficiency with a special burden on the less advantaged.

A related argument is that America has such bad policies because income inequality means policy is badly skewed toward the interests of the wealthy. But it is hardly obvious that the degree of wealthy or elite control of government has gone up over time. Most of the federal budget, or state budgets for that matter, is taken up by broadly popular programs, namely Medicare, Medicaid, Social Security, and defense spending; for state governments the list is Medicaid, K–12 schooling, roads, and prisons. Only Medicaid is less than fully popular here, and that unpopularity is often with poorer red-state voters, not so much with elites. Wealthy elites do have greater say over regulations and the minute details of individual policies, but it is not obvious that it has increased over time and with higher income inequality. For instance, some of the biggest increases in regulation have come in the environmental area, where regulation is often driven by popular sentiment. To some extent, the lax financial regulation leading up to the Great Recession was driven by the desire to spread homeownership to lower-income buyers, another relatively popular goal driven by the desire for votes.

Overall there is good evidence that the policy preferences of highly educated elites are closer to what economic science suggests are truly popular preferences.[12] Furthermore, the influence of wealthy elites is not nearly as strong as it is made out to be, especially in an age of social media. I am writing this piece in early 2016, a year when wealthy donors supposedly were "buying" the election for Scott Walker or maybe Jeb Bush or Marco Rubio—that isn't exactly how things are working out. More generally, less and less of federal and state budgets is up for discretionary reallocation at all, but rather most of it is spent by formula, on various benefit schemes or otherwise mandated expenditures, such as prisons. Again, that is not a sign of elite domination of politics, although to some extent it does represent the strong electoral influence of the elderly, and also of suburban parents.

Another claim is that high income or wealth inequality is bound to lead to political revolution, instability, riots in the streets, or some other set of negative consequences. Yet the data don't show this. The most violent period in recent American history was something like 1963–73, which came right after and during America's most significant period of robust middle-class income growth. Overall, the research does not suggest definitive conclusions, but there is at least as much evidence suggesting that rising expectations are a more important cause of instability than is income inequality.[13]

In sum, America has serious problems of inadequate education, lack of retraining, and some quite bad policies in particular areas. In most cases that disaggregation is a better way of understanding what is going on rather than emphasizing inequality at the macroeconomic level. The *gap* between rich and poor is neither the major driver of the actual problems nor the most important symptom of the most significant problems. Lack of opportunity in absolute terms is the main symptomatic problem.

Most generally, we probably cannot know what is the optimal income distribution in society.[14] Moral philosophers have debated this question for centuries, without making much definite progress on it; in part this is because "inequality" is a statistical residue with several possible meanings and causes, rather than an ultimate moral value. It is true that there are good arguments for some income redistribution, including the utilitarian and the political stability arguments, but our society already engages in a fair amount of redistribution, not always efficiently of course. I do not mean to endorse universal moral skepticism, or advocate that we throw up our hands, or refuse to judge social outcomes at all. It's just that the question of how much inequality is justified in the aggregate isn't such a useful way to proceed. Instead, by breaking inequality down into its constituent problems of low skills, thwarted opportunities, and bad schooling, we can find micro areas where good policy or better institutions can boost both efficiency and most plausible conceptions of social justice. The resulting changes in the distribution of wealth are probably philosophically desirable as piecemeal changes, even if we don't have, and probably can never have, overarching standards for exactly how much inequality a society should be willing to tolerate.

How Should Policy Respond?

This is obviously a major issue, and not every aspect of it can be considered here. But let's think of a few areas where laws and regulations might be changed to increase opportunity and to improve levels of well-being for less fortunate individuals. In the process inequality will sometimes but not always go down, again noting that additional wealth creation, even if it benefits most people, will elevate some people more than others.

Health Care. When it comes to health care, the greatest tragedy is that many people die or suffer great pains and disabilities without any real chance of a cure. The cure or treatment just doesn't exist. We don't usually think of that as an "insurance" problem, but it is—those people have insufficiently useful insurance, no matter what their workplace or governmental coverage may stipulate.

We often forget that by far the biggest inequality is between the living and the dead. Overall recent research has indicated that the health benefits of health insurance are lower than we had thought, while the health benefits of innovation and new pharmaceuticals are higher than we had thought. So the federal government could, through a mix of higher subsidies and lesser regulation for health care innovation, promote both absolute well-being and egalitarian ideals, properly specified.[15]

Occupational Licensing. An ever-growing percentage of American occupations are covered by state and local licensure, often over 30 percent.[16] Occupational licensing may well make sense for professions where people's lives are at stake, such as medicine. But do we really need state-level occupational licensure for interior decorators and barbers, among other occupations? There is a good case for doing away with most of these legal restrictions. It would improve both efficiency and equity, under most reasonable standards, even if it does not always increase measured income equality.

Education. This is not the place to survey all possible options for education. Needless to say many of the experiments with charter schools are succeeding, as many charter schools are exhibiting above-average performance and seem also to be serving up replicable lessons. Overall there should be more state and local experimentation in K–12 education in the United States; fortunately, the country is headed in this direction, but much more could be done. Individuals who receive substandard educations simply have a much harder time later making up for that difference in starting points.

Cheaper Rent and Lower Home Prices. These days it is harder for Americans to migrate successfully to some of the most economically dynamic American cities, in large part because of high rents and restrictive building codes, stemming from the NIMBY mentality. For a low-skilled worker, the higher wages in New York or San Francisco do not always make up for the much higher rental costs.[17]

In the 1950s, a typical apartment in New York City rented for about $60 a month, or adjusting for inflation about $530 a month; today that is closer to the cost of a parking space in Manhattan.[18] If it were cheaper to move into major American cities, more Americans would have an easier path toward a higher salary and a brighter future. Economists Chang-Tai Hsieh and Enrico Moretti have argued that the American economy could become much richer if more workers could move from the low-productivity cities to the high-productivity cities; that would increase income mobility, too. Hsieh and Moretti estimate that lower rents, through building deregulation, could increase American GDP by almost 10 percent. A lot of those gains would go to Americans who cannot currently afford to move to San Francisco and other high-productivity cities.[19]

Discontinue or Ameliorate the War on Drugs. America now has over two million of its citizens in jail, many more than in 1970, and that too is a rather drastic form of inequality. That is the largest jail population in the entire world and also the highest incarceration rate. So one partial remedy for inequality would be to lower the jail population, and in part that could be done by decriminalizing the possession and sale of drugs. On the negative side, this would mean drugs would be available more cheaply for the children of upper-income and middle-income families, and some social costs would result from that. Still, the monopolies of drug gangs would disappear, inner cities probably would become more peaceful, and the prison population would fall and probably would be less racially inequitable as well. Obviously this is a major issue with numerous angles, but it is hardly obvious that current drug policy has been a major success. Improving these policies—in whatever direction a more sustained analysis might call for—could go a long way toward remedying the kinds of states of affairs that bother most egalitarians.

End Crony Capitalism. Numerous federal and state government programs transfer incomes away from lower-income individuals and toward corporations or toward the wealthy. A simple example would be farm subsidies, which currently have a direct fiscal cost of about

$20 billion a year and raise the price of milk (and other foodstuffs) rather than lowering it. There are dozens or indeed hundreds of instances of corporate welfare in the United States, ranging from stadium subsidies to special tax breaks to the Export-Import Bank, and many, many more; we should consider abolishing as many of these programs as possible.

Summary Remarks

The United States has some very real problems, in particular with respect to some of its low- and middle-income citizens. But the concept of inequality is not the best conceptual starting point for finding or evaluating potential solutions.

Notes

1. Council of Economic Advisers, *Economic Report of the President*, Executive Office of the President, 2015, https://www.whitehouse.gov/sites/default/files/docs/cea_2015_erp.pdf.

2. Jonathan Haidt, *The Righteous Mind: Why Good People Are Divided by Politics and Religion* (New York: Vintage, 2013).

3. See Harry G. Frankfurt, *On Inequality* (Princeton, NJ: Princeton University Press, 2015); Harry G. Frankfurt, "Economic Inequality Is Not Immoral," Bloomberg View, August 27, 2015; and George Sher, *Equality for Inegalitarians* (Cambridge, UK: Cambridge University Press, 2014).

4. Frankfurt, "Economic Inequality Is Not Immoral."

5. See the papers from the *Journal of Happiness Studies* 6, no. 4 (2005), for instance: Ruut Veenhoven, "Return on Inequality in Modern Society? Test by Dispersion of Life-Satisfaction Across Time and Nations," *Journal of Happiness Studies* 6, no. 4 (2005): 457–87.

6. Raj Chetty et al., "Is the United States Still a Land of Opportunity? Recent Trends in Intergenerational Mobility" (working paper, National Bureau of Economic Research, January 2014).

7. For one set of very recent estimates showing that income and wealth inequality are lower than is often suggested, see Jesse Bricker et al., "Measuring Income and Wealth at the Top Using Administrative and Survey Data,"

Brookings Institution, March 10, 2016, http://www.brookings.edu/about/projects/bpea/papers/2016/bricker-et-al-income-wealth-top. On consumption inequality in particular, see the discussion in Alan J. Auerbach, Laurence J. Kotlikoff, and Darryl R. Koehler, "US Inequality, Fiscal Progressivity, and Work Disincentives: An Intragenerational Accounting" (working paper, National Bureau of Economic Research, February 2016).

8. Branko Milanovic, *Global Inequality: A New Approach for the Age of Globalization* (Cambridge, MA: Belknap Press at Harvard University, 2016).

9. On these issues, see Milanovic, *Global Inequality*; and Tomáš Hellebrandt and Paolo Mauro, "The Future of Worldwide Income Distribution" (working paper, Peterson Institute for International Economics, April 2015).

10. Thomas Lemieux, "Increasing Residual Wage Inequality: Composition Effects, Noisy Data, or Rising Demand for Skill?" *American Economic Review* 96, no. 3 (2006).

11. For a survey of these arguments, see Tyler Cowen, *Average Is Over: Powering America Beyond the Age of the Great Stagnation* (New York: Dutton, 2013).

12. Bryan Caplan, *The Myth of the Rational Voter: Why Democracies Choose Bad Policies* (Princeton, NJ: Princeton University Press, 2008).

13. See Frederick Solt, "Economic Inequality and Democratic Political Engagement," *American Journal of Political Science* 52, no. 1 (2008): 48–60; and Jonathan Krieckhaus et al., "Economic Inequality and Democratic Support," *Journal of Politics* 76, no. 1 (2014): 139–51. Arguably these cross-national studies are inconclusive for the American context, but a lack of a clear conclusion is precisely what I am suggesting here.

14. Murray N Rothbard, *Egalitarianism as a Revolt Against Nature, and Other Essays* (Auburn, AL: Ludwig Mises Institute, 2000), https://mises.org/library/egalitarianism-revolt-against-nature-and-other-essays.

15. On the benefits of insurance being lower than we had thought, see Amy Finkelstein, Nathaniel Hendren, and Erzo F. P. Luttmer, "The Value of Medicaid: Interpreting Results from the Oregon Health Insurance Experiment" (working paper, National Bureau of Economic Research, 2015). On the benefits of pharmaceutical innovation being higher, see Frank R. Lichtenberg, "The Effect of Pharmaceutical Innovation on Longevity: Patient-Level Evidence from the 1996–2002 Medical Expenditure Panel Survey and Linked Mortality Public-Use Files" (working paper, National Bureau of Economic Research, 2012).

16. US Department of the Treasury, Office of Economic Policy, Council of Economic Advisers, and US Department of Labor, *Occupational Licensing: A Framework for Policymakers*, The White House, July 2015.

17. On the latter point, see Peter Ganong and Daniel Shoag, "Why Has Regional Convergence in the US Stopped?" (working paper, Harvard Kennedy School, June 2012).

18. Tom Streithorst, "Why Your Rent Is So High and Your Pay Is So Low," *Los Angeles Review of Books*, August 4, 2015.

19. Chang-Tai Hsieh and Enrico Moretti, "Why Do Cities Matter? Local Growth and Aggregate Growth" (working paper, National Bureau of Economic Research, May 2015).

Should We Be Concerned About Income Inequality in the United States?

MELISSA S. KEARNEY
University of Maryland

Income inequality is neither all good, nor all bad. Inequality will arise in a capitalist society that rewards work, talent, and ingenuity. It incentivizes individuals to be economically productive and forgo leisure for human capital development and economic activity. But while it can do much to stimulate productivity and efficiency, it also creates inequities that challenge collective notions of justice and fairness and, if left unchecked, undermines our social fabric and collective productivity. So it is neither all good, nor all bad, and the challenge is to figure out whether current income gaps and inequality trends have gone so far that they are imposing real costs on society.

In this essay I will offer my conclusion that yes, we do need to worry about income inequality in the United States, for two particular reasons. First, many of the key trends that have been driving income inequality in this country are threatening the economic security of large segments of Americans, in particular, those with lower levels of skill and education. To the extent that today's income inequality reflects underlying forces that will continue to erode the economic security of less educated Americans, we need to be concerned, and we need to act.

Second, I worry about the impact that persistent income gaps are having on the fabric of our society and the outcomes of children from low-income homes. Some will point out that what matters most is equality of opportunity, not equality of outcome. I am sympathetic to that view, to a point. We need to realize that the large and persistent inequality of outcomes across segments of society is eroding the promise of opportunity for many.

As I describe below, children born to low-educated, low-income parents are falling increasingly behind their higher-income peers. They are completing lower levels of education, which, given economic trends, will make their chances of achieving economic security and advancement that much smaller. The possibility of poverty traps and self-reinforcing inequality across population segments cannot be ignored.

Some Background Observations

I start with the essentially irrefutable observation that income inequality has indeed increased dramatically in the United States during recent decades. The economic growth experienced since 1975 has not translated into shared prosperity, as it did in earlier decades. During the period of economic prosperity between 1947 and 1979, families in every quintile experienced more than 100 percent growth in family income, according to Census income data.[1] In stark contrast, between 1979 and 2012, income gains were vastly different for families at different points in the income distribution, with average percentage gains monotonically increasing up the distribution, ranging from losses at the low end to tripling at the top end.

Government tax and transfer programs have mitigated the inequality resulting from changes in market income. The Census estimates cited above do not fully capture the effect of government tax and transfer payments because, although some cash transfers are included, Census household income measures do not include taxes paid or tax credits received, nor do they adjust for in-kind benefits, such as Medicaid. The Congressional Budget Office has made adjustments along these lines and finds that, based on a more comprehensive measure of post-tax, post-transfer income, between 1979 and 2007, income grew by 275 percent for the top 1 percent of households, 65 percent for the next 19 percent, just under 40 percent for the next 60 percent, and 18 percent for the bottom 20 percent.[2]

There are a variety of reasonable ways to calculate these estimates, but regardless of the exact numbers, there is really no denying that despite the beneficial effects of redistributive tax and transfer policies, recent increases in our nation's prosperity have been going disproportionately to those at the top of the income distribution.

Importantly, if it were the case that our nation had high levels of income inequality but also high rates of income mobility—both within an individual's lifetime and across generations—then we would view income inequality very differently. As it turns out, social mobility in the US is not as high as most of us were probably raised to believe. We are a nation that celebrates "rags to riches" stories, but the data indicate that our rates of social mobility are in fact lower than most European countries. I hasten to acknowledge that, although it is often assumed that higher levels of income inequality lead to lower levels of social mobility, that need not be the case.[3] However, as I describe below, my own research and my reading of related evidence have led me to the conclusion that we probably do need to worry about the role that sustained income gaps play in eroding upward mobility for those born to economically disadvantaged circumstances.

Finally, it should never cease to astound us that in the midst of all this income growth at the upper end of the distribution, some 44 million Americans, about 15 percent of individuals in this country, live in a household with income below the official poverty threshold. Sure, the official poverty threshold is an arbitrary number, but we can all agree that it is very low. It is about $11,000 for an individual and $24,000 for a family of two adults and two children.

Some people manage to make ends meet by supplementing their low reported cash income with transfer payments and in-kind benefits from the government, charities, churches, friends, and relatives. Yet, many do not. In the United States, one in seven people struggle with hunger. Roughly 50 million Americans are living in food insecure households, including some 32 million adults and 15 million children.[4]

We cannot ignore these statistics. Let me repeat just one—15 million children in this country do not have adequate food to eat.

We should take that as a moral imperative, but also recognize that these children are not in a position to thrive in school and develop their human potential. That is an economic imperative as well.

As a practical answer to the question of whether we need to worry about income inequality and associated challenges, we need no more evidence than the surprising turn of events in the 2016 presidential campaign to see that extraordinary numbers of Americans are feeling like our current economic "system" is not working for them. If for no other reason than for the sake of preserving political support for the fundamental basis of our capitalist and open society, it seems imperative that we address the impacts that income inequality and the associated economic challenges are having on our society. Since it is too easy to stop there, I will spend the remainder of this essay emphasizing two specific issues related to income inequality that I believe call for our collective attention and policy action.

Inequality as a Symptom of Structural Changes in the Labor Market

The rise in income inequality has been largely driven by increases in earnings inequality, which reflect structural changes in the labor market that threaten the economic security of low- and middle-skilled Americans. What concerns me is not so much how much income the most highly educated are making, but rather, how much less the less-educated now make. These earnings and employment gaps between those with higher and lower levels of skills and educational attainment are arguably more relevant to the lives of most Americans than is the rise in the income share going to the very top percentiles of the population.[5]

On average, a college graduate now makes twice the wage of a high school graduate. Since the mid-1970s, those with the highest levels of education—more than 16 years—have seen their wages rise steadily. Those with exactly a college degree or some college have seen some improvement, but not to the same extent. High school graduates and those with less than a high school degree experienced declining real wages through the late 1970s and 1980s, and after some rebounding in the early 1990s, their wages have remained fairly stagnant since.[6] Less than 70 percent of prime-age men with a high school degree or less now work full-time.[7] These statistics reflect structural challenges that were with us before the recent recession and do not show any immediate signs of significant reversal.

There is not a simple one-dimensional explanation for these trends. A number of economic forces have combined to weaken the economic position of those with lower levels of education, in particular men, while enriching those individuals who possess skills and talents that are in shorter supply. Technological developments have enhanced the productivity of those with certain skill sets, including professionals and those in many service-sector occupations, while replacing the need for many routine labor tasks.[8] Globalization has expanded the scope for firm revenues and product markets, which enhances the market value and income of top entrepreneurs, CEOs, and entertainers.[9] Trade with China has brought the domestic benefit of lower-priced goods, but it has hurt those who were earning fairly high wages producing manufactured goods in the US.[10] At the same time, the decline of the real value of the minimum wage and diminished union representation among US workers has exacerbated the weakened economic position of low- and middle-wage workers.[11]

In terms of the impact of technological developments, so-called techno-optimists will point out that recent developments, including the proliferation of smart machines, networked communication, and digitization, have the potential to transform the economy. But sluggish productivity growth and the fact that the median American male worker's wage rose by just 3 percent from 1979 to 2014 call into question just how positive any such transformation will be for the typical American worker. It is often noted that previous periods of technological advancement also brought winners and losers and that, even though the transition period might be tough for some workers, after a period of adjustment, new jobs will be created and ultimately the benefits will be widespread. But there is no guarantee.

How this plays out for the American worker in the long run will largely depend on how labor supply responds in terms of education. In their 2008 book *The Race Between Education and Technology,*

Claudia Goldin and Lawrence Katz make the case that the US economy prospered during the 20th century in large part because advances in the educational attainment of the US population kept pace with the technological advances that were increasing the relative demand for skilled workers. Because there was an increasing supply of educated Americans to meet the increasing demand for skills, inequality did not rise dramatically, and economic gains were broadly shared. But, they observe that in the latter part of the century, the advance of technology and the corresponding demand for high-skilled workers has accelerated more rapidly than the supply of skills.[12]

Will the majority of US workers obtain a level of education and skill that will enable them to prosper in the modern economy? What will we as a society choose to do for those individuals who simply cannot achieve those skills? What if there simply aren't enough high-paying jobs for everyone? I worry about a future reality in which some highly skilled segment commands increasingly high wages, and the rest of the population is engaged in low-paying service-sector jobs, presumably offering personal services and the like to those with high incomes.

Some will counter that if we have a society with great wealth created by a few particularly productive people, then the challenge is not one of economic productivity, but rather of distribution. One might argue that as long as we redistribute the largess, then all of society can benefit. But to my mind, a society where only a small share of individuals are engaged in meaningful employment, and the rest rely on transfers from the rich, is more dystopian than not.

Related Policy Aims. We need to address these challenges with multiple approaches. First, we need a concerted, sustained effort at massively upgrading skills and improving the educational system, from preschool through institutions of higher education. Second, we need a stronger system of supports for low-wage and out-of-work individuals.

Some observers from the left bristle at the education prescription, saying that the education story is tired and that we need stronger worker institutions. This is a false dichotomy. Workers would benefit from both. But I think that undoubtedly the single best thing we can do to put more Americans in a position of economic strength and security is to equip them with the skills they need to thrive in today's modern global economy.

Not only will it be imperative to increase the overall educational attainment of a larger share of the American population, but also the provision of education will have to be effective and appropriately tailored to the demands of today's global, technology-demanding economy. Our system of primary and secondary school education will need to perform better, in terms of educating our students in math and science, teaching them to write and communicate persuasively, and giving them opportunities to develop their skills of team cooperation and leadership.

Some students will benefit from targeted training in industry-specific skills. But, given that the labor market is dynamic, workers will need to be adaptive and have sufficient general skills such that they can productively move across jobs as the workplace evolves. There will also have to be ample opportunities for lifelong learning, as the skill demands of the economy change. The notion of higher education as being something that an individual engages in just once in one's early 20s will surely become obsolete.

Critics of this view that education must play a key role in addressing the challenges associated with recent inequality and wage trends have argued that increasing educational attainment is not the answer because it will not appreciably reduce the level of overall inequality. To some extent this is true because a large share of earnings inequality occurs above the median, and changing college shares will not substantially affect those differences. But, it would certainly improve the economic position of those at or near the bottom.

In a 2015 Hamilton Project analysis, Brad Hershbein, Larry Summers, and I simulated what would happen to the distribution of earnings if one out of every 10 men age 25–64 who did not have a college degree were to obtain one—a sizeable increase in college attainment.[13] (We focus on men because low-skilled men have seen the largest drops in employment and earnings over the past few decades.) That simulation's results demonstrate that increasing educational attainment would reduce inequality in the bottom half of the earnings distribution, largely by pulling up the earnings of those between the 25th and 50th percentiles (after adjusting for likely general equilibrium effects on wages). In fact, increasing the share of men with a BA by 10 percent would nearly completely erase the decline in median male earnings between 1979 and 2013 and would cut the decline at the 25th percentile by one-third.

Importantly, increasing the skill level of our potential workforce is a long-term proposition. Many will struggle through the transition, and others will simply face too many barriers to developing a high level of skills. Therefore, we need to accompany this effort with an expanded system of supports for low-wage and out-of-work individuals. Potential policy levers include an expanded earned income tax credit and a reasonable increase in regional minimum wages.

We also need to support those who can't work or can't find work. Increasingly, transfer payments are tied to work, as with the earned income tax credit and work requirements implemented as part of the 1996 welfare reform legislation. This has very desirable work incentive properties, but it does raise the issue of how we support out-of-work individuals. We need expanded support that offers some basic level of food, housing, and medical assistance. Researchers have documented that the introduction and subsequent expansions of the food stamp and Medicaid programs have long-term benefits to the health and human capital of affected individuals.[14] These programs must continue to be supported with dedicated funding.

Asserting that basic income supports will undermine incentives to work and lead to lower levels of economic productivity is false and counterproductive. Individuals need to have a basic level of health and security to pursue educational and employment opportunities. In many respects, we are not on the efficiency/equity frontier. We have the opportunity to promote a more equitable society that will ultimately lead to a collectively more productive population of workers and a more dynamic, robust economy.

Inequality as a Cause of Social Problems

A second element of inequality that should concern us is the divergent experiences and outcomes that we are seeing for children born to parents with lower and higher levels of education. Changes in marriage patterns have combined with rising earnings inequality to create an even larger divergence in household-level income inequality and striking differences in the way that children from poor and rich households are growing up.

The sociologist Sara McLanahan called attention to the "diverging destinies" of children born to women with the least and highest levels of education, noting that "children born to the most-educated women are gaining resources, in terms of parents' time and money, while those born to the least educated women are losing resources."[15] This divergence reflects several factors, but two key drivers are that the least educated women are largely raising their children alone on low incomes and that the highest educated women are not only pulling in high incomes themselves these days but also marrying high-earning men. In other words, demographic, cultural, and labor market forces are combining to create separate and very unequal family lives for children from low and high socioeconomic status (SES) backgrounds.

Forty percent of births are now outside marriage; the rate is an astounding 70 percent among African Americans. But this is not just a racial divide. It is very much a divide between education classes: 61.7 percent of births to women with a high school degree or less are nonmarital. In contrast, 9.6 percent of births to women with a college degree or more are outside marriage.[16] This matters because numerous studies show that children who grow up in two-parent, married homes do better on a host of educational, behavioral, and long-term economic outcomes. As long as marriage continues to bring children the benefits of stability and the resources of two persons as compared to one—in the form of income, time, energy, and networks, among others—growing up in a home with two married parents will benefit children.

And it is not just family structure that is different across education and income groups. Research has documented that higher-income parents spend more time with their children[17] and are more likely to engage in positive parenting practices.[18]

Academic and behavioral gaps appear early in life. By the time kids get to kindergarten, there are large differences in school readiness, and these differences persist. Sean Reardon of Stanford University has documented that by age six, children from families in the 90th percentile of the income distribution and those in the 10th already exhibit a gap of one standard deviation on math and reading tests. This gap is barely diminished by the age of 18, leaving it equivalent to several extra years of secondary schooling.[19]

Income gaps in educational performance between children from low- and high-income families have grown over time, largely because the kids at the top are pulling away. We need to equip our most capable students to do as well as they can, but we also need to recognize that income inequality has led to such dramatic resource gaps between kids from different backgrounds that the notion of equal opportunity is now far from a reality. Children born to highly educated, high-income parents are doing better and better, and the kids at the bottom are being left behind. We need to address this dimension of inequality if we are going to have an inclusive capitalist society where an individual has a reasonable chance of economic success regardless of his or her circumstances at birth.

Arthur Okun warned about the batter who goes up to the plate with two strikes already against him.[20] I worry that this is how many of our nation's children are starting out in their "at bat" of life. The odds are stacked against them, and the relative deficit they experience is larger than ever.

In addition, evidence suggests that persistent income gaps make the disadvantages of a low-SES background even greater. As bad as it is to be poor, being poor in a more unequal place appears to be worse. In a recent paper for the *Brookings Papers on Economic Activity* series, Phillip Levine and I document that children from low-educated homes, boys in particular, are more likely to drop out of school when they grow up in parts of the country that have persistently high levels of lower-tail income inequality (defined as the gap between the 50th and 10th percentiles of income). We test for a large set of potentially confounding factors, and the data provide robust evidence that there is something about the income gap itself that is related to the decision of boys from lower socioeconomic backgrounds to drop out of school.[21]

We interpret the findings as being consistent with—albeit not a conclusive demonstration of—a model of decision making in which a persistently wide gap between the bottom and middle of the income distribution negatively affects the perceived likelihood of economic success through human capital investments. This could occur either through impeded opportunity in actuality or through an effect on perceptions, shaped by a variety of factors experienced throughout one's childhood. These implications are consistent with recent research showing that the community children grow up in has important causal effects on their outcomes, with the effect sizes being largest for children who experience the neighborhood from a younger age.[22]

The fact that boys appear to respond to greater levels of income inequality by dropping out of school more often is consistent with a growing body of evidence suggesting that boys suffer greater educational and labor market consequences from family and economic disadvantage.[23] However, these patterns do not necessarily mean that low-SES girls are not affected by the economic disadvantage or conditions around them. They might simply respond on different margins. For instance, Levine and I find that low-SES girls in more unequal places are significantly more likely to become young, unmarried mothers.[24]

These findings have implications for the potential of disadvantaged youth to achieve upward mobility and the types of policies that are likely to be successful. Furthermore, they reflect a plausible channel through which higher rates of income inequality might causally lead to lower rates of social mobility.

My summary judgment on this issue is that there is good reason to worry that going forward, children from lower-income backgrounds will have an even harder time climbing the economic ladder than children from earlier generations. Although recent papers have showed that social mobility has not been declining in recent decades, those data are necessarily backward looking. We do not yet know what social mobility will look like for kids born this decade. If we do not act, I worry that it will be even lower than it is currently.

Related Policy Aims. We need to invest much more heavily in our nation's children, who are the future of our country. We need to bolster and expand funding for those programs that are as much about investing in the health and human potential of the next generation as they are about immediate transfers of income and consumption. Again, I point to the importance of SNAP (formerly Food Stamps) and Medicaid. Children cannot learn if they are hungry or sick.

We need to invest in targeted expansions of child care funding and early childhood education programs. To get the most benefit from our invested dollars, we should focus on providing early childhood education and high-quality day care to the millions of children who would not otherwise have access to such environments. I worry that the policy interest in "universal preschool" will mean resources are spread thin, yielding very little marginal benefit per dollar spent. The academic research showing positive effects of early childhood interventions such as Perry Preschool is based on evidence from intensive programs targeted to low-income children. Our policy commitment should be to increasing access to high-quality early childhood environments for low-income children.

We also need programs aimed at decreasing the prevalence of nonmarital births and improving the home environment and parenting practices of poor families. There is some evidence that parenting interventions might show promise, but really, much more work is needed here to figure out what types of policies and programs will help strengthen families. The results from the pro-marriage initiatives of the Bush administration were disappointing, but we can't take from that that there is nothing policy can do. We must gather lessons from policy and program interventions that are designed to encourage positive fatherhood and strengthen family interactions.

Ideally, improvements in the economic prospects of low-skilled men would turn some of this around, by improving the "marriageability" of these men.[25] This brings us back again to the challenges I discussed earlier: the decline in the economic position of less-skilled men. It is an open question how much of the rise in nonmarital childbearing among less-educated segments of the population is driven by economic versus cultural factors, but my best guess is that they are reinforcing, and both sets of forces are at play.

We need to invest in adolescents and improve the economic trajectory of children from low-income backgrounds. Successful interventions would focus on ways for low socioeconomic youth to increase the likelihood of achieving economic success. Those interventions should focus both on improving the actual return to investing in human capital, as well as improving perceptions of what is possible for them. College scholarship programs for low-income high school graduates, for instance, may make college a better investment for low-income youth and increase the return associated with graduation from high school. But it could also alter the student's perception that going to college is the sort of activity that they can achieve. Other such interventions might take the form of mentoring programs that connect youth with successful adult mentors or school and community programs that focus on establishing high expectations and providing pathways to graduation.

Concluding Observations

Too often the political debate oversimplifies the choices before us when dealing with the aforementioned challenges. It is too simple to assert that high levels of income inequality reflect the promise of capitalism and do no harm. A standard economist view is that inequality incentivizes individuals to invest in their own education and work harder. This is true only to a point. Eventually large income gaps leave those at the bottom so far behind that they and their children don't have a reasonable chance at catching up. But, it is also too simple to argue for policies that reduce inequality by taxing the rich at very high rates and transferring a lot of money to the poor, without acknowledging the disincentive effects that would accompany too heavy a hand in that direction.

Ultimately, we need to invest in our collective human potential, and that means devoting policy attention and fiscal resources to investments that foster the health, well-being, and productive capacity of broader segments of our population. By taking dedicated, concrete steps to address the root causes and associated symptoms of income inequality, we will put our nation on a more solid path toward sustained and widely shared economic prosperity.

Notes

1. Russell Sage Foundation, "Chartbook of Social Inequality," http://www.russellsage.org/research/chartbook/percentage-change-family-income-1947-1975-and-1975-2012.

2. Congressional Budget Office, *Trends in the Distribution of Household Income Between 1979 and 2007*, October 25, 2011, https://www.cbo.gov/publication/42729.

3. For instance, the fact that the US has a high level of income inequality and a relatively low level of social mobility could simply reflect something about our underlying population. We have a very diverse population with different traits and levels of ability and work ethic. Combine that heterogeneity with the role of both nature and nurture, and we might expect that the children of highly successful people will become highly successful adults, and similarly for less economically successful adults and their offspring.

4. Feeding America, "Feeding America," http://www.feedingamerica.org/.

5. Regarding the increasing income share going to the top 1 percent, I don't think we as scholars or economic observers have a very good sense for how much of the rising income share of this very top group reflects real economic and utility value that these "superstars" are creating versus how much of it is a "rent grab," coming from changed social norms and a breakdown in labor-supporting institutions. This is still very much an open question. See Jon Bakija, Adam Cole, and Bradley T. Heim, *Jobs and Income Growth of Top Earners and the Causes of Changing Income Inequality: Evidence from U.S. Tax Return Data*, Mimeo, April 2012, http://web.williams.edu/Economics/wp/BakijaColeHeimJobsIncomeGrowthTopEarners.pdf.

6. David H. Autor, Lawrence F. Katz, and Melissa S. Kearney, "Trends in U.S. Wage Inequality: Revising the Revisionists," *Review of Economics and*

Statistics 90, no. 2 (2008): 300–23.

7. Melissa Kearney, Brad Hershbein, and Elisa Jacome, "Profiles of Change: Employment, Earnings, and Occupations from 1990–2013," The Hamilton Project, April 20, 2015, http://bit.ly/295IDdD.

8. David H. Autor, Frank Levy, and Richard J. Murnane, "The Skill Content of Recent Technological Change: An Empirical Exploration," *Quarterly Journal of Economics* 118, no. 4 (2013): 1279–333.

9. See Xavier Gabaix and Augustin Landier, "Why Has CEO Pay Increased So Much?" *Quarterly Journal of Economics* 123, no. 1 (2008): 49–100.

10. David H. Autor, David Dorn, and Gordon H. Hanson, "The China Shock: Learning from Labor Market Adjustment to Large Changes in Trade," *Annual Review of Economics,* forthcoming.

11. See David H. Autor, Alan Manning, and Christopher L. Smith, "The Contribution to the Minimum Wage to U.S. Wage Inequality over Three Decades: A Reassessment," *American Economic Journal: Applied Economics* 8, no. 1 (2016): 58–99; and David Card, Thomas Lemieux, and W. Craig Riddell, "Unions and Wage Inequality," *Journal of Labor Research* (2004): 25.

12. Claudia Goldin and Lawrence F. Katz, *The Race Between Education and Technology: The Evolution of U.S. Educational Wage Differentials, 1890 to 2005* (Cambridge, MA: Harvard University Press, 2008).

13. Melissa Kearney, Brad Hershbein, and Lawrence H. Summers, "Increasing Education: What It Will and Will Not Do for Earnings and Earnings Inequality," The Hamilton Project, March 30, 2015, http://bit.ly/29318Ra.

14. D. Almond, H. Hoynes, and D. W. Schanzenbach, "Inside the War on Poverty: The Impact of Food Stamps on Birth Outcomes," *Review of Economics and Statistics* 93, no. 2 (2011): 387–404; David Brown, Amanda Kowalski, and Itahi Lurie, "Medicaid as an Investment in Children: What Is the Long-Term Impact on Tax Receipts?" (working paper 20835, National Bureau of Economic Research, 2015); and Laura Wherry et al., "Childhood Medicaid Coverage and Later Life Health Care Utilization" (working paper 20929, National Bureau of Economic Research, February 2015).

15. Sara McLanahan, "Diverging Destinies: How Children Fare Under the Second Demographic Transition," *Demography* 41, no. 4 (2004): 607–27.

16. Melissa Kearney and Philip Levine, "The Marriage Premium for Children," July 2016.

17. Jonathan Guryan, Eric Hurst, and Melissa Kearney, "Parental Education and Parental Time with Children," *Journal of Economic Perspectives* 22, no. 3 (2008): 23–46.

18. A. Kalil, R. Ryan, and M. Corey, "Diverging Destinies: Maternal Education and the Developmental Gradient in Time with Children," *Demography* 49, no. 4 (2012): 1361–83.

19. Sean Reardon, "The Widening Academic Achievement Gap Between the Rich and the Poor: New Evidence and Possible Explanations," in *Whither Opportunity? Rising Inequality and the Uncertain Life Chances of Low-Income Children,* ed. Greg J. Duncan and Richard J. Murnane (New York: Russell Sage Foundation Press, 2011).

20. Arthur Okun, *Equality and Efficiency: The Big Tradeoff* (Washington, DC: Brookings Institution Press, 1985).

21. Melissa S. Kearney and Philip Levine, "Income Inequality, Social Mobility, and the Decision to Drop-Out of High School," *Brookings Papers on Economic Activity*, March 2016.

22. Raj Chetty, Nathaniel Hendren, and Lawrence F. Katz, "The Effects of Exposure to Better Neighborhoods on Children: New Evidence from the Moving to Opportunity Experiment" (working paper no. 21156, National Bureau of Economic Research, May 2015).

23. See M. Bertrand and J. Pan, "The Trouble with Boys: Social Influences and the Gender Gap in Disruptive Behavior," *American Economic Journal: Applied Economics* 5, no. 1 (2013): 32–64; and David Autor et al., "Family Disadvantage and the Gender Gap in Behavioral and Educational Outcomes" (working paper 15-16, IPR Northwestern, October 2015).

24. Melissa S. Kearney and Phillip Levine, "Income Inequality and Early, Non-Marital Childbearing," *Journal of Human Resources* 49 (Winter 2014): 1–31.

25. William J. Wilson, *The Truly Disadvantaged: The Inner City, the Underclass and Public Policy* (Chicago: University of Chicago Press, 1987).

About the Authors

Dean Baker is codirector of the Center for Economic and Policy Research, which he cofounded in 1999. His areas of research include housing and macroeconomics, intellectual property, Social Security, Medicare, and European labor markets. He is the author of several books, his latest being *Getting Back to Full Employment: A Better Bargain for Working People* (Center for Economic and Policy Research, 2013). He has also published work in a variety of academic and policy journals, as well as popular outlets. He has worked as a senior economist at the Economic Policy Institute and as an assistant professor at Bucknell University. He has served as a consultant to the World Bank, the Joint Economic Committee of the US Congress, and the OECD's Trade Union Advisory Council. He holds a Ph.D. in economics from the University of Michigan.

George J. Borjas is the Robert W. Scrivner Professor of Economics and Social Policy at the Harvard Kennedy School. He was awarded the Institute for the Study of Labor (IZA) Prize in Labor Economics in 2011. He is a research associate at the National Bureau of Economic Research and a research fellow at IZA. Dr. Borjas is the author of several books, including *Immigration Economics* (Harvard University Press, 2014); *Heaven's Door: Immigration Policy and the American Economy* (Princeton University Press, 1999); and the widely used textbook *Labor Economics* (McGraw-Hill, 2016), now in its seventh edition. His latest book is *We Wanted Workers: Unraveling the Immigration Narrative* (W. W. Norton, Fall 2016). He has also published around 150 articles in books and scholarly journals. Dr. Borjas was elected a fellow of the Econometric Society in 1998 and a fellow of the Society of Labor Economists in 2004. He holds a Ph.D. in economics from Columbia University.

Richard V. Burkhauser is the Sarah Gibson Blanding Professor of Policy Analysis in the Department of Policy Analysis and Management at Cornell University and a senior research fellow at the Lyndon B. Johnson School of Public Affairs at the University of Texas at Austin. His professional career has focused on how public policies affect the economic behavior and well-being of vulnerable populations, such as older persons, people with disabilities, and low-skilled workers. He has published widely on these topics in journals of demography, economics, gerontology, and public policy and is the coauthor of *The Declining Work and Welfare of People with Disabilities* (AEI Press, 2011). He was the 2010 president of the Association for Public Policy Analysis and Management. He holds a Ph.D. in economics from the University of Chicago.

Peter Cappelli is the George W. Taylor Professor of Management at the University of Pennsylvania's Wharton School and director of Wharton's Center for Human Resources. His recent research examines changes in employment relations in the US and their implications. He is a research associate at the National Bureau of Economic Research and has previously been a faculty member at Massachusetts Institute of Technology, the University of Illinois, and the University of California, Berkeley. He has served on numerous boards and commissions, including as codirector of the US Department of Education's National Center on the Educational Quality of the Workforce. He has authored several books, including *Why Good People Can't Get Jobs: The Skills Gap and What Companies Can Do About It* (Wharton, 2012) and *Will College Pay Off? A Guide to the Most Important Financial Decision You'll Ever Make* (PublicAffairs, 2015). He holds a Ph.D. in labor economics from Oxford University.

Miles Corak is a full professor of economics with the Graduate School of Public and International Affairs at the University of Ottawa and a visiting professor with the Department of Economics at Harvard University during the 2015–16 academic year. His publications focus on labor markets and social policy, including child poverty, access to university education, social mobility, and unemployment. He joined the University of Ottawa in 2007 with 20 years experience in the Canadian federal government, most of that time spent as a research director at Statistics Canada, and has also held visiting appointments with UNICEF, the University of London, Princeton University, and the Russell Sage Foundation. Dr. Corak maintains his own blog at MilesCorak.com and can be found on Twitter @MilesCorak.

Tyler Cowen is the Holbert L. Harris Chair of Economics at George Mason University and serves as chairman and general director of the Mercatus Center at George Mason University. A dedicated writer and communicator of economic ideas who has written extensively on the economics of culture, Dr. Cowen is the author of several books, his latest being *Average Is Over: Powering America Beyond the Age of the Great Stagnation* (Dutton, 2013). He is widely published in academic journals, including the *American Economic Review*, *Journal of Political Economy*, *Ethics*, and *Philosophy and Public Affairs*. He also writes regularly in popular media and is coauthor of the popular economics blog "Marginal Revolution." Dr. Cowen holds a Ph.D. in economics from Harvard University.

Mary C. Daly is senior vice president and associate director of research at the Federal Reserve Bank of San Francisco, where she specializes in employment and wage dynamics, economic inequality and mobility, relative income and subjective well-being, disability and economic well-being, and disability policy in industrialized nations. She is also a research fellow with the Institute for the Study of Labor, a member of the editorial board for *Industrial Relations*, and a fellow with the National Academy of Social Insurance. She has published extensively in a variety of academic journals and is the coauthor of *The Declining Work and Welfare of People with Disabilities* (AEI Press, 2011). She holds a Ph.D. in economics from Syracuse University.

Martin Feldstein has been a professor of economics at Harvard University since 1969. He served as president and CEO of the National

Bureau of Economic Research from 1977 to 1982 and from 1984 to 2008. From 1982 through 1984, he was chairman of the Council of Economic Advisers and President Reagan's chief economic adviser. He served as president of the American Economic Association in 2004. In 1977, he received the John Bates Clark Medal of the American Economic Association, a prize awarded every two years to the economist under the age of 40 who is judged to have made the greatest contribution to economic science. Dr. Feldstein has been a director of several major public corporations.

Jason Furman is the 28th chairman of the Council of Economic Advisers. In this role, he serves as President Obama's chief economist and a member of the cabinet. He has also served as principal deputy director of the National Economic Council and assistant to the president. Previously, Dr. Furman worked at the Council of Economic Advisers and National Economic Council during the Clinton administration, at the World Bank, as a senior fellow at the Brookings Institution and the Center on Budget and Policy Priorities, and in visiting positions at various universities, including New York University's Wagner Graduate School of Public Policy. He has conducted research on many topics, including fiscal policy, tax policy, health economics, Social Security, and domestic and international macroeconomics. He is the editor of two books on economic policy and the author of numerous articles in academic journals and related publications. He holds a Ph.D. in economics from Harvard University.

Harry J. Holzer is the John LaForge SJ Professor at the McCourt School of Public Policy at Georgetown University. He is also an institute fellow at the American Institutes of Research and a nonresident senior fellow in economic studies at the Brookings Institution. He is a former chief economist at the US Department of Labor. He serves on the boards of directors for the Economic Mobility Corporation and the National Skills Coalition. He has written or edited 12 books and more than 50 articles in peer-reviewed journals. His research and writing focuses on the low-wage labor market and policies designed to help low-wage workers. He holds a Ph.D. in economics from Harvard University.

Glenn Hubbard, a former chairman of the President's Council of Economic Advisers, is currently the dean of Columbia Business School and a visiting scholar at AEI. He specializes in public and corporate finance and financial markets and institutions. He has written more than 100 articles and books, including three textbooks, on corporate finance, investment decisions, banking, energy economics, and public policy. He has served as a deputy assistant secretary at the US Department of the Treasury and as a consultant to, among others, the Federal Reserve Board and the Federal Reserve Bank of New York. He holds a Ph.D. in economics from Harvard University.

Melissa S. Kearney is a professor in the Department of Economics at the University of Maryland, where she has been on the faculty since 2006, and a nonresident senior fellow at the Brookings Institution. She is also a research associate at the National Bureau of Economic Research (NBER), a faculty affiliate of the Notre Dame Lab for Economic Opportunities (LEO), and an affiliated scholar of the MIT Abdul Latif Jameel Poverty Action Lab (J-PAL). Past positions include director of the Hamilton Project at Brookings, Mellon Fellow at Brookings, and assistant professor at Wellesley College. Dr. Kearney's research focuses on issues of social policy, poverty, and inequality and has been published in leading economics journals. She holds a Ph.D. in economics from the Massachusetts Institute of Technology.

Robert Z. Lawrence is the Albert L. Williams Professor of International Trade and Investment at the Harvard Kennedy School, a senior fellow at the Peterson Institute for International Economics, and a research associate at the National Bureau of Economic Research. He currently serves as faculty chair of the Practice of Trade Policy executive program at Harvard Kennedy School. He served as a member of the President's Council of Economic Advisers from 1998 to 2000. Dr. Lawrence has also been a senior fellow at the Brookings Institution. His research focuses on trade policy, and he has authored several books on issues related to trade and globalization. He has served on the advisory boards of the Congressional Budget Office, the Overseas Development Council, and the Presidential Commission on United States–Pacific Trade and Investment Policy. He holds a Ph.D. in economics from Yale University.

Bhash Mazumder is a senior economist and research adviser in the economic research department and the executive director of the Chicago Federal Statistical Research Data Center at the Federal Reserve Bank of Chicago. His research has been focused on intergenerational economic mobility, the long-term effects of poor health early in life, and black-white gaps in human capital development. Dr. Mazumder's research has been published in academic journals such as the *Journal of Political Economy*, *American Economic Review*, *Quantitative Economics*, *American Economic Journal: Applied Economics*, and *Review of Economics and Statistics*. He oversees the operations of a research center enabling access to census microdata on behalf of a consortium of research institutions. He holds a Ph.D. in economics from the University of California, Berkeley.

Robert A. Moffitt is the Krieger-Eisenhower Professor of Economics at Johns Hopkins University and holds a joint appointment with the Bloomberg School of Public Health. He researches the economics of poverty and welfare programs for the poor and the economics of the labor market. He has been the chief editor of the *American Economic Review*, a Guggenheim Fellow, a member of the American Academy of Arts and Sciences, a national associate of the National Academy of Sciences, a fellow of the Econometric Society, and a recipient of a MERIT Award from the National Institutes of Health. He holds a Ph.D. in economics from Brown University.

Casey B. Mulligan is a professor in economics at the University of Chicago. In the past, he has served as a visiting professor teaching public economics at Harvard University, Clemson University, and the Irving B. Harris Graduate School of Public Policy Studies at the University of Chicago. He is affiliated with the National Bureau of Economic Research, the George J. Stigler Center for the Study of the Economy and the State, and the Population Research Center.

His research covers capital and labor taxation, the gender wage gap, Social Security, voting, and the economics of aging. He has authored several books, the most recent of which is *Side Effects and Complications: The Economic Consequences of Health Care Reform* (University of Chicago Press, 2015). He holds a Ph.D. in economics from the University of Chicago.

Pia M. Orrenius is a vice president and senior economist at the Federal Reserve Bank of Dallas and adjunct professor at the Hankamer School of Business at Baylor University. She is also a research fellow at The Tower Center for Political Studies at Southern Methodist University and the IZA Institute for the Study of Labor in Bonn, as well as an adjunct scholar at the American Enterprise Institute. At the Dallas Fed, Dr. Orrenius manages the regional economy group focusing on economic growth and demographic change. Her academic research focuses on the labor market impacts of immigration, unauthorized immigration, and US immigration policy, and her work has been published in academic journals including the *Journal of Labor Economics*, *Journal of Development Economics*, and *Labour Economics*. She is coauthor of *Beside the Golden Door: U.S. Immigration Reform in a New Era of Globalization* (AEI Press, 2010). Dr. Orrenius was senior economist on the President's Council of Economic Advisers from 2004 to 2005. She holds a Ph.D. in economics from the University of California, Los Angeles.

Timothy M. Smeeding is the Lee Rainwater Distinguished Professor of Public Affairs and Economics at the University of Wisconsin–Madison. He was director of the university's Institute for Research on Poverty from 2008 to 2014. He was the founding director of the Luxembourg Income Study from 1983 to 2006. Dr. Smeeding's recent work has been on social and economic mobility across generations, inequality of income, consumption and wealth, and poverty in national and cross-national contexts. He has published many books on these topics, the most recent of which is *SNAP Matters: How Food Stamps Affect Health and Well Being* (Stanford University Press, 2015). His research is widely published in a variety of academic journals. He holds a Ph.D. in economics from the University of Wisconsin–Madison.

Betsey Stevenson is an associate professor of public policy at the Gerald R. Ford School of Public Policy at the University of Michigan, with a courtesy appointment as an associate professor of economics in the College of Literature, Science, and the Arts. She is a research associate with the National Bureau of Economic Research, a fellow of the Ifo Institute for Economic Research in Munich, and an honorary associate professor of economics at the University of Sydney. She served as a member of the President's Council of Economic Advisers from 2013 to 2015 and as the chief economist of the US Department of Labor from 2010 to 2011. Dr. Stevenson's research focuses on the impact of public policies on the labor market and explores women's labor market experiences, the economic forces shaping the modern family, and the potential value of subjective well-being data for public policy. She holds a Ph.D. in economics from Harvard University.

Michael R. Strain is director of Economic Policy Studies and resident scholar at AEI. His research interests include labor economics, public finance, and social policy, and his papers have been published in both academic and policy journals. He also writes regularly for popular audiences on a variety of topics in economics and public policy, and he is frequently interviewed by major media outlets. Before joining AEI, he worked in the Center for Economic Studies at the US Census Bureau and in the macroeconomics research group at the Federal Reserve Bank of New York. He holds a Ph.D. in economics from Cornell University.

Justin Wolfers is a professor of public policy in the Gerald R. Ford School of Public Policy and a professor of economics in the College of Literature, Science, and the Arts at the University of Michigan. His research interests include labor economics, macroeconomics, political economy, economics of the family, social policy, law and economics, and behavioral economics. Most recently, he was an associate professor of business and public policy at the University of

Pennsylvania and a visiting professor at Princeton University. He is a research associate with the National Bureau of Economic Research, a research affiliate with the Centre for Economic Policy Research in London, and an international research fellow at the Kiel Institute for the World Economy in Germany. He holds a Ph.D. in economics from Harvard University, where he was a Fulbright, Knox, and Menzies Scholar.

Madeline Zavodny is a professor of economics at Agnes Scott College in Decatur, Georgia, and a research fellow at the Institute for the Study of Labor in Bonn. She was formerly an associate professor of economics at Occidental College and a research economist at the Federal Reserve Bank of Atlanta and the Federal Reserve Bank of Dallas. She is also an adjunct scholar at the American Enterprise Institute. She is coauthor of *Beside the Golden Door: U.S. Immigration Reform in a New Era of Globalization* (AEI Press, 2010). Her research on the economics of immigration has been published in many journals, including the *Journal of Labor Economics*, *Industrial and Labor Relations Review, Research in Labor Economics*, and *Journal of Policy Analysis and Management*. She holds a Ph.D. in economics from the Massachusetts Institute of Technology.

The American Enterprise Institute

Founded in 1943, AEI is a nonpartisan, nonprofit research and educational organization based in Washington, DC. The Institute sponsors research, conducts seminars and conferences, and publishes books and periodicals.

AEI's research is carried out under three major programs: Economic Policy Studies, Foreign and Defense Policy Studies, and Social and Political Studies. The resident scholars and fellows listed in these pages are part of a network that also includes adjunct scholars at leading universities throughout the United States and in several foreign countries.

The views expressed in AEI publications are those of the authors and do not necessarily reflect the views of the staff, advisory panels, officers, or trustees.